Revised edition | # On their own
in reading

How to give children independence in analyzing new words

by **William S. Gray,** *University of Chicago*

Senior Author of The New Basic Readers

With the collaboration of Staff Editors from the Language Arts Department

Scott, Foresman and Company

To all who from their scientific knowledge of the English language or from their experience in teaching boys and girls to read have contributed to this revision of *On Their Own in Reading*.

William S. Gray

Foreword

I doubt there has ever been a time when learning to read
and teaching reading have seemed more important or
aroused more debate. How does one learn to read? How
can and should the reading of English be taught to children
by adults? How can children who have begun to read go on
with accuracy and suitable reward ("happiness" if that is
your *summum bonum*)?

There are surely various ways of learning to read.
Outside of school we can observe children learning to read
by themselves or being taught by brothers and sisters. Maga-
zines, roadside signs, and television play a part. A real
rock-ribbed conservative can argue: those who are destined
to read will read! Why bother?

This, however, is not the American way. We believe
that every citizen should be literate, and that the way to
guarantee national literacy is to require that every child
attend school and be taught to read. It is a large order,
and the mental and physical variation among children
being what it is, the problems are never ending, the suc-
cesses and the slow-ups.

A large part of a child's first two years in school
is given to reading and writing, and much of the remaining years of grammar school, which is to say "reading and
arts of communication school." This represents a lot of
time and a lot of tax-money. It is quite right that we should
ask ourselves and the teachers: is everything being done
in the best way? Isn't there a wonderful modern short
cut? Phonemes, semantemes, morphemes, intimes; word
counts, meaning counts, nose counts, no-counts. These are
new? Surely there is an easier way to teach reading now,
even though I can't seem to get my television to work right.

No one's answers to these questions interest me more than Dr. William S. Gray's. His well-known book *On Their Own in Reading* was written for teachers of those children who might be said to be predestined to read and of those who can acquire this grace with the help of intelligent teaching. The progress of both groups is facilitated. Students are fortunate who have had the advantage of a pedagogy ordered by his firm though sympathetic principles, his imaginative and practical progression in the analysis of English words. I wish that I had been taught by Dr. Gray.

He has now revised *On Their Own in Reading* in recognition of many new studies of the language arts, of communication. Anyone acquainted with his magnificent Unesco study, *The Teaching of Reading and Writing*, will expect to find here another classical study, marked by an almost unique experience, wide sympathy and hard sense (a reticence of ego, a distrust of the dramatic). This is such a book.

In this new edition, Dr. Gray's guidance is perhaps more expert, but he has found no easy answer. Midst the vexations of English spelling and the irregular forms that our children must learn to read, he gives the Puritan's comfort: do not despair. Children learn to speak and to understand these words—most of them anyway—before they learn to read them. Begin by teaching them to read the language they know. This is no foreign tongue to them. *This is their language already.* They have taken to it like ducks to water. By word analysis you can teach them step by step to command it in letters black on white as they do now in terms of sound. —Well, this is what he says to me! And may he forgive my putting words into his wise mouth.

His comfort is intellectual in these premises: (1) that children already know the language on the level that one should teach them and (2) that teachers can benefit, and children progress, by the orderly analysis of our word stock.

To these Dr. Gray adds a third proposition: that by an intelligent use of an English dictionary—a use exceedingly well presented in a new chapter for this edition—older children acquire a ready tool to ascertain, on their own and for as long as they live, the meaning and use of the English language. This may well be the most important skill that can be taught in school—for it gives each individual ready access to. . . . What shall we say? To all that part of life that resides in written words? It is more than that, for written words stimulate and are in turn affected by spoken words. Let's just say Reading and Writing and Listening. Pronounce them slowly, and say them twice, and add Amen.

W. Cabell Greet
Barnard College
Columbia University

Contents

Explanation of terms

The terms in this section are neither fully nor technically defined; rather they are explained in light of their use in this book. Definitions of these terms by various scholars in the field of language might differ considerably, principally in technical detail. It would be well for a teacher of reading to acquaint herself with present-day studies in linguistic research. A knowledge, for example, of how vowel and consonant sounds are formed, how they are classified, and why they are so classified will prove valuable. However, a teacher should keep in mind that an English-speaking child who is learning to read does not need to know how consonant and vowel sounds are formed and how they are classified. One of his problems in learning to read is to associate sounds that he knows with the letters that represent them in printed words.

Accent (also referred to as *stress*)—the degree of relative loudness with which a syllable is spoken. In words of two or more syllables, one syllable is accented or stressed more than the other or others. A shift in accent can affect meaning as these pairs of words illustrate: *con'tract, con tract'; pres'ent, pre sent'; ob'ject, ob ject'*. Syllables may be spoken with at least three degrees of accent as indicated below:

Primary accent—the loudest accent or stress; for example, the first syllable in each of these words is said with a primary accent or stress: *sec're tar'y, prim'rose'*. Note the mark used to denote primary stress.

Secondary accent—the next loudest accent or stress; for example, the second syllable in each of these words is said with a secondary accent or stress: *home'sick'*, *en cy'clo pe'di a*. Note the mark used to denote secondary stress.

Unaccented syllable—the syllable said with the least loud accent or stress; for example, the first syllable in the words *ap prove'*, *re main'* and the last two syllables in the word *con'fi dent* are unaccented. Note that no accent mark is used to denote unaccented syllables.

Affix—a prefix, a suffix, or an inflectional ending.

Compound—a word composed of two or more words that combine their meanings to make a new word. A compound may be written as one word, written as two or more words, or hyphenated (*steamboat, dime store, merry-go-round*). English compounds are distinguished from phrases mainly by reduced stress on one of the words. For example, say the sentences given below and note the difference in stress between *bluebird* and *blue bird*. This difference in stress indicates a difference in meaning.

I saw a bluebird yesterday (*bluebird* is a compound meaning "a specific kind of bird"). The stress pattern is that of a primary accent on *blue* and a secondary accent on *bird*.

I saw a strange blue bird at the zoo (*blue bird* is a phrase meaning "any kind of bird that is blue"). The word *bird* is stressed more strongly than it is in the compound.

Consonant—a speech sound that is produced by interrupting or modifying the outgoing air or breath by some organ of articulation such as the lips, teeth, tongue, hard and soft palates. Twenty-four consonant sounds are commonly recognized. These consonant sounds are those heard at the beginning of the following words: *bad, do, fat, go, he,* *jam, kind, land, me, no, pan, run, sit, tell, very, will, yet, zero, child, she, thin, then;* at the end of *long;* and in the middle of *pleasure*. In written English consonant sounds are represented by letters of the alphabet. There is not a one-to-one correspondence between consonant sounds and the letters that represent them. Although many letters usually stand for only one sound, *b* and *p*, for example, other letters may represent more than one sound, the letter *g* (*girl, giant*) and the letter *s* (*sit, his, sure*), for example. Still other letters may represent the same sound, the letters *g* and *j* (*gem, jam*), for example, and the letters *c, k,* and *q* (*car, kind, quit*).

Consonant blend (also called *consonant cluster*)—two or more consonant sounds that occur together without intervening vowel sounds, for example, the two initial sounds in *play* (pl) and in *bribe* (br) and the three initial sounds in *scream* (skr); the three medial sounds in *astride* (str); and the three final sounds in *glimpse* (mps). In this book, the sounds represented by the letters *l, r,* and *s* are presented as common "blenders."

Derived form (also called *derivative*)—a word that is composed of a root plus a prefix or suffix or both, for example, *unhappy, happiness, unhappiness.*

Diphthong—a succession of two vowel sounds that are joined in a single syllable under a single stress. A diphthong is made by a continuous glide of the tongue from one vowel position to the other. The vowel sounds heard in *boy* and *toil* and in *house* and *cow* are diphthongs. The vowel sounds heard in such words as *bait, beat, boat,* and especially in *bite* are often classified as diphthongs. In this book only the vowel sounds heard in *boy* and in *house* are referred to as diphthongs.

Ending—see *Inflectional ending.*

Homograph—a word with the same spelling as another word but with a different meaning and origin, for example, *mail* meaning "letters" and *mail* meaning "armor"; *bow* (bō) meaning "a tie" and *bow* (bou) meaning "to bend."

Homonym—a word with the same pronunciation as another but with a different meaning, origin, and usually, spelling, for example, *steak* and *stake.* (Homographs that are pronounced alike are homonyms—"*fair* play," "state *fair.*")

Inflected form—a word to which an inflectional ending has been added. An inflectional ending (-*s*, for example) may be added to a root word (*lights*), to a derived form (*lighters*), or to a compound (*headlights*).

Inflectional ending—a meaningful element (-*s*, -*es*, -*'s*, -*ed*, -*ing*, -*er*, -*est*, for example) that is affixed to the ends of words to form plurals and the possessive case of nouns (*boys*, *churches*, *boy's*); the past tense, the third person singular, present indicative, and the present participle of verbs (*walked*, *walks*, *walking*); and the comparison of adjectives or adverbs (*bigger*, *biggest; sooner, soonest*).

Meaning unit—a root word, a prefix, a suffix, an inflectional ending. These meaningful parts of words are often referred to as *morphemes*, a morpheme being the smallest meaningful unit in the structure of words. For example, *rain*, a root word, is a meaning unit or morpheme. *Rainy* is composed of two morphemes, the root *rain* and the suffix -*y;* *raincoats*, a compound, is composed of three morphemes, the roots *rain* and *coat* and the inflectional ending -*s.*

Morpheme—see *Meaning unit.*

Phoneme—the smallest unit of sound by which we can tell one thing that is said from anything else that might be said. Knowledge of consonant sounds and vowel sounds as phonemes is essential to word analysis. Equally valuable is knowledge of another kind of phoneme, accent. There are three phonemes (or units of sound) in the word *bat*—the consonant phoneme represented by the letter *b*, the vowel phoneme represented by the letter *a*, and the consonant phoneme represented by the letter *t*. The initial consonant phoneme differentiates such words as *bat, cat, chat, fat, hat, mat, pat, rat, sat, that, vat*. The medial vowel phoneme differentiates such words as *bat, bet, bit, bought, but*. The final consonant phoneme differentiates such words as *bat, bad, bag, back, ban, bang, bash, bath*.

In a word like *permit*, a shift in accent from the first syllable (*per′mit*) to the second syllable (*per mit′*) distinguishes noun from verb meaning.

Phonetic analysis—a means by which a reader analyzes a printed word to determine its pronunciation. He uses visual clues in printed words as aids in determining consonant and vowel sounds, syllabic divisions, and accented syllables. He must be able to hear phonemes (consonant and vowel sounds and accent) accurately, to associate consonant and vowel sounds with letters of the alphabet, and to blend these sounds into syllables and the syllables into words with appropriate accent.

Prefix—a meaningful element that is affixed to the beginning of a root word or a derived or inflected form, for example, *re-* in *repay*, *un-* in *untruthful*, *pre-* in *precooked*. A prefix combines its meaning with that of the word to which it is affixed.

Primary accent—see *Accent.*

Root word (also called *root*)—the center or base to which prefixes, suffixes, and inflectional endings may be added. For example, *play* is the root word in *playing, played, plays, player; talk* in *talkative; polite* in *politeness, impolitely.* The identification of a root word in a derived or inflected form enables a child to associate core or root meaning with the form. He then can combine the root meaning with that of the affix to determine the meaning of the total form. The word *root* in this book refers to English roots; for example, *invent* is a root word in English although it comes from two Latin roots *in* and *venire.* A child would therefore identify *invent* as the root in *invention, inventive,* and *inventor.*

Schwa—the vowel sound heard in most unstressed syllables in English, for example, the sound represented by the letters *a, e, i, o,* and *u* in the unaccented syllables of *sofa, problem, April, ballot,* and *circus.* This sound is represented by the schwa symbol (ə) in many dictionaries, including all the Thorndike-Barnhart dictionaries. (Some dictionaries do not restrict the use of this symbol to unstressed syllables.)

Secondary accent—see *Accent.*

Stress—see *Accent.*

Structural analysis—the means by which a reader identifies meaning units (morphemes) in words and sees relationships between inflected or derived forms and their roots. Structural analysis is concerned with the identification of root words, prefixes, suffixes, and inflectional endings.

Suffix—a meaningful element that is affixed to the end of a word (the word may be a root, an inflected form or a derived form). For example, the suffix *-er* is added to *follow* to make *follower;* the suffix *-ly* is added to *admitted* to make *admittedly;* the suffix *-ness* is added to *cloudy* to make *cloudiness.* A suffix combines its meaning with that of the word to which it is affixed. Most suffixes have a grammatical function; for example, *-er* added to a verb (*teach*) makes a noun (*teacher*); *-y* added to a noun (*wind*) makes an adjective (*windy*).

Syllable—a word or part of a word in which a vowel sound is heard. In most dictionaries an entry word is divided into visual syllables, **ti ny, nerv ous,** for example. These written syllabic divisions indicate where a word may be divided at the end of a line of writing. Written syllables may or may not correspond to spoken syllables as the pronunciations (tī′ ni) and (nėr′ vəs) illustrate.

Voice—sound made by vibrating the vocal cords with air forced from the lungs. If there is no vibration of the vocal cords in the production of a sound, that sound is referred to as unvoiced or voiceless. All vowel sounds are voiced. Voiced consonant sounds are those heard at the beginning of *bad, do, go, jam, very, then, zoo, man, no, lake, run, yes, wet,* and at the end of *sing* and of *rouge.* Unvoiced (or voiceless) consonant sounds are those heard at the beginning of *pet, to, keep, child, fat, thin, sit, shut,* and *hat.*

Vowel—a speech sound for whose production the oral passage is comparatively unobstructed so that the breath stream can flow from the lungs to the lips and beyond without audible friction and without being disturbed or cut off at any point. A vowel sound carries one of the three degrees of accent.

There is a difference of opinion among authorities as to the number of vowel sounds heard in English and the way in which they should be classified. This book, like the

Thorndike-Barnhart dictionaries, recognizes nineteen English vowel sounds. These vowel sounds are those heard at the beginning of the following words: *at, age, air, are, end, eat, earn, it, ice, odd, oak, or, oil, out, up, use;* in the middle of *put* and of *rule;* and in the first syllable of *about.* (This book adheres to the traditional terminology of calling the vowel sounds heard in *ate, eat, ice, oak, use* "long" vowel sounds and those heard in *am, end, it, odd, up* "short" vowel sounds. Although this terminology does not indicate accurately the relative length of vowel sounds, it is adhered to because it is simple for children to use as they learn to associate vowel sounds with letters.)

Vowel sounds are represented in written English by letters of the alphabet. A letter does not always represent the same vowel sound; the letter *a,* for example, may represent the vowel sounds heard in *hat, age, care, father, many, ago,* and *all.* The same vowel sound may be represented by various letters or spellings; for example, the vowel sound heard in *end* may be represented by the spellings shown in the words *many, said, says, let, bread, heifer, leopard, friend, bury.* (The letters *y* and *w,* although they commonly represent consonant sounds, may also represent vowel sounds. A child associates the initial sound in *yes* and *yawn* with the letter *y;* the initial sound in *wet* and *wash* with the letter *w;* and he refers to these sounds (y), (w) as consonant sounds. He also associates the letter *y* with the vowel sounds heard in *fly* and *hymn* and at the end of *funny,* and he may regard the letter *w* as representing a vowel sound when it combines with the letter *o* to stand for the diphthong heard in *cow.*)

Word—a speech sound or series of sounds having meaning and used as a unit of language. A word may consist of a single morpheme (*joy, friend*) or of a combination of morphemes (*joyfully, unfriendliness*).

Chapter one | # The role of
word perception in reading

A child who is ready to read knows the sound and meaning of hundreds of words, and he knows how these words are put together in phrases and sentences to convey ideas. In short, he expresses and receives ideas through the medium of spoken language. Soon he will learn to respond to these same words in print, a process known as reading.

In order to read—to receive ideas from printed language—a child must associate sound and meaning with printed words. Teaching him to do so raises some challenging questions. Should a child be expected to memorize the printed forms of all the words that are in his oral vocabulary? That task, most of us would agree, is neither possible nor necessary, since there are ways of identifying many words independently. But how shall we teach a child to figure out new words for himself, and when? What kind of words, if any, can most beginning readers be expected to attack while reading? Should all word-attack skills be taught by the end of the primary grades? Does the term "word analysis" mean "sounding out" new words, or is there more to it than that? Is the child who is adept at identifying new words for himself necessarily a good reader?

It is the purpose of this book to answer such questions by (1) pointing out the relationship of word perception to reading, (2) discussing various aids to word perception, (3) presenting an overview of a program in word analysis, (4) giving procedures for teaching children how to analyze unfamiliar words that they encounter while reading.

Four components of the reading process

To understand the relationship of word perception to reading, we should consider first what happens when a person fully interprets what he reads. Although most of us probably think of reading as a kind of unified response to the visual stimulus of printed words, we can distinguish four main components in the interpretation of printed matter. Briefly stated, they are (1) word perception, (2) comprehension of the ideas represented by the words, (3) reaction to these ideas, (4) assimilation or integration of the ideas with previous knowledge or experience.

Word perception

Obviously one of the first steps in learning to interpret printed words is to recognize that each one represents a spoken word in our language. As adults, however, most of us are not word-by-word readers. Our eyes move rapidly along the lines, taking in whole phrases at a single glance. We are scarcely aware that we are identifying individual words by their general configuration and by using context clues to arrive at meaning. Should we read "Mr. Hanson was elected to the school board," we get the idea immediately because our word perception has been instantaneous and automatic. Even in a hasty reading we did not think, for example, that the last word was *beard* or *broad;* neither makes sense in the sentence. Awareness of context also helped us assign instantly the appropriate meaning to the word. Not for a second did we wonder whether *board* meant "a piece of wood" or "get on a train." Word perception, then, means identifying words accurately and associating with each the meaning that the author had in mind.

As we perceive words in sentences and paragraphs, we fuse their meanings into a stream of related ideas. The way we achieve understanding of what we read on a given occasion depends on the type of material that we are reading and on our purpose in reading it. As we read fiction and biography, for example, we form vivid mental images of the setting and people. We recognize the emotions and motives of the characters and often identify ourselves with them. Sometimes we read between the lines to grasp implied meanings, see relationships, or sense the writer's purpose (and often his prejudices and feelings). We may associate with the subject at hand everything we have experienced or learned that will help clarify the ideas of an author. Then, if we are competent readers, the ideas, impressions, and imagery we receive are usually those that the author intended to communicate.

Comprehension of ideas

If we are intelligent, interested readers, we cannot help reacting in some fashion to the ideas and imagery we receive from reading any more than we can help reacting to spoken language. We may respond to a book or a selection with only mild interest. Or it may arouse in us delight, enthusiasm, curiosity, nostalgia, sorrow, indignation, or horror, to name but a few emotional reactions that all of us have had. The strength and validity of any reader's intellectual or emotional reaction depend in large measure on his background of experience. I may consider a book about Portugal extremely informative and recommend it highly. Someone who has spent several years in that country may consider the same book inadequate and misleading. Since his reaction is based on broader knowledge and experience, it is more valid than mine. Reaction,

Reaction to these ideas

then, means responding to and reflecting on ideas we have read, evaluating these ideas, and accepting or rejecting them on the basis of our evaluation.

Combining new ideas with old

Most people would agree that full interpretation of what is read goes beyond reacting intellectually and emotionally to what the author says. The ideas that we have evaluated and accepted often add to our knowledge; they frequently give us new insight into ourselves and others. They can provide new interests and change our attitudes. From a good book we can derive comfort, pleasure, inspiration. Whatever we have gained—new wisdom, interests, or appreciations—changes us in some way. In short, much of what we read affects us whether we are aware of it or not; for the vicarious experiences we gain from reading are sometimes more significant than actual experiences. As we assimilate the experiences and ideas obtained through reading and integrate them with those we already have, our total experience is broadened. This fusion of new ideas with old is perhaps the most significant component of the total reading act.

Interdependency of the four components

The components of the interpretative or reading process are interrelated and mutually dependent. We can comprehend a writer's ideas only if we can identify the printed words he uses and can associate with these words the meaning the writer had in mind. I may "sound out" (albeit incorrectly) the following: "Mi piace leggere."[1] But unless I know Italian, I am neither perceiving individual words nor comprehending the total meaning they represent. The validity of our reaction to an author's ideas and their influence on our lives and thinking depend, in turn, on accurate comprehension of his meaning. Then, too, the ideas

[1] "I like to read."

and vicarious experiences we acquire through reading form a large part of the background of meaning that we bring to the perception of words. In short, what we *take from* one reading experience gives us more to *take to* the next one.

In the final analysis then, word perception is the all-important base of the reading process. We cannot expect children or adults to comprehend, react to, or be influenced by the ideas of any author if they are unable to identify the printed words that convey the ideas. Obviously one of the major goals of a good reading program is to teach children to perceive printed words. To do so, teachers should be aware of what is involved in word perception. The next chapter deals with four major aids to word perception and points out how children grow in their ability to use them. The chapter also discusses the relationship of word analysis to word perception and the role of word analysis in reading.

Chapter two | What is involved
in word perception

Because their perception of words is usually automatic, few adults have occasion to think of the ways in which they identify words while reading. However, let us take time to consider what enables a mature reader to respond to most printed words accurately and quickly and what additional means he may use to identify an unfamiliar word when he meets one. Once we have determined what the aids to word perception are, we will consider how children learn to use them.

How printed words are identified

In efficient, rapid word perception the reader relies almost wholly on context clues and word-form clues. Awareness of sentence context (and often of general context) and a glance at the general configuration of a word enable the reader to respond instantly with the meaning the author had in mind when he wrote the word. This type of word perception occurs in most of the reading done by expe-

Instantaneous word perception

rienced, mature readers. For example, you had no difficulty perceiving the words in this and the preceding paragraph. You did not stop to study the form of separate words. Nor did you analyze words by consciously noting root words, prefixes, and suffixes or by "sounding them out," syllable by syllable. It is highly unlikely that you consulted a dictionary for the pronunciation or the meaning of any word. Why not? Every word was familiar—you have used each one yourself and have seen it in print thousands of times; you know its meaning (or meanings). Therefore you were free to comprehend the ideas conveyed by the words, react to these ideas, and add them to what you already know about the subject, providing of course you consider them worth while.

Suppose, however, you encounter this sentence: "The annulet on his coat of arms proclaimed him a fifth son." Unless the word *annulet* is in your vocabulary, it probably stops you, at least momentarily. From sentence context you infer that an annulet is some kind of symbol; in short, you use context clues to get a general meaning for the word. Because a glance at the word does not reveal a word that you know, you may try word analysis. But study of the word form reveals no familiar ending, prefix, suffix, or root (structural analysis); so you divide the word into syllables and determine vowel sound and accent (phonetic analysis). When you arrive at a pronunciation, you wonder about it, since you cannot remember ever seeing or hearing this word. If you are in a hurry, you may be satisfied with your tentative pronunciation and with a general meaning ("some kind of symbol"). Nevertheless your perception of the word *annulet* is uncertain and incomplete. To find out exactly what it means and to check its pronunciation, you will have to consult the dictionary.

If context furnishes no clue to the general or specific meaning of an unfamiliar word, the dictionary is a reader's

Delayed word perception

only recourse. The word *assagai* in the sentence "Kent showed us the assagai he had brought from Africa" serves as a good example. If you have never seen or heard the word, no amount of guessing or word analysis is likely to reveal its meaning or pronunciation.

Four major aids to word perception have been mentioned: (1) memory of word form, (2) context clues, (3) word analysis (structural and phonetic), (4) the dictionary. The first two, as already noted, function automatically in most of the reading we do to ensure instantaneous word perception. When fluent word perception is stopped by an unfamiliar word, however, we may consciously use one or more of the four aids.

So far we have been concerned with the way these methods of word perception function in adult reading. Now let us turn our attention to the way children first learn to recognize printed words and to the ways these four methods of perceiving words help young readers grow in ability to remember known words and to identify new ones.

Four major aids to word perception

Promoting growth in word perception

Although all printed words are strangers to him, a child who is ready to read has learned to respond to and to use hundreds of spoken words. No two children, however, have the same oral vocabulary or the same background of experiences. That is why a teacher of reading devotes a great deal of effort (especially in the primary grades) to helping children enlarge and enrich their oral vocabularies. She knows that if a child, from the very beginning, is to regard reading as something more than merely pronouncing words, he must know the meanings of the printed words that he is asked to read and be able to use them in his own speech. Otherwise, he will have to try to associate an un-

Relationship between a child's oral vocabulary and reading

known pronunciation and meaning with an unfamiliar printed form. We do not expect an adult to make this three-way association of unknowns without the aid of a dictionary. Therefore until a child can use a dictionary, we should not expect him to read words whose spoken forms he has never heard or used. Even though he may "sound them out" correctly, he is merely exercising his eyes and vocal cords; he is not reading.

The first printed words a child learns to recognize are usually presented to him as wholes in context. Words that children learn in this way are called sight words. To make sure that every child will associate both sound and a specific meaning with a sight word the first time he sees it, the teacher initiates an oral discussion in which the word is used informally with the same meaning it has in the story that pupils are about to read. During the discussion, as she uses the word in a sentence, the teacher shows its printed form (usually on a word card at early levels). For example, if the new words were *Sandy* and *jump*, she might say, "One day Jim wanted his dog Sandy to learn a new trick; so he held a piece of meat over Sandy's head and said, 'Jump, Sandy, jump.'" While saying these words, the teacher would present their printed forms and then ask children to read them with her. Thus direct associations of sound, meaning, and word form are established when pupils see a printed word for the first time.

How a child first learns to identify printed words

For at least two reasons much of a child's early success in reading depends on his mastery of an initial stock of sight words: ability to identify these sight words enables him to read his pre-primers and primer fluently; he will also use his ever-growing stock of sight words as a basis for understanding the relation between letters and sounds (phonetic analysis) and the function of root words, inflectional endings, prefixes, and suffixes (structural analysis). These understandings will enable him to attach sound

Importance of an ever-increasing sight vocabulary

and meaning to many unfamiliar printed words while reading. At Primer or Book One level when the child has a
sight vocabulary of one hundred to one hundred fifty words,
he begins to attack new words on his own through the use
of word analysis. Even so, throughout the primary grades
and until a child can use a dictionary, the teacher should
continue to present as sight words those new words that
the young reader could not be expected to attack independently because (1) he has not yet developed the pre-
requisite skills of phonetic and structural analysis or (2)
the new words do not lend themselves to word analysis
(*aisle, whose, cough,* for example). The teacher will also
continue to present as a sight word any word whose pronunciation and meaning are likely to be unfamiliar.

One of the ways that a basic reading program ensures
mastery of a stock of sight words (and later of new words
that children figure out independently or look up in a dictionary) is by a planned, sequential pattern of introducing
and maintaining vocabulary. For example, in one primer
that is widely used there is never more than one new word
on a page and never more than five new words in a story.
Once a word has been introduced, it is repeated at least
nine times at spaced intervals in the book, the first five uses
being close together as an aid to mastery. Furthermore,
words are not dropped but are repeated and maintained
in succeeding books in the series of basic readers. This
kind of control over the introduction and repetition of
printed words, especially in the primary grades, makes it
possible for children to bring to the level of instantaneous
perception a large number of highly useful words.

In addition to vocabulary control, an effective basic
reading program provides specific techniques for helping children remember sight words. It also assumes responsibility
for teaching pupils to figure out or analyze new words independently and to use the dictionary. In short, one of the

Vocabulary control as an aid to instantaneous word perception

major goals of reading instruction is to help children develop competence in perceiving printed words easily and efficiently. This can best be accomplished by developing the ability to remember word forms and to use context clues, word analysis, and the dictionary.

Memory of word form

When a printed word is completely familiar, we respond to it automatically and are scarcely aware of the details of its form. This kind of response is based on memory of word forms, one of the major word-perception abilities used in rapid, fluent reading. In most instances, memory of word forms is based on (1) the habit of scrutinizing new or relatively unfamiliar word forms, (2) the ability to call up a mental picture or image of a word form, (3) the association of meaning with printed words.

Before a child can remember a printed word and associate it correctly with its meaning (or meanings), he must look carefully at its details, noting how it differs in form from other printed words that he knows.

Scrutiny of word form

Even before a child begins to read, he prepares for scrutinizing printed words by looking carefully at pictured objects on many pages in books especially made to provide readiness for reading. He is led to note and discuss first gross and later minute differences in form, size, position, etc. In so doing, he acquires and refines a vocabulary for thinking about form and arrangement that he will soon apply to printed words. For example, children might be asked to look carefully at a row of pictured chairs that differ only in the way they are facing. As youngsters note and discuss which chair backs are *to the left* and *to the right*, they use the kind of scrutiny and vocabulary they will later use to notice and think about the difference between such letters as *b* and *d* and consequently between such words as *big* and *dig*, *bark* and *dark*.

When a child first begins to read, his attention is called to the spaces between words. He learns to look at a word from left to right; he not only makes gross discriminations between words on the basis of their general configuration but also notes the distinctive characteristics of words. Is the word long or short? Does it have letters that are tall or that extend below the line? The length of the word *grandfather*, the two *e*'s in *feet*, or the first and last letters in *happy* may be the visual characteristics that beginning readers use to identify these words.

As a child begins to encounter words that are very similar in appearance, he learns to compare their details and to note minute differences that distinguish one word from another. Words like *eat* and *cat*, *bean* and *bear*, *but* and *tub*, *then* and *than*, *from* and *form* may be easily confused by a child who is not looking closely or noting the serial order of letters. Because independent word analysis is based on close scrutiny of the arrangement of letters in a word, it is important that pupils form the habit early of comparing the details of printed words and of noting minute differences in form. Obviously, sensitivity to word meaning and sentence context must go hand in hand with such visual discriminations.

As a child matures in reading ability, he uses scrutiny of form to note relationships between such words as *courteous* and *discourteous*, even though the longer word may contain a prefix or suffix with which he is not yet familiar. Words like *different* and *difference*, *establish* and *establishment*, *friend*, *unfriendly*, and *friendship*, he decides, are related not only in form but in meaning.

The ability to call up a clear visual image (a mental picture) of a known word is closely related to the habit of scrutinizing word forms to remember details. The child who has carefully observed the details of a known word can usually develop the ability to call up a mental image

Imagery of word form

of that word and to compare its form with that of a word that is before him in print.

In the early stages of reading when a child sees the word *looking* and thinks of *look* with *ing* added or sees *pick* and thinks, "That word looks like *stick* except at the beginning," a part of a word calls to his mind a known visual form. Then, too, young readers often use the initial consonant as a clue to the whole word. The initial consonant *r*, for example, combined with meaning clues from a picture may be all that a child needs to recognize the word *red* in the context "a big red car."

Children learn early to rely on consonant letters as quick clues to recognizing words, since consonants form the distinguishing framework of most words. The ease with which one can image total words from consonant letters alone or from other kinds of partial word forms is illustrated by the following:

Sh_ p_t tw_ n_ck_ls _n h_r b_nk.

She is saving money for a birthday present.

As a child progresses, he becomes adept at using imagery of known word forms to help him identify new words. He may recognize the new word *bump* because, as he scrutinizes it, he compares it with his mental image of the known word *jump*. Later, derived forms like *unconcern, adaptation, brilliancy* arouse in his mind images of their roots *concern, adapt, brilliant*. If he misreads a word (*contact* for *contract*, for example), ability to compare his mental image of the word *contact* with his scrutiny of the printed word *contract*, coupled with meaning clues, helps him correct his error.

The ability to image word forms enables a child to think of words that illustrate a particular language understanding or principle. For example, experience with many two-syllable words like *otter, fellow, rudder,* and *channel* helps children generalize that two like consonant letters following the first vowel letter in a word are a visual clue to a short vowel sound in an accented first syllable. Once pupils have made this generalization, ability to image known word forms should help them think of other two-syllable words that illustrate this visual clue to accent and vowel sound.

Association of meaning with word form

If every time a child sees or hears a word in different contexts he associates meaning with it, he automatically strengthens his memory of that word. He might, for example, see the word *line* many times before encountering a sentence like "The driver grabbed the lines and shouted to the horses," which requires the reader to associate the meaning "reins" with the word *lines.* Only as a child has many opportunities to encounter familiar words used with new meanings and to meet totally new words will he increase his speaking and reading vocabularies.

Before children begin to read, a teacher helps them strengthen and increase their associations of meaning with spoken words. For example, with the stimulus of pictured situations and their teacher's skillful questions, pupils reinforce understanding of such necessary but abstract words as *good, kind, funny,* and *selfish.*

In the initial stages of learning to read, a child is required to associate only known meanings with printed words; for in his beginning books he meets only printed forms that stand for words he has heard and spoken for a long time. Most of these words have fairly concrete meanings and denote action (*come, run*) and position (*here, there, in*) or name things and people (*car, Mother*).

Before long, however, a youngster begins to encounter words that are not in his speaking vocabulary. Such words, of course, should be used in oral discussion before pupils are asked to identify them in print. A third-grader, for example, may find authors using the word *scurry* instead of *run*, *alarm* instead of *frighten*. As he adds such words to his reading vocabulary, he often adds them to his speaking vocabulary. At the same time he is learning new meanings for familiar word forms. A city child may know the meaning of "fair play" and "fair weather" but may need an explanation of *fair* in the phrase "the county fair."

Throughout the middle grades, children's associations of meaning with words not only increase rapidly but are sharpened and refined. As sensitivity to shades of meaning develops, boys and girls begin to notice how an author uses particular words to evoke vivid imagery or emotional response. Each of the words *peer*, *stare*, *gaze*, and *peek*, for example, denotes a different way of looking at someone or something. *Notorious* and *famous* both mean "well-known," but the first suggests unfavorable or undesirable qualities that the other does not.

At middle- and upper-grade levels, through discussion of real and fictional situations, pupils become sensitive to the meaning of abstract terms like *responsibility*, *loyalty*, *ingenuity*, and *brotherhood*. Many children become curious about words, mull them over, and make deliberate efforts to add them to their speech.

Context clues

The reader who seeks and uses context clues is demanding meaning from the printed page. The use of context clues is based on two understandings of language: (1) a word may have more than one meaning (and pronunciation); (2) meaning (and sometimes pronunciation) must be determined in light of context. Only through the use of context clues can a reader associate appropriate meaning with a visual form like *bank*, as the phrases "money in the bank," "on the bank of the stream," "bank the fire," and "the third bank of seats" prove. Similarly, meaning and pronunciation of words like *tear, wind, wound,* and *bow* depend on the context in which they are used—"a tear in the eye," "a tear in a coat," "to tear down a building."

Through the use of pictures at the pre-reading level, children are trained to expect meaning from books. The guidance suggested for many pages in reading-readiness books promotes the kind of thinking that children must engage in if they are to use context clues while reading. One procedure frequently employed is to ask pupils what they think will happen next in a story.

At early reading levels meaning clues furnished by pictures and sentence context are especially valuable to a child as aids to the identification of printed words. A picture of three horses on a page may help the young reader identify the words *three horses* in a story. Should he misread the word *cat* by calling it *eat* in the sentence "Tom fed the cat," awareness of context helps him correct his error. As soon as a child learns to associate sounds with some of the letters, he uses context clues to check phonetic analysis. The only way, for example, that he can be sure which sound the letters *oo* stand for in the new word *foot* or *boot* is to ask himself, "Does this sound like a word I know, and does it make sense in the sentence?" Very early, then, children learn to combine scrutiny of form and phonetic clues with context clues and to use the latter as the final check on their identification of new words.

By about third grade most children use the context of both sentence and paragraph to figure out meanings that they have not previously associated with a printed word. They also use context clues to check variant meanings of prefixes and suffixes. When a child first learns the prefix *un-*, for example, he may assume that it always means "not." However, meaning clues tell him that in the context "The boy untied his shoes" the derived form *untied* does not mean "did not tie" but rather denotes an action opposite to that expressed in the root word *tie*. As his vocabulary grows, a child is increasingly able to use context clues to discriminate between variant meanings and uses of word forms like *pound* and *light* and between forms like *close* and *lead* whose meanings and pronunciations can be determined only in light of context ("close a door," "close to the door"; "heavy as lead," "lead a band").

In the middle and upper grades (indeed, throughout life) a reader continues to use context clues (pictorial and verbal) to check word analysis, to discriminate between similar word forms, and to derive new meanings independently. He uses context clues to determine the accent as well as the meaning of many words—*per'mit, per mit'; ob'ject, ob ject'; con'duct, con duct'*, etc. When a pupil begins to use a dictionary, he learns that he must use context clues to choose the appropriate definition of a word.

Experience soon teaches the alert reader that an unfamiliar word may be defined or explained in subsequent context. He discovers, too, that the general context or subject matter of a selection is a clue to the meaning of many words. For example, the word *pitcher, batter, plate,* or *rhubarb* would mean one thing in an article about baseball and something quite different in a cookbook.

[Context clues are perhaps the most important single aid to word perception.] Regardless of whether a child identifies a printed word quickly or stops to figure it out, he must be sure that it makes sense in the sentence. The youngster who is satisfied to read "Tim went into the horse" for "Tim went into the house" is obviously not using context clues. However, we should not forget that scrutiny of form must accompany the use of meaning clues. Careful scrutiny of the details of form helps children remember words; and, like the use of context clues, it is fundamental to word analysis.

Word analysis

Word analysis involves analyzing an unfamiliar printed word for clues to its sound and meaning. Frequently instantaneous word perception is blocked by a word that a child cannot readily identify from a glance at its configuration and by the use of context clues. When this happens, he should have at his command systematic methods of attacking the unfamiliar word. If the word is in his speech, the child's ability to apply what he has learned about word analysis will often enable him to identify what at first glance appeared to be a totally strange word form.

Word analysis is of two kinds—structural and phonetic. The two are interrelated and are used in combination to attack a new word. A young reader, seeing a word like *leaf* or *buzz* for the first time, uses structural analysis when he decides that the word has no inflectional ending, prefix, or suffix. He is then ready to use phonetic analysis to arrive at its pronunciation.

Frequently, of course, the new words that children encounter are inflected or derived forms. Suppose, for example, a second-grader encounters in context the new word *neatly* ("new" in the sense that he has never before seen it in print). If he has had systematic training in word analysis, he has learned to scrutinize the total word form for familiar meaning units—a root word, an inflectional ending, a suffix (structural analysis). His scrutiny of the word *neatly* reveals the familiar suffix *-ly*. The child then mentally "takes off" the suffix and searches for clues to the sound of the root word (phonetic analysis). He has learned that when two vowel letters occur together in a word, the first often stands for a long vowel sound and the second is silent. Applying this principle, he comes up with the correct pronunciation of the root *neat* to which he now reattaches the suffix *-ly*. Once he has identified the word *neatly*, he recognizes that it is one he has heard and used many times. The stumbling block in the sentence has been removed; he is free to go on interpreting the printed page. To sum up, the child has successfully used structural and phonetic analysis to identify a word on his own while reading.

As has been noted, structural analysis is the means by which a child identifies meaningful parts of words—

Structural analysis

roots, inflectional endings, prefixes, and suffixes. Ability to use structural analysis is based on two fundamental understandings of language. One of these is that a root word retains one of its basic meanings in inflected and derived forms and in compounds. For example, one meaning of the root word *play* is present in its inflected forms *plays* and *playing;* in its derived forms *replay* and *player;* in the compounds *plaything* and *playmate.* The other understanding fundamental to structural analysis is that prefixes, suffixes, and inflectional endings are meaningful parts of words. For example, in the derived form *unable* the prefix *un-* means "not"; in the derived form *unwrap* it means "the opposite of." The suffix *-er* often means "a person or thing that _____," as in the derived forms *singer* and *freezer.* The endings *-s* and *-es* may mean "more than one," as in the inflected forms *boys* and *bushes.*

The first structural elements, other than root words, that most children learn to recognize in print are such simple endings as *-s, -ed, -ing* added to known roots. (Chapter Three, pages 53-62, contains a discussion of the major skills and understandings involved in structural analysis and of the sequence in which they are presented.)

Children use phonetic analysis to associate sounds with the letters in printed words and hence to derive the pronunciation of words. Although English spelling is often

inconsistent, there are clues to pronunciation in the spelling of the majority of words—certain types of letter patterns that occur repeatedly. These clues should be presented gradually and systematically as soon as children know a fair number of printed words that illustrate how the clues to sound function.

Ability to use phonetic analysis is based on two fundamental understandings of the relationship between spoken and written language—understandings that children acquire over a period of years as their reading vocabularies increase. One is that consonants, vowels, and accent are basic elements of sound (phonemes) which, when blended in innumerable ways, make words that express meaning. Notice, for example, how changing one consonant or vowel sound or shifting the accent alters meaning in these pairs of words: *run, sun; hat, hut; ob'ject, ob ject'*. The other understanding basic to phonetic analysis is that in printed words there are certain visual clues that aid in determining consonant sounds, vowel sounds, syllabic divisions, and accent. For example:

When final *e* follows the letter *c* or *g*, *c* usually stands for the *s* sound and *g* for the *j* sound, as in the words *dance* and *huge*.

A single vowel letter in the middle of a one-syllable word or accented syllable usually stands for a short vowel sound, as in *had* and *lad'der*.

Two like consonant letters in the middle of a two-syllable word are a clue to an accented first syllable and to a short vowel sound in that syllable, as in *hap'pen, bliz'zard*, and *ten'nis*.

An easy way for children to start using phonetic analysis is to substitute one initial consonant for another in attacking a one-syllable word. A child who has learned to associate sound with most of the consonant letters can identify in context the printed word *hall*, for example, if he knows the word *ball*. (In Chapter Three, pages 34-53, the major skills and understandings of phonetic analysis and the sequence in which they are presented are discussed in detail.)

The dictionary

There are many unfamiliar words that children encounter in their reading—especially from middle-grade levels on—to which the application of structural and phonetic analysis will be of little or no help. Word analysis breaks down when an unfamiliar printed word is not in a child's vocabulary. If he has never heard or used the word, he will have to ask someone how it is pronounced and what it means or consult a dictionary. Then, too, some words do not lend themselves to word analysis. If, for example, you had never seen in print the words *sough, hough, sou, chamois,* and *patois,* would you be able to identify them through word analysis?

The dictionary may be used in two ways as an aid in identifying unknown words encountered in reading. It may serve as a check on the meaning and pronunciation of a word that the reader has tentatively arrived at through the use of context clues and word analysis. Or it may be the only efficient method of determining the meaning and pronunciation of an unfamiliar word.

The dictionary, then, is an indispensable aid to word perception as soon as children begin to encounter numbers of words whose pronunciations, meanings, and printed forms are unfamiliar. We must remember, however, that a dictionary is likely to be a mysterious and formidable volume unless children are taught how to use it. Even though the dictionary is not usually introduced until fourth grade, the understandings pupils in the primary grades acquire about the variant meanings of words, the use of context clues, and the use of structural and phonetic analysis prepare them for learning how to use the dictionary. (For a discussion of specific skills and understandings necessary to successful use of the dictionary, see Chapter Three, pages 62-65, and Chapter Seven.)

The importance of word analysis

Thus far we have discussed what is involved in reading and have noted that word perception (attaching sound and meaning to printed words) is a very important component of the reading process. We have also discussed the four major aids to word perception—memory of word form, context clues, word analysis, and the dictionary. The remainder of this book, with the exception of the last chapter on the dictionary, will be devoted to word analysis, the means by which a child learns to attack unfamiliar printed forms that represent familiar spoken words.

When we remember that the average child in first grade uses hundreds, even thousands, of words in his speech, we realize what an impossible task it would be to expect him to learn the printed form of each one of these words as a separate item. It is not only impossible but unnecessary, since our written language operates on an alphabetic principle. That is, twenty-six letters in various combinations and patterns stand for the sounds in spoken words. If children are to read independently, they must become familiar with the clues to sounds (consonant sounds, vowel sounds, and accent) that occur in the spelling of words. Unless youngsters learn how to analyze words—to see how letters are used to represent sounds, to recognize root words, endings, prefixes, and suffixes as meaningful parts of words—they will be reduced to guessing when they encounter unfamiliar printed words.

Word analysis is not the "be-all and end-all" of word perception, but it is an important means to that end. To deprive a child of the skills and understandings that enable him to figure out new words on his own while reading is to retard him in reading. A good reading program not only helps children acquire these skills and understandings but also provides youngsters with many opportunities to apply them. For example, there are books in which all the new words can be attacked independently by children who have acquired the skills of structural and phonetic analysis that have been presented by a given level. Such books give young readers a chance to clinch their newly acquired skills while reading interesting stories and provide the teacher with a realistic way of measuring progress.

The ultimate goals in word perception are (1) to bring to the level of instantaneous perception a maximum number of highly useful words that are common to different types of materials that a child wants and needs to read and (2) to develop understandings, skills, and abilities that enable him to attack unfamiliar words independently and thus be on his own in reading. This book, as its title indicates, is primarily concerned with the second goal. By discussing in detail what is involved in a program in word analysis, Chapter Three shows how this second goal may be realized.

Chapter three | A program
in word analysis

A teacher of reading might well ask such questions as "What skills and understandings should be developed in a good program in word analysis? In what sequence should these skills and understandings be developed? Why is a teaching sequence necessary?" It is the purpose of this chapter to answer such questions by describing a program in word analysis in some detail. For most children, this program will probably encompass grades one through eight. It may also be used with high-school students who have not acquired independence in recognizing printed words.

An effective program in word analysis

As we have noted in Chapter Two, word analysis entails careful scrutiny of an unfamiliar word (1) to determine whether it has an ending, prefix, or suffix (structural analysis) and (2) to identify visual clues to its pronunciation (phonetic analysis). The two types of analysis, although shown on separate charts (pages 39 and 55) and discussed separately in this chapter, should not be thought of as isolated parts of word analysis. A child learns to combine structural and phonetic analysis as he attacks new words. He develops the habit of scrutinizing an unfamiliar word to see whether it is a root word or a root word plus a known structural element before using phonetic analysis to arrive at the pronunciation of the word. In this chapter, however, phonetic analysis is discussed before structural analysis, one reason being that at early levels there is much emphasis on hearing sounds in spoken words and on associating these sounds with letters in printed words.

An effective program in word analysis should be carefully planned to develop in sequence the skills and understandings that enable a child to attack independently unfamiliar printed words that are in his oral vocabulary. Obviously, the program should progress from the simple to the complex. In phonetic analysis, for example, a child should first learn to identify a given sound before he is asked to associate it with any letter. He should then learn to associate that sound with the letter (or letters) that most commonly represents it before he is expected to associate this sound with other letters. For example, he should associate the sound heard at the beginning of *fat* with the letter *f* before he is expected to associate this sound with the letters *ph* and *gh* (*phone, laugh*).

The skills and understandings taught at any level should be basic to those that follow and should keep pace with the kinds of words that a child meets in his reading. For example, a second-grader needs to be able to analyze words like *earliest* and *north* but not words like *repetitious* and *unanimity*. A seventh- or eighth-grader, however, should be capable of analyzing the last two words.

A good program is based on a scientific knowledge of the language and never introduces a "gimmick" or "rule"

Proceeds from simple to complex

Keeps pace with children's needs

Is based on a scientific knowledge of the language

that the child has to unlearn as he progresses in reading. For example, the letters *ap* may "say" (ap) in many words like *cap, map,* and *lap.* But because of syllable division and accent in longer words (*apron, maple, approach,* for example) this "rule" certainly cannot be applied to many words of more than one syllable.

Guides children in forming generalizations

The understandings that children apply in analyzing words should not be presented as rules. They should be generalizations that pupils make under guidance while studying known words that illustrate a given understanding. For example, instead of being told that in one-syllable words a single vowel letter usually stands for a short vowel sound unless the letter comes at the end of the word (*end, wet, we*), children should be helped to make this generalization for themselves after they have studied the arrangement of vowel and consonant letters in known words. They should be encouraged, too, to find words in a story they have just read that illustrate or support the generalization.

Provides for application of generalizations

After children have made a generalization on the basis of words that they recognize in print, they should have many opportunities through guided exercises and through specially prepared materials to apply it to new words in context. Only then will they be likely to establish the habit of trying to analyze unfamiliar words that they encounter in independent reading.

Growth in the use of phonetic analysis

Essential abilities

Phonetic analysis is a means by which a child figures out the pronunciation of an unfamiliar printed word. It requires ability to (1) hear and identify consonant sounds, vowel sounds, syllables, and accent, (2) associate vowel and consonant sounds with letters of the alphabet, (3) use visual clues in printed words that aid in determining consonant and vowel sounds, syllabic divisions, and accent, (4) blend consonant and vowel sounds into syllables and syllables into meaningful word wholes with appropriate accent.

Obviously children neither acquire nor master the major abilities mentioned above all at one time or in a short period of time. Careful consideration of these abilities leads to the conclusion that the order in which the phonetic elements are taught is an important factor in determining the kind of word analysis that can be used at any level of growth. In keeping with the principle of proceeding from the simple to the complex, it would seem that consonants should be taught before vowels and that vowels should be taught on the basis of one-syllable words before accent and its effect on vowel sounds can be introduced. Let us consider some of the reasons for presenting consonants, vowels, and accent in this sequence.

Sequential introduction of phonetic elements and development of abilities

In English there is not a one-to-one correspondence between consonant and vowel sounds and the letters of the alphabet that represent them in printed words. We have only twenty-six letters in our alphabet to represent many more sounds. Obviously some letters must represent more than one sound. The letter *a*, for example, represents the vowel sounds heard in the words *hat, hate, hard, care, all, any,* and *alone*. The same sound may also be represented by different letters. Notice how many different spellings represent the same vowel sound in the words *age, aid, gaol, gauge, say, break, vein, eight,* and *they*.

Consonants are taught first

There is a more regular correspondence between consonant sounds and letters than between vowel sounds and letters. It is easy for a child to associate a consonant sound with a given letter because most consonant letters represent only one sound. When a child sees the letter *b, f, k, l, m, n, p,* or *t*, for example, in a word, he knows what sound to associate with that letter. It is easier for a child to acquire the understandings given below on the basis of consonants rather than vowels, since the relationship between consonant sound and letter is less complex than it is between vowel sound and letter.

> A letter may represent more than one sound, for example, the g in *give* and in *giant;* the c in *cake* and in *cent;* the s in *this* and in *is.*

> The same sound may be represented by different letters, for example, the initial sound in *germ* and in *jump;* the initial sound in *can* and in *keep.*

> Letters may be silent in words, for example, the k in *knot;* the w in *wren;* the l in *talk.*

Consonant letters are important in word perception because they form the distinguishing framework of printed words. For example, look at the two lines that are given below. Which of the two can you read easily?

W_ L k_d th_ p_gs _nd ch_ck_ns. ✓

__e _i__ _a_ _u__ u_ _o_e. ✓

Vowel letters are omitted in the first line; in the second line consonant letters are omitted. The first line, "We liked the pigs and chickens," is easily read because the eye readily recognizes words from their distinguishing framework of consonant letters. But it is usually impossible to identify words from their vowel letters alone. Who would recognize the second line as "The wind can push us home"?

Another reason for teaching consonants first is that a knowledge of the sounds that even a few consonant letters commonly represent can be used almost immediately by a beginning reader to help him recognize unfamiliar printed words in context. He may use just the initial consonant and meaning clues to identify words like those that are italicized in the phrases "*fat* pig," "bat the *ball*," "house on the *hill*." Then, too, the first method of word attack that children can use profitably is that of substituting one initial consonant for another. A child who knows the word *get* or *pet* as a sight word, for example, can identify independently new words like *met*, *net*, and *wet* by comparing them mentally with the known word and substituting within the word whole the sound represented by each initial consonant. This method of word analysis is called consonant substitution.

Vowels are taught next

When children can discriminate between vowel sounds (long, short, *r*-controlled, etc.) and associate them with vowel letters, they see that any vowel letter stands for more than one sound. They should then learn how to determine which vowel sound to try first in an unfamiliar word. Here again a knowledge of consonants is essential, since it is often the vowel-consonant pattern that furnishes the clue to vowel sound. To determine the vowel sound in a one-syllable word, for example, a child learns to examine not only the vowel letter or letters but also any consonant letters that may follow. A consonant letter after the only vowel letter in a word usually provides a clue to the vowel sound (a "short" sound or an "*r*-controlled" one, as in *hem* and *her*). The lack of a consonant letter is usually a clue to a "long" vowel sound, as in *he*.

Accent is the last phonetic element to be learned

When a child can associate appropriate vowel and consonant sounds with the letters he sees in simple one-syllable words and can blend these sounds into word wholes, he is ready for the analysis of longer words. He should next learn to hear syllables and accent and should note how accent affects vowel sounds. As shown on the chart on page 39, in phonetic analysis a child uses visual clues to syllabication and to accent in analyzing two-syllable words. Later, to analyze multisyllabic words, he acquires understanding of patterns of accent and learns to use suffixes as clues to primary accent.

The chart on the next page shows how a child progresses in phonetic analysis from the analysis of one-syllable words to the analysis of complex derived forms. The types of words that children can be expected to analyze are shown at the left of the chart; at the right are shown increasingly mature methods of analyzing these words to determine their pronunciation.

Three major stages of progress in the use of phonetic analysis are indicated, and within each stage the most significant methods of analysis are shown. During the first stage children learn to attack one-syllable words, first by using consonant substitution and then by using visual clues to vowel sound. At the second stage of progress children learn to attack two-syllable words by using visual clues to syllabication and to accent. Pupils can then apply to the accented syllable the understandings of consonants and vowels that they acquired at the first stage of progress. During the third and most mature stage of progress pupils learn to analyze multisyllabic words by refining and extending their knowledge of consonants, vowels, and accent.

Of course children do not learn everything about phonetic analysis before learning to use structural analysis. Each stage of progress in the use of phonetic analysis is paralleled by a stage of progress in the use of structural analysis (see page 55). For example, at the first stage of progress in word analysis when a child is learning to associate consonant sounds with letters, he is also learning to identify roots and inflectional endings. As he develops understandings about vowel sounds and letters, he is learning to identify suffixes as units of meaning and to recognize roots in inflected or derived forms in which the spellings of the roots change.

A discussion follows of the major phonetic skills and understandings and of the way they function at each stage of progress shown on the chart.

Three major stages of progress in phonetic analysis

Stages of progress in phonetic and structural analysis parallel each other

Stages of progress in phonetic analysis

Types of words that can be attacked are shown at the left. Increasingly mature methods of analysis needed to study these words for clues to sound are shown at the right.

First stage

One-syllable words					that can be attacked by
let	(pet)	sad	(sat)		using consonant substitution
add	hi	arm	pain	wake	using visual clues
end	me	her	sleet	these	to vowel sound
hit	by	bird	tie	slide	
bus	go	hurt	hoe	cube	

(handwritten annotations: "end" with "1", "R", "2 V.", "silent e")

Second stage

Two-syllable words					that can be attacked by
	lad der	la dy	la dle		using visual clues
	slen der	me ter	peb ble		to syllabication
	tin der	ti ny	thim ble		and vowel sound
	mot to	mo tor	no ble		
cannon	nickel	ramble	explode	obtain	using visual clues
letter	jacket	eagle	parade	indeed	to accent and
furrow	buckle	bottle	provide	conceal	vowel sound
	regretted	competing	trumpeter		
	referring	refusal	traveling		*suffix*
	allotted	promoted	pivoted		

Third stage

Multisyllabic words				that can be attacked by
medicine	opossum	represent	appendicitis	identifying patterns
accident	determine	pioneer	encyclopedia	of accent
confident	intelligent	interrupt	electromagnet	
moment	momentous	triumph	triumphal	noting that accent
symbol	symbolic	harmony	harmonious	may shift in
popular	popularity	excel	excellence	a derived form
-ion	-ity	-ic or -ical		using suffixes
definition	nationality	symbolic		as visual clues
repetition	popularity	scientific	-ate	to primary accent
information	originality	historical	domesticate	
			certificate	
-ian	-ial	-ious	obligate	
Bostonian	torrential	laborious		
vegetarian	official	malicious		
politician	equatorial	repetitious		

First stage of progress

Readiness for phonetic analysis

Before children begin actual reading, they should have many experiences in listening to the sounds that occur in spoken words and in discriminating between them. For example, they should be able to distinguish between spoken words that do and do not rhyme and to contribute examples from their own vocabularies of words that rhyme with a word that the teacher pronounces. They should also be able to hear and to discriminate between initial, medial, and final sounds (phonemes) in spoken words. The teacher might say such pairs of sentences as those given below in which the difference in meaning is due to the difference in one phoneme in each pair. As she says a sentence, she asks pupils to point to the picture that describes what she says.

> The clown is standing on a wire.
> The clown is standing on a tire.
>
> Bob is holding a rock.
> Bob is holding a rake.
>
> The kitten is jumping over a puddle.
> The kitten is jumping over a puzzle.
>
> Tom is looking at a map.
> Tom is looking at a man.

Auditory perception of significant sounds is basic to phonetic analysis and should be emphasized throughout a program in word analysis.

Consonant substitution

As shown by the first examples given in the chart on page 39 (see below), the first use a child makes of phonetic analysis is dependent on his knowledge of consonants.

let (pet)	sad (sat)		using consonant substitution

As soon as a child can associate a few consonant sounds with the letters that represent them, he learns to analyze an Knowledge of consonants enables a beginning reader to attack words unfamiliar word that looks like a word he knows except for an initial or final consonant letter. For example, if a child knows the word *pet*, he can analyze the word *let* by noting that it looks like *pet* except for the first letter. He then substitutes the sound that the letter *l* represents for the initial consonant sound in *pet* and arrives at the pronunciation of *let*. If he knows the word *sat*, he can arrive at the pronunciation of *sad* by substituting the sound that the letter *d* represents for the final consonant sound in *sat*. This type of phonetic analysis is called consonant substitution. First-graders can learn this type of analysis and become proficient in its use.

To use consonant substitution effectively, a child must be able to recall the visual form of a word that is like the Known words are the basis of analysis word to be analyzed except for the initial or final consonant letter. He must also be able to associate a consonant sound with the initial or final consonant letter and to blend this sound with the remaining sounds in the word. Early in the first grade most children learn to recognize the printed forms of a number of words that can provide a basis for consonant substitution. As children study these sight words under guidance, they learn to associate consonant sounds with the letters that commonly represent them. At the same time pupils develop basic understandings about the relation of sound to printed symbol. They note that a consonant letter may stand for more than one sound (the *s* in *bus* and in *has*, for example) and that a consonant letter may be silent in a word (the *l* in *walk*, one of the *l*'s in *tell*, the *k* in *know*, for example).

A child should not establish the habit of analyzing a new word by sounding his way through it from left to right —letter by letter. Nor should he establish the habit of thinking of sounds in isolation rather than as parts of a word whole. One of the values of abundant practice in consonant substitution is that of developing the ability to blend sounds rapidly and smoothly into words. This blending of a consonant sound with the remaining sounds in a word provides readiness for the next level of growth in phonetic analysis—identifying a vowel sound in a one-syllable word and blending this sound with consonant sounds to make a meaningful word in context.

Consonant substitution provides practice in blending sounds

Visual clues to vowel sound

When a child has developed proficiency in associating consonant sounds with most of the letters that represent them and in using consonant substitution to attack printed words, he should next learn to associate vowel sounds with the letters that represent them. Working with known words, he learns to discriminate between vowel sounds (long, short, *r*-controlled, etc.) and to associate them with vowel letters. In so doing, he develops the understanding that all vowel letters represent more than one sound; the letter *i*, for example, may represent the vowel sound heard in *it*, *ice*, or *bird*. The child is now ready to learn which vowel sound to try first in an unfamiliar one-syllable word. As he does so, he develops awareness that it is often the relative position of consonant and vowel letter that furnishes the clue to vowel sound. Most children learn to use visual clues to vowel sound in the second grade.

A vowel letter represents more than one sound

To promote awareness of visual clues to vowel sound in the spelling of one-syllable words, the teacher writes a group of known words that illustrate one of the visual clues and asks pupils to listen to the vowel sound as they pronounce each word. Then children are encouraged to look beyond the vowel letter in each word to see whether they can discover the clue to vowel sound. Gradually, as pupils work with different groups of known words, they should learn to identify the visual clues to vowel sound

The spelling of a word often gives a clue to the vowel sound

illustrated by the groups of words shown on the section of the chart (page 39) that is reproduced below.

add	hi	arm	pain	wake	using visual clues
end	me	her	sleet	these	to vowel sound
hit	by	bird	tie	slide	
bus	go	hurt	hoe	cube	

Position as a clue to vowel sound

As pupils' attention is directed to the vowel and consonant letters in many known words like *add, at, end, egg, it, him, on, box, up, bus,* and *me, she, by, fly, go, no,* they see for themselves that a single vowel letter at the beginning or in the middle of a word is likely to stand for a short vowel sound. If the vowel letter occurs at the end of a word, it probably stands for a long vowel sound.

The consonant r as a clue to vowel sound

On the basis of known words like *arm, barn, park, her, herd, term, bird, girl, first, north, fort, corn, burn, curl, fur,* pupils note that if the consonant letter *r* follows the vowel letter, the vowel letter probably does not stand for a short vowel sound but for an *r*-controlled sound.

Two vowel letters together as a clue to vowel sound

By studying known words like *pain, sleet, goat, pay, key, beat, tie* in which there are two vowel letters together, pupils conclude that the first vowel letter usually represents a long vowel sound and the second vowel letter is silent.

Final e as a clue to vowel sound

On the basis of known words like *wake, ate, these, hide, ripe, note, home, cube,* and *use,* children are led to generalize that if there are two vowel letters in a word, one of which is final *e* preceded by a consonant letter, the first vowel letter usually represents a long vowel sound and the final *e* is silent.

When a child has become familiar with any one of these visual clues to vowel sound, he should be expected to use it to figure out the pronunciation of new one-syllable words that he encounters in his reading.

As a child associates vowel sounds with letters, he should extend to vowels the basic understandings that he has developed on the basis of consonants. For example, a letter may represent more than one sound as in *at, ate,* and *car;* the same sound may be represented by different letters as in *hike* and *my,* as in *her, bird,* and *burn,* as in *boy* and *toil;* letters may be silent in words, the final *e,* for example, in such words as *wake, slide, note.*

Children should be encouraged to extend their understanding of visual clues to vowel sound as their reading vocabularies increase. For example, on the basis of such known words as *else, pulse, dance, fringe,* and *twelve,* pupils should be able to generalize that two consonant letters plus final *e* following a single vowel letter are often a clue to a short vowel sound. Scrutiny of such groups of known words as *high, night, bright; kind, find, mind; old, cold, told* alerts pupils to spelling patterns that are additional clues to long vowel sounds.

Additional clues to vowel sound

Second stage of progress

Up to this point, children have applied their knowledge of consonant and vowel sounds and the letters that represent them primarily in the analysis of one-syllable words. If pupils are to progress in reading, they should learn how to apply visual clues to vowel sound in two-syllable words. To do so, they must learn how to divide printed words into syllables. For example, knowing that the first syllable in *ladder* is *lad* but that in *lady* and *ladle* it is *la* helps a reader know whether to try a long or short vowel sound first in these syllables.

Applying previous learnings to the syllable

Before children attempt to divide printed words into syllables, they should learn to hear syllables in spoken words and to identify a syllable as a word or a part of a word in which one vowel sound is heard. They should also become aware of the fact that in words of two or more syllables, one syllable is stressed or accented more than the other or others. When pupils become adept at discriminating be-

Hearing syllables, accent, and the schwa sound

tween accented and unaccented syllables in spoken words, attention should be focused on the vowel sound heard in the majority of unstressed syllables—the schwa sound. Through listening to themselves as they pronounce such known words as *sofa, problem, April, pilot,* and *circus,* pupils develop the understanding that any vowel letter may stand for the schwa sound in an unstressed syllable.

Visual clues to syllabication

When children can distinguish syllables in spoken words and can identify the accented ones, they are ready to deter-

Identifying a syllable visually mine syllabic divisions in printed words. Again, consonant letters play an essential part in visual analysis to determine pronunciation. By studying the vowel-consonant patterns in such groups of known words as those shown on the portion of the chart that is reproduced below, pupils note visual clues that aid in determining syllabic divisions.

lad der	la dy	la dle	using visual clues
slen der	me ter	peb ble	to syllabication
tin der	ti ny	thim ble	and vowel sound
mot to	mo tor	no ble	

As pupils pronounce words like *ladder, scamper, slender, mitten, winter, cotton, mustard,* and *puppet,* they note that a short vowel sound is heard in the first syllable of each. They know that in one-syllable words a vowel letter

Two consonant letters following the first vowel letter usually stands for a short vowel sound if it is followed by a consonant letter (other than *r*). Attention is next directed to the two consonant letters in the middle of each word, and children are led to see that the first of the two consonants probably ends the first syllable because they hear a

One consonant letter following the first vowel letter short vowel sound in that syllable. A similar study of words like *lady, meter, tiny, motor,* and *pupil,* in which a long vowel sound is heard in the first syllable, leads pupils to decide that if they see only one consonant letter after the first vowel letter in a word, that consonant letter probably begins the second syllable.

By noting the vowel sound in the first syllable of words like *ladle, pebble, rifle, thimble,* and *noble* and by scrutinizing the vowel-consonant patterns, pupils generalize that if a word ends in the letters *le* preceded by a consonant letter that consonant letter probably begins the second syllable. ✓

The letters le preceded by a consonant letter

As pupils progress, they will add other visual clues to syllabication to the major ones already noted. For example, on the basis of such known words as *cypress, apron, secret,* children learn that syllables in a word do not often break between consonant blends (*cy press, a pron, se cret*). On the basis of such known words as *cricket, buckle, chicken,* pupils are led to generalize that the letters *ck* go with the preceding vowel to form a syllable (*crick et, buck le, chick en*), and thus are a clue to short vowel sounds.

Additional clues to syllabication

As children learn to divide printed words into syllables, they should be developing two related understandings about accent: (1) accent affects vowel sounds, (2) visual clues that aid in determining vowel sound usually apply only to accented syllables. For example, although the letters *pa* form the first syllable of each of the words *paper* and *parole,* the letter *a* stands for a long vowel sound only in the word *paper,* in which the syllable *pa* is accented (pā′pər). In *parole* the *a* in the unaccented syllable *pa* stands for the schwa sound (pə rōl′). At this level pupils may determine which syllable to accent in an unfamiliar printed word by stressing first one syllable and then the other until they arrive at a pronunciation that "makes sense" in context.

Understanding that accent affects vowel sounds

Most children are now ready to build upon the understandings of accent mentioned in the preceding paragraph. The next level in phonetic analysis is concerned primarily with an understanding that is too often neglected in the teaching of word analysis—there are visual clues to accent in the spelling of many two-syllable words.

Visual clues to accent

Pupils who have acquired the phonetic understandings discussed so far should increase their knowledge of accent.

Determining the accented syllable They should now begin to notice clues to accent in the spelling of two-syllable root words and of inflected and derived forms of two-syllable roots. As they study such groups of known words as those shown on the section of the chart that is reproduced below, pupils are led to notice how certain vowel-consonant patterns furnish clues to accent.

cannon	nickel	ramble	explode	obtain	using visual clues
letter	jacket	eagle	parade	indeed	to accent and
furrow	buckle	bottle	provide	conceal	vowel sound
	regretted	competing	trumpeter		
	referring	refusal	traveling		
	allotted	promoted	pivoted		

Visual clues to accent are extensions of the visual clues to vowel sound and to syllabication that pupils learned to use at previous levels. By pronouncing such known words as *cannon, letter, puppet, furrow*, and by scrutinizing the vowel and consonant pattern in the spelling of the words, pupils **Two like consonant letters following the first vowel letter** note that two like consonant letters following the first vowel letter are a clue to an accented first syllable and to a short vowel sound in that syllable (except when the vowel sound is controlled by *r*).

By pronouncing and noting the spelling of such known words as *nickel, jacket, buckle*, pupils see that the letters *ck* **The letters ck** are a clue to an accented first syllable and to a short vowel sound in that syllable.

A study of such known words as *ramble, eagle, bottle* **A consonant letter plus le** leads pupils to note that when the final syllable ends in *le* preceded by a consonant, that syllable is usually unaccented.

Two visual clues to long vowel sound are utilized as clues to accent. As pupils study such words as *explode, parade, obtain, indeed,* they are led to note that final *e* preceded by a single consonant letter or two vowel letters together in the last syllable are clues to an accented final syllable and to a long vowel sound in that syllable.

Final *e* or two vowel letters together

With such words as *regretted, propeller, allotted, referring,* pupils not only extend their previous phonetic learnings to include accent but they combine their phonetic knowledge with a knowledge of structural analysis. They use two like consonant letters before an ending or suffix as a clue to an accented final syllable in the root word and to a short vowel sound in that syllable (except when the vowel sound is controlled by *r*).

Two like consonant letters before an ending or suffix

With separate groups of known words like *competing, refusal, promoter,* and *trumpeter, traveling, pivoted,* pupils note that a single consonant letter following a single vowel letter before an ending or suffix (that begins with a vowel) may be a clue either to a dropped final *e* and to a long vowel sound in an accented final syllable of the root or to an unaccented final syllable of the root. Pupils note that this single consonant letter is never a clue to a short vowel sound in an accented final syllable of the root.

A single consonant letter before an ending or suffix

In preparation for the third stage of progress, pupils should be led to note patterns of accent in two-syllable words and in compounds and to hear and identify secondary accent. Pairs of sentences like those given below illustrate a common pattern of accent in two-syllable words. As pupils study such sentences, they note that the accent in words like *record, contest, object, permit* can be determined only in context (when used as nouns, such words are accented on the first syllable; when used as verbs, on the second).

Patterns of accent in two-syllable roots and in compounds

I keep a *record* of what I earn.
I *record* my earnings in this book.

Joe entered the *contest.*
We did not *contest* the judge's decision.

By pronouncing such words as *homesick, railroad, steamboat, waterfall, sharpshooter,* children are led to note that a common pattern of accent in compounds is that of a primary accent on or within the first word and a secondary accent on or within the second word (*home'sick', rail'road', steam'boat', wa'ter fall', sharp'shoot'er*). With compounds, pupils are introduced to secondary accent, which they need to identify before they progress to the phonetic analysis of multisyllabic words.

Third stage of progress

Accent and the multisyllabic word

By the end of the second stage of progress, children should have a basic knowledge of how consonants, vowels, and accent function in words and should be able to use this knowledge to analyze independently unfamiliar printed words of two syllables. In the middle grades pupils encounter increasing numbers of words that contain more than two syllables. Before they can successfully analyze such multisyllabic words, they will need to learn more about accent. A trial-and-error method of determining the accented syllable in a multisyllabic word can easily end in discouragement. Too often the very length of a "long" word discourages a young reader, and he will skip the word even though it is in his oral vocabulary. The knowledge that there are patterns of accent in multisyllabic words just as there are visual clues in many two-syllable words can help him identify accented syllables in unfamiliar printed words. As a native speaker of English he unconsciously uses these patterns of accent. He needs only to be made aware of them so that he can use them in analyzing unfamiliar multisyllabic words.[1]

---

[1]Any English word spoken in isolation possesses a definite stress pattern. In running speech the accent pattern of an individual word may or may not be preserved. Also there are regional variations in accent. For the purpose of word attack, however, the stress pattern of an individual word is important if the word is to be recognized.

Patterns of accent in multisyllabic words

The groups of words shown on the section of the chart that is reproduced below illustrate basic patterns of accent that pupils need to identify if they are to analyze multisyllabic words successfully.

medicine	opossum	represent	appendicitis	identifying patterns
accident	determine	pioneer	encyclopedia	of accent
confident	intelligent	interrupt	electromagnet	

By first studying such groups of known words as *medicine, accident, confident, opossum, determine, intelligent* (each word should contain only a primary accent), pupils learn that in words of three or more syllables the first or second syllable is accented (*med′i cine, ac′ci dent, con′fi dent, o pos′sum, de ter′mine, in tel′li gent*).

Pupils are next led to note that in such words as *represent, pioneer, interrupt, appendicitis, encyclopedia, electromagnet* the accent on the first or second syllable is a secondary one (*rep′re sent′, pi′o neer′, ap pen′di ci′tis, en cy′clo pe′di a, e lec′tro mag′net*). Attention is also called to the fact that there is one unaccented syllable between the two accented syllables. Thus pupils become aware of another pattern of accent in multisyllabic words—a secondary accent (on the first or second syllable), an unstressed syllable, a primary accent. Knowledge of this pattern of accent becomes especially useful when pupils learn to use suffixes as visual clues to primary accent.

As boys and girls progress, their attention should be called to other patterns of accent in multisyllabic words. For example, they will encounter some words like *superintendent* and *representation* in which there are two unstressed syllables between the secondary and the primary accent (*su′per in tend′ent, rep′re sen ta′tion*). They will likely encounter a few words like *individuality* and *super-*

An accent (primary or secondary) occurs on the first or second syllable in multisyllabic words

ficiality in which there are two secondary accents (*in'di vid'- u al'i ty, su'per fi'ci al'i ty*). They will note also that in such words as *secretary, supervisor, necessary* the primary accent occurs first, then an unstressed syllable followed by a syllable that carries a secondary accent (*sec're tar'y, su'per vi'sor, nec'es sar'y*).

From this point on in phonetic analysis, you will notice that the understandings of accent are all applicable to derivatives. This is just another instance of what has already been stated—structural and phonetic analysis cannot be thought of as completely separate strands. However, the skills and understandings discussed here are primarily phonetic, since they help a reader get the pronunciation of words.

Accent may shift in a derived form

Shifting accent in derivatives

After pupils have become familiar with patterns of accent in multisyllabic words, they are led to compare the accented syllables in root words with those in their derived forms. As they do so, pupils will note that in many instances the root does not retain its original pronunciation in a derived form. Accent often shifts, and as a result vowel sounds often change; for example, note the roots and their derived forms that are given on the section of the chart that is reproduced below.

moment	momentous	triumph	triumphal	noting that accent
symbol	symbolic	harmony	harmonious	may shift in
popular	popularity	excel	excellence	a derived form

By listening to the accented syllables in pairs of words like those shown on the chart, pupils develop the understanding that although the root in a derived form retains some kind of accent, the primary accent within the root word often shifts to another syllable when a suffix is added (*mo'ment, mo men'tous; sym'bol, sym bol'ic; pop'u lar, pop'u lar'i ty;* etc.). Pupils should also note that a shift in accent causes a change in vowel sound. These understandings, coupled with knowledge of common accent patterns, are basic to the use of visual clues to primary accent in multisyllabic words.

Suffixes as visual clues to primary accent

Clues to accent in derivatives

In the upper grades, boys and girls are sure to encounter many derivatives that look formidable and hard to pronounce. However, many of these derivatives are not difficult to say if a person knows where to put the primary accent. As the derivatives on the last section of the chart indicate (see below), eight commonly used suffixes are reliable clues to primary accent.

Boys and girls learn to recognize visual clues to primary accent in the same way that they learned to recognize other visual clues—on the basis of known words. When pupils know many words that end in the suffixes shown on the section of the chart below, they are ready to note that there are clues to pronunciation in many derived forms.

-ion	*-ity*	*-ic* or *-ical*		using suffixes
definition	nationality	symbolic		as visual clues
repetition	popularity	scientific	*-ate*	to primary accent
information	originality	historical	domesticate	
			certificate	
-ian	*-ial*	*-ious*	obligate	
Bostonian	torrential	laborious		
vegetarian	official	malicious		
politician	equatorial	repetitious		

By listening for the primary accent as they pronounce a group of words ending in one of the suffixes shown on the chart, for example, *definition, repetition, information, exhibition, introduction, recitation, comprehension,* pupils are led to generalize that the primary accent usually falls on the syllable before the suffix *-ion.* In like manner, pupils learn that (1) the primary accent usually falls on the syllable before the suffix *-ity, -ic, -ical, -ian, -ial,* or *-ious* and (2) the primary accent usually falls on the second syllable before the suffix *-ate.*

Anyone who knows these clues to primary accent in derivatives is not likely to be discouraged by such "tongue twisters" as *unanimity, inimical, tragedian, ignominious, enigmatical,* and *managerial.*

Growth in the use of structural analysis

Because many words that pupils encounter at all grade levels are inflected and derived forms, ability to use structural analysis is essential. Based on visual scrutiny of total word form, structural analysis is the means by which a reader identifies meaning units within a word and associates total meaning with an inflected or derived form.

Identifying meaning units within word wholes

Visual scrutiny of a word may reveal that it is (1) a root word—*work,* for example; (2) a root word plus an inflectional ending—*works, working, worked;* (3) a root word plus a prefix—*rework, overwork,* or plus a suffix—*worker, workable,* or plus both a prefix and suffix—*unworkable;* (4) a compound—*workshop, homework.*

As a child learns to identify roots and affixes, he gradually develops two understandings that are basic to structural analysis: (1) a root word retains its meaning in inflected, derived, and compounded forms, and (2) affixes are meaningful parts of words.

Three major stages of progress in structural analysis

The chart on page 55 shows how pupils progress in structural analysis from identifying root words and simple inflectional endings to using affixes and the position of words in context as quick clues to meaning. Three major stages of progress are indicated. The types of words that pupils can be expected to analyze structurally at each stage are shown at the left of the chart. The methods of analysis are shown at the right.

Each of the three major stages of progress in structural analysis parallels a stage of progress in phonetic analysis. During the first stage of progress, as a child learns to use phonetic analysis to attack one-syllable words, he learns to use structural analysis to identify root words, inflectional endings, and suffixes as meaning units. At the second stage of progress, while he is learning to analyze two-syllable words phonetically, he is learning to use structural analysis to identify prefixes as meaning units and is acquiring understanding of the grammatical function of suffixes.

As has been stated previously, when a child has completed the second stage of progress in phonetic analysis, he has acquired basic understandings of the way consonants, vowels, and accent function in words. By the end of the second stage of progress in structural analysis, a pupil has developed understandings of roots, inflectional endings, suffixes, and prefixes that are fundamental to structural analysis. At the third stage of progress, while pupils learn to analyze multisyllabic words for clues to their pronunciation (phonetic analysis), they are developing mature skills and understandings that enable them to analyze the structure of increasingly complex derivatives.

A discussion follows of the major skills and understandings of structural analysis and of the way they function at each stage of progress shown on the chart.

First stage of progress

Before children begin to read, their attention should be focused on hearing structural units in words and noting their function. Through the medium of pictures and guided oral language activities, pupils are prepared for structural analysis of printed words. For example, they become consciously aware that the sound (s) or (z) is added to count-

Readiness for structural analysis

Stages of progress in structural analysis

Types of words that can be analyzed are shown at the left. Increasingly mature methods of analysis needed to analyze the structure of these words are shown at the right.

First stage

Simple inflected, compound, and derived forms of known roots	that can be analyzed by
Inflected forms He *walks* to school with his *friends.* The cat ate the *dog's* food. She *washes* the *dishes.* We were *playing* ball when Mother *called.*	identifying root words and inflectional endings as meaning units
Compounds I lost my *raincoat* on the *playground.*	
Derived forms It was a *rainy* day. She spoke *softly.* The *farmer* drove to town.	identifying root words and suffixes as meaning units
Inflected forms bigger earliest baking *Derived forms* muddy busily driver	identifying the root in an inflected or derived form in which the spelling of the root changes

Second stage

Derived forms of known or unknown roots	that can be analyzed by
I was *unable* to *unlock* the door. It is *impossible* to cut the grass in an hour. A person who steals is *dishonest.*	identifying prefixes and root words as meaning units
We *publish* books for children. (verb) I am a *publisher* of children's books. (noun)	recognizing the grammatical function of suffixes as an aid to meaning

Third stage

More complex derived forms of words	that can be analyzed by
"negative" *prefixes* *noun-forming suffixes* incomplete unconscious interpreter suggestion irregular disapprove translator performance illegal nonstop darkness existence imperfect settlement growth	identifying affixes in terms of meaning or function
colony: colonial, precolonial, colonist, colonize, colonization *divide:* division, subdivision, divisible, indivisible, divisor	recognizing a root common to many derivatives in which pronunciation changes may occur
The *friendly* girl spoke *kindly* to the stranger. She works as an *assistant;* she is an *assistant* clerk. We watched the *rehearsal* of the *musical* comedy.	using position of words in sentences and word endings as clues to meaning

less words to indicate "more than one"—*cat, cats; pocket, pockets; dog, dogs; friend, friends.* Through listening to and using in their own speech such verb forms as *walks, walked, walking* and such forms of comparison as *big, bigger, biggest,* pupils also become aware that the endings *-s, -ed, -ing, -er,* and *-est* carry meaning.

Root words and inflectional endings as meaning units

The first use a child makes of structural analysis occurs when he meets printed words that are formed by the addition of simple endings to known words. For example, a child who has mastered *car* as a sight word reads "Tom saw two cars." *Cars* is a new printed word for him; but if he knows that *-s* is often added to a word, his visual survey should tell him that this is the word *car* with *-s* added to it and that *cars* means "more than one car."

| *Inflected forms* | He *walks* to school with his *friends.*
The cat ate the *dog's* food.
She *washes* the *dishes.*
We were *playing* ball when Mother *called.* | identifying root words
and inflectional endings
as meaning units |
| *Compounds* | I lost my *raincoat* on the *playground.* | |

As indicated on the first part of the chart (page 55), which is reproduced above, children first use structural analysis to identify root words and the inflectional endings *-s, -'s, -es, -ed,* and *-ing* as meaning units. For example, in the printed word *friends,* a child identifies the known root word *friend* and the inflectional ending *-s.* He recognizes that the ending *-s* added to the root word *friend* makes a word that means "more than one friend." He also recognizes that the *-s* added to *walk* in "He *walks* to school . . ." indicates something quite different because he uses such verb forms as "I *walk*" and "He *walks*" in his speech. The child also learns to identify known roots in compounds and

Known roots and simple endings

develops the understanding that two root words may combine their meanings to form a compound. If he can read the words *rain* and *coat*, for example, he should be able to identify the form and meaning of the compound *raincoat*.

Suffixes as meaning units

When a child is familiar with simple inflectional endings, he next learns to identify suffixes as meaningful parts of words. He also learns to recognize the inflectional endings *-er* and *-est* of comparison and develops the understanding that the spelling of a root word may change in an inflected or derived form. The section of the chart that is reproduced below illustrates this kind of growth in structural analysis.

Derived forms	It was a *rainy* day. She spoke *softly*. The *farmer* drove to town.			identifying root words and suffixes as meaning units
Inflected forms	bigger earliest baking	*Derived forms*	muddy busily driver	identifying the root in an inflected or derived form in which the spelling of the root changes

Such suffixes as *-y*, *-ly*, and *-er* of agent, which children encounter frequently in derived forms as they read, **Known roots and suffixes** may be used to develop understandings of suffixes as meaning units. For example, when such derivatives as *painter, farmer, toaster* are part of their reading vocabularies, children are led to note that the suffix *-er* is added to a root word to make a word that means "a person who_____" or "a thing that_____."

Attention is also called to the endings *-er* and *-est* of comparison. As children note how a root and its inflected forms (*long, longer, longest*, for example) are used, they are led to generalize about the meaning of the endings.

On the basis of such known inflected and derived forms as *bigger, earliest*, and *driver*, children learn that the spelling of a root word often changes when an ending or a suffix is added. For example, the final consonant may be doubled as in *bigger, muddy, shopping;* the final *y* may be changed to *i* as in *earliest, busily, cried;* the final *e* of a root word may be dropped before an ending or a suffix as in *baking, driver, greasy.* By studying such words in sentences, children strengthen the understanding that the meaning of the root is present in an inflected or a derived form even though the spelling may change.

Second stage of progress

A child who has developed understanding of inflectional endings and suffixes as meaningful parts of words is ready to take the next step in structural analysis, that of noting that prefixes, like endings and suffixes, are added to root words to make new words.

Prefixes as meaning units

The italicized words on the section of the chart (page 55) that is reproduced below are examples of prefixes (*un-, im-, dis-*) that most pupils first learn to identify as meaningful parts of words. At the same time children also increase their understanding of suffixes as units of meaning as they learn to identify such suffixes as *-ish, -ful, -less, -ness.*

I was *unable* to *unlock* the door. It is *impossible* to cut the grass in an hour. A person who steals is *dishonest.*	identifying prefixes and root words as meaning units

Known roots
and prefixes
As a child's attention is focused on the meaning of derivatives that he knows (*impolite, impatient, impossible,* for example), he recognizes that a prefix (*im-*) added to the beginning of a root word (*polite, patient, possible*) combines its meaning ("not") with that of the root word. He notes also that prefixes may be added to inflected and derived forms (*unlocked, dishonesty,* for example).

The grammatical function of suffixes

When pupils have had much experience in identifying suffixes as meaningful parts of words, they are ready for the understanding that most suffixes have a grammatical function (see the section of the chart that is reproduced below). At this level children continue to learn such new affixes as the prefixes *re-* and *fore-* and the suffixes *-or* and *-ward*.

We *publish* books for children. (verb) I am a *publisher* of children's books. (noun)	recognizing the grammatical function of suffixes as an aid to meaning

The grammatical function of suffixes as an aid to meaning

Pupils develop the understanding that suffixes have a grammatical function by noting how a root and its derived form are used in paired sentences like those shown on the chart. The root *publish*, for example, is used as a verb; the derived form *publisher* is used as a noun. Adding the suffix *-er* to a root that is a verb makes a derived form that is a noun. As pupils note how other roots and their derived forms are used in sentences, understanding is developed that although a root word retains one of its basic meanings in a derived form, the grammatical function of a derived form (its part of speech) is usually different from that of the root.

Since many suffixes do not have a clear-cut lexical meaning, the grammatical function of suffixes is stressed from this point on. A suffix signals that the derivative is a noun, verb, adjective, or adverb. A knowledge of the function of a word within the sentence helps a reader get meaning from the sentence.

By the end of the second stage of progress, children have developed skills and understandings that are basic to structural analysis. They know that root words, prefixes, suffixes, and inflectional endings are units of meaning, and they can combine the meanings of the component parts of a derived or inflected form to arrive at the meaning of the whole. At the next stage of progress pupils will learn many new affixes and will refine and extend the basic skills and understandings developed thus far in structural analysis.

Third stage of progress

As boys and girls learn increasing numbers of affixes (-*ship*, -*ment*, -*able*, -*ible*, -*ous*, -*al*, etc.) and work with many derivatives, they constantly reinforce two basic structural understandings: (1) endings, suffixes, and prefixes are meaningful parts of words; (2) root words are meaning units in derived forms.

Classification of affixes by meaning or function

Grouping prefixes and suffixes

Throughout the middle and upper grades, boys and girls are adding many prefixes and suffixes to their oral and reading vocabularies (the prefixes *in-, il-, ir-, trans-, semi-, a-, be-, over-, out-, under-, non-* and the suffixes *-ion, -ance, -ence, -th,* for example). Pupils strengthen the understandings that prefixes and suffixes are meaning units and that suffixes have a grammatical function as they note that certain prefixes and certain suffixes fall into related groups (see the section of the chart that is given below).

"negative" prefixes		noun-forming suffixes		identifying affixes
incomplete	unconscious	interpreter	suggestion	in terms of meaning
irregular	disapprove	translator	performance	or function
illegal	nonstop	darkness	existence	
imperfect		settlement	growth	

As pupils learn new affixes and work with many derivatives, they see that certain prefixes and certain suffixes can be classified in groups on the basis of lexical or grammatical meaning. For example, the prefixes *in-, ir-, il-, im-, un-, dis-,* and *non-* all carry a negative meaning ("not" or "the opposite of"). The suffixes *-er, -or, -ness, -ment, -ion, -ance, -ence, -th* make derivatives that are nouns.

Derivatives based on a common root

Recognizing derivatives based on a common root

By this time, most pupils are familiar with many derived forms that come from a common root. These derivatives may show more complex changes than a dropped final *e*, a final *y* changed to *i*, or a final consonant doubled in the root. The spelling of the root or its pronunciation (or both) may change as indicated on the section of the chart below.

colony: colonial, precolonial, colonist, colonize, colonization	recognizing a root common to many derivatives in which pronunciation changes may occur
divide: division, subdivision, divisible, indivisible, divisor	

In analyzing such forms as those shown on the chart, pupils build on an understanding that was introduced at the first stage of progress (although the spelling of a root word often changes in derived and inflected forms, a meaning of the root word is present in these forms). From studying sentences in which roots like *divide* and several derived forms like *division, divisible, indivisible, divisor* are used, pupils learn that, even though the pronunciation and the spelling of a root word may change in a derived form, root meaning relates the words to each other.

This understanding enables a reader to figure out in context the meaning of many derived forms of known root words even though the root may have undergone a radical change. An alert reader who knows the roots *deceive, admit, pursue*, and *accurate*, for example, should have little difficulty inferring the meaning of such derived forms as *deceptive, admission, pursuit*, and *accuracy* in context.

Position of words and endings as clues to meaning

Boys and girls are now ready to build upon the understanding that suffixes have a grammatical function by noting how the position of a derived form in a sentence may furnish clues to meaning. They should also learn to identify increasing numbers of affixes, for example, *mis-, in-, en-, em-, pre-, co-, inter-, super-, ultra-, -ist, -ic, -ical, -ty, -ity, -ive, -ian, -ial, -ious, -hood, -some, -fy, -ize, -ee, -ess, -age, -ery, -ary.*

The *friendly* girl spoke *kindly* to the stranger.
She works as an *assistant;* she is an *assistant* clerk.
We watched the *rehearsal* of the *musical* comedy.

using position of words in sentences and word endings as clues to meaning

---

Position of words in sentences as an additional clue to meaning

The sentences shown on the section of the chart that is reproduced above are examples of the kind of sentences that pupils work with to arrive at the understanding that word endings and the position of words are often clues to sentence meaning. For example, a derivative that ends in the suffix *-ly* (*friendly*) occurring before a noun nearly always serves to describe the noun (adjective). A derivative ending in the suffix *-ly* (*kindly*) occurring after a verb usually tells "how" or "in what manner" something was done (adverb). Words ending in the suffix *-ant* or *-al* (*assistant, rehearsal, musical*) may be nouns or adjectives.

One way to prove to boys and girls that word endings and position of words in context are useful in getting meaning is to have them read a bit of nonsense like the following and tell what "ideas" they get from it, even though most of the words are not in the dictionary.

The toomly bulters stamified a maratant,
Who lumarized most bightfully.
He was so trassible and dairitant
That they fled naftly to their snightity.

Word analysis and the dictionary

As children's reading horizons expand, a dictionary becomes an indispensable tool for learning the meanings and pronunciations of totally unfamiliar words or for checking the accuracy of word meanings and pronunciations that have been tentatively arrived at by using context clues and word analysis. For example, if a child encounters in a book the expression "a fortuitous meeting of two sailors at the quay," neither the context nor the application of word-analysis skills is likely to help him with the meaning or pronunciation of the words *fortuitous* and *quay* unless these words are already in his vocabulary. He needs to consult a dictionary.

During the middle grades most children learn to use a dictionary. The skills that are essential to using a dictionary fall into three categories—those needed to (1) locate an entry word, (2) choose the appropriate definition of an unfamiliar word and adapt that definition to context, and (3) translate pronunciation symbols into a spoken word. The skills and understandings in word analysis that most pupils acquire in the primary grades provide background and readiness for using a dictionary. For example, most inflected forms of words (*parrying, canopies, hindered*) are not main entries in a dictionary. Ability to identify root words in inflected forms helps a child locate a word. As a child learns to interpret dictionary pronunciations, he builds upon what he has already learned in phonetic analysis and increases his knowledge of the relationship between sound and symbol. Throughout the middle and upper grades, word-analysis skills and dictionary skills supplement each other.

Using the dictionary for meaning

Most children are introduced to the dictionary in the fourth grade. For the first few weeks, they use it primarily to learn the meanings of words. (At the same time, however, they are gradually developing skill in using it to get the pronunciation of words.) Since a reader's motive in turning to the dictionary for the meaning of a word is usually to discover the total meaning of a passage containing that word, pupils should not be asked to look up meanings of lists of words. What would it profit a child, for example, to find the definitions of words like *galley, litter, amphibian,* or *counsel* out of context?

Throughout the middle grades, pupils should develop ability to adapt the appropriate definition of an unfamiliar word to the context in which it appears. To use a dictionary for meaning, children must master four levels of difficulty in adapting defined meanings to context:

Simple substitution: If a child consults the dictionary for the meaning of *attempt* in the sentence "The man will *attempt* to free the boy," he can simply substitute the definition "try" for the word *attempt* in context with no rewording of the definition or of the original sentence.

Inflectional adaptation: Many unfamiliar words occur in inflected form, for example, "The noise *startled* me." Once a child has located the root *startle* and has selected the definition "frighten," he realizes that to adapt it to the context in which *startled* appears, he must add an inflectional ending, making it "frightened."

Transposition of words: When a child looks up a word like *aggravate* as it occurs in "The weather *aggravated* my cold," he finds that he cannot substitute the appropriate definition "make worse" directly, nor can he merely change the word *make* to *made.* He must transpose the words of the original context and of the definition, for example, "The weather made my cold worse."

Complete paraphrasing: Often, to understand the meaning of a sentence like "A *skeptical* look came over Tom's face as he listened to my story," a child must read all the definitions of *skeptical.* Then, to grasp the meaning of the original sentence, he must completely paraphrase it and the words of the definitions for *skeptical.* He might arrive at something like the following: "Tom looked as if he doubted the truth of my story as he listened to it."

Using the dictionary for pronunciation

To use the dictionary for the pronunciation of words, pupils apply their knowledge of consonants, vowels, and accent as they learn to associate sounds with new visual symbols—with vowel letters combined with diacritical marks, with the schwa, and with the accent mark. Children must acquire the following understandings if they are to interpret dictionary pronunciation symbols: (1) printed pronunciations are recordings of sound; (2) each symbol stands for a sound; (3) the clue to the sound that each symbol stands for is the key word or words given for that sound in whatever dictionary or glossary is being used.

Children who have acquired these understandings are not likely to think it strange that the spelling of a word and its printed pronunciation in the dictionary often look quite different—for example, *assertion* (ə sėr′shən), *incredulous* (in krej′ů ləs), *deign* (dān). Neither are they confused by the fact that various dictionaries and glossaries use different pronunciation symbols as illustrated by the following printed pronunciations for the word *rumor* found in various elementary dictionaries and glossaries: (rü′mər),\′rüm-r\, (rōō′mẽr), (ru̯′mor).

The remainder of this book is devoted to specific procedures for developing a program in word analysis and in the use of a dictionary. Chapter Four gives procedures in word analysis that aid the child in analyzing independently one-syllable root words and their inflected and derived forms. Chapter Five presents procedures for independent attack of two-syllable root words and their inflected and derived forms, and Chapter Six lists procedures for analysis of multisyllabic words. Chapter Seven gives procedures for teaching children to use a dictionary.

Chapter four | Word analysis at
the first stage of progress

This chapter and the remaining ones in this book give specific procedures for developing in sequence the skills and abilities that children need to attack words independ-

Major emphasis on one-syllable words

ently. The procedures in this chapter are recommended for teaching children to analyze one-syllable words with or without inflectional endings or suffixes. Development of the skills and abilities necessary to analyze these words marks the first stage of progress in phonetic and structural analysis as indicated on the charts on pages 39 and 55.

Using consonants in phonetic analysis

The first application that most children make of phonetic analysis is using consonant substitution to identify in print an unfamiliar one-syllable word. They learn to analyze an unfamiliar word that looks like a word they know except for a single consonant letter, a two-letter consonant symbol (*ch, sh, th, ng*), or a consonant blend at the beginning or end of the word.

As pupils use consonant substitution, they strengthen the fundamental understanding that consonant sounds are phonemes; that is, we use them to distinguish between meanings (*lip, sip, tip, ship*, etc.). Eventually this understanding

Fundamental understandings of language are established is extended to include vowel sounds and accent. As pupils work with consonant sounds and letters, they also develop understanding of the relationship between sound and letter. They notice that a consonant letter may stand for more than one sound, that a sound may be represented by different letters, that letters may be silent in words. These understandings, too, will later be extended to vowels.

To use consonant substitution, children must be able to (1) hear accurately the sounds that single consonant letters (*p, b, d, t*, etc.), that consonant blends (*bl, pr, st*, etc.), and that two-letter consonant symbols (*ch, sh, th, ng*) stand for in words; (2) associate appropriate sound with a consonant letter or letters; (3) apply their understanding of the relationship between consonant sounds and letters in attacking new words; (4) blend sounds into word wholes.

Auditory perception of rhyme and consonants

One of the first steps in a program of phonetic analysis should be that of promoting the ability to hear speech sounds and to discriminate between them. At readiness and pre-primer levels, children should be given training in identifying rhyme and in hearing and discriminating between initial, medial, and final consonant sounds.

Readiness for identifying speech sounds The first procedures check auditory acuity and build readiness for identifying rhyme and consonant sounds.

1. Ask children to close their eyes. Have one child speak and ask the others to tell who has spoken.
2. Have children close their eyes. Tap on the wall or radiator and ask children to tell what you tapped on.
3. Play two notes on the piano and ask pupils to tell whether the second note was higher or lower than the first.
4. Tap twice softly and once loudly and ask the class to tell whether the first tap was loud or soft.

5. Tap rhythmically several times with loud and soft taps. Have children imitate the rhythm and sound.

The next nine procedures are only a few of those that may be used to promote ability to hear rhyme.

1. Display pictures of a cake and a rake, for example, and say the words *cake* and *rake* as you point to each picture. Have children repeat the words, and explain that we say these two words rhyme because they sound alike except at the beginning.

Then display pictures of a lock and a book. Have children note that the words *lock* and *book* do not rhyme. Repeat these procedures with other pairs of pictures, the majority of which represent rhyming words.

2. Before reading a jingle like the following, ask pupils to listen for words in the jingle that rhyme with the word *thick*.

> Jack be nimble,
> Jack be quick,
> Jack jump over the candlestick.

After children have identified the words that rhyme, repeat this procedure with other jingles.

3. Say groups of three words, two of which rhyme, *car*, *play*, *star*, for example. Ask which words in each group rhyme.

4. Say sentences like those given below in which two words rhyme. Ask pupils to identify the rhyming words.

> I climbed the hill with Bill.
> I lost my shoe at the zoo.
> The little fox hid in a box.

5. Encourage pupils to think of rhyming words on their own and to make up rhymes. To get them started, you might say that you saw some funny things that made a rhyme. You saw a mouse in a house and a dog on a log. Where might pupils see a goat (in a boat)? an elf (on a shelf)? a

bear (in a chair, on the stair)? Continue with "The bear in the chair had a pear," "The goat in the boat had a coat," and so on. Then have pupils contribute their own rhymes.

6. When children know a few sight words, write a known word like *run* on the board and pronounce *fun* and *play*. Ask children to tell which word rhymes with the word on the board.

7. Distribute pages containing pairs of pictures with a known word beneath each pair. The word should rhyme with the name of one of the pictures, for example, pictures of a boy and a rabbit with the word *toy*. Have children underline the picture whose name rhymes with the word.

8. Write an unfinished couplet on the board (for example, "See the talking bunny! He is very _____."). Ask children to read the lines silently and to think of a word that will finish the rhyme. When the rhyming word has been suggested, read the couplet aloud, using that word, and have children decide whether or not the words rhyme. Continue with other couplets.

9. Write a sentence about a story that pupils know and ask them to supply a rhyming line that will complete the idea as told in the story. For the first line you might write "Johnny Cake had lots of fun." Children might then contribute a line like "Making all the people run."

Identifying initial consonant sounds

As children grow in their ability to identify rhyming words, their attention should be focused on hearing and discriminating between single consonant sounds in the initial position in words. In general, a child should be able to hear a consonant sound accurately and to produce this sound in his own speech before he is asked to associate the sound with a printed letter. Since consonant sounds are integral parts of words, children should seldom be asked to hear them or to produce them in isolation. In using any procedure suggested for promoting auditory perception, pronounce words naturally without overarticulation or distortion.

The following procedures are suggested for helping children hear and discriminate between initial consonant sounds in words. Although the examples are for the most part based on the sound that is represented by the letter *b* as in the word *bet*, the same procedures may be used for other single consonant sounds.[1] In presenting these sounds, avoid words that begin with a blend (*brick, black, quit, dwarf*, etc.) but accept such words if children suggest them.

1. Pronounce such pairs of words as *bee, bunny; back, tack; big, pig; big, boy*, and ask pupils to tell whether the words in each pair sound alike or different at the beginning.
2. Give pupils an assortment of pictures—a ball, bacon, a piano, an airplane, etc. Say the word *bird* and ask pupils to select the pictures whose names begin with the sound heard at the beginning of *bird*.
3. Pronounce three words, two of which begin with the same consonant sound, for example, *butter, sand, bank*. Have pupils tell which two sound alike at the beginning.
4. Pronounce two or three words that begin with the sound represented by the letter *b*. Ask pupils to give other words that begin with the same sound. (Accept such words as *blue, brown*, and *bread* if pupils suggest them.)
5. Ask pupils to look around the classroom and to name everything and everyone they see whose name begins with the same sound as the word *back*.
6. Say sentences like those given below. Ask children to tell which words in each sentence sound alike at the beginning.

> Tom and Bob played ball on the beach.
> Betty burned the biscuits she was baking.
> Ben bought butter and bananas.
> Bill put his book on a bench behind the door.

[1] The consonant sounds heard at the beginning of the words *cat* or *kind*, *chin, do, fat, go, hill, jar* or *giant, let, man, no, pan, run, sit* or *cent, she, top, thin, then, valentine, will, yes, zoo* are considered single consonant sounds in this book.

Next, say, "Bill put his book on a bench. What else that begins with the same sound as *book* could Bill put on a bench (*ball, bat,* etc.)?" Repeat with other sentences.

7. Tell children that Billy Baker was a boy who put anything in his big box that began with the same sound as Billy and Baker. He put a banana, a buffalo, and a bicycle in his big box. Would he put a boat in his box? a peanut? a balloon? a kite? Invite children to think of other things that Billy Baker would put in his big box. Suggest that each child repeat the sentence "Billy Baker put a _____ in his big box" as he names an object.[1]

8. Suggest that children pretend that they like to do things or eat things that begin with the same sound as their names. Choose a child, Patty, for example, and say that Patty likes to paint pictures and eat pickles. What else would she like to do (pick petunias and poppies, polish the piano, put pennies in her purse)? What else would she like to eat (peanuts, pancakes, potatoes)? Continue similarly with other children, letting each child tell what he likes to do and eat and having the class contribute any other examples.[1]

Identifying final consonant sounds

Procedures 1-8 on pages 70-71 may be adapted for helping children identify single consonant sounds at the end of words (for example, the sound heard at the end of the words *hid, red, add, bud* and the sound heard at the end of the words *like, back, soak, walk*).

When children can identify and discriminate between consonant sounds at the beginning and at the end of spoken words, their attention should be focused on consonant sounds in the medial position.

To introduce auditory perception of medial consonant sounds, you might ask pupils to listen to the consonant

[1]This procedure is adapted from the book *Learn to Listen, Speak, and Write,* Book 1¹, by Marion Monroe, Ralph G. Nichols, and W. Cabell Greet (Chicago: Scott, Foresman and Company, 1960).

sound heard at the beginning of *bird* and at the end of *tub*. Then pronounce the word *rabbit* and ask pupils where they hear this sound in *rabbit*. Next, pronounce a group of words, two of which contain the same consonant sound in the middle (*ribbon, supper, pebble*, for example) and ask children to say the two words that have the same consonant sound in the middle. Continue with other groups of words.

Identifying medial consonant sounds

To strengthen ability to hear likenesses and differences in consonant sounds, use pairs of sentences like those given below in which the difference in meaning is due to the difference in one consonant phoneme. Say each pair of sentences and ask whether they mean the same. Which words are different? How are they different?

Consonant sounds are important to meaning

I like ham.
I like jam.

I don't want mush for breakfast.
I don't want much for breakfast.

We looked at the camel.
We looked at the cattle.

Other pairs of words that may be used in sentences to promote auditory perception of consonant sounds in words are *dish, fish; shell, bell; ham, hash; snake, snail; lesson, lemon; bubble, buckle.*

Visual-auditory perception of rhyme and consonants

With a background of auditory perception of rhyme, which has been developed by such procedures as those suggested on pages 68-69, a child is prepared to learn that some words that *sound* alike except at the beginning also *look* alike except at the beginning. That is, he is ready for visual-auditory perception of rhyming words. In helping him develop this concept, the teacher is building readiness for

Rhyming words often look alike except at the beginning

initial consonant substitution. (If a child knows the printed word *had*, he can identify the new words *bad*, *sad*, and *mad* by substituting the sounds that the letters *b*, *s*, and *m* stand for and by blending these initial sounds with the other sounds in the words.)

The next group of procedures is suggested for developing visual-auditory perception of rhyme. (The words used in these procedures should be known sight words.)

1. Write the words *pay*, *say*, and *pet* on the board. Ask children to pronounce them and to tell which two rhyme. Underline the rhyming words *pay* and *say*. Lead pupils to note that these words look alike except at the beginning. Proceed in the same way with other sets of words.

Hearing and scrutinizing rhyming words

2. List on the board the words *he*, *run*, *my*. Next write the word *by*. Have a child pronounce *by*, and then ask him to find a word in the list that rhymes with it. Direct attention to the fact that the word *by* looks and sounds like *my* except at the beginning. Proceed with other words that rhyme with the remaining words on the board.

3. After writing such words as *hat*, *sat*, *tar*, *fat*, *nut*, *mat*, ask children to pronounce them and to indicate those that look and sound alike except at the beginning.

4. Write an unfinished sentence like the following: "The boy has a new _____." Underline the word *boy* and have children choose from the following three words the one that rhymes with the underlined word: *cat*, *ball*, *toy*. Continue in the same way with other sentences and rhyming words.

Once children have learned to identify single consonant sounds, they should next learn to associate these sounds with the letters that commonly represent them.[1] This is

---

[1] The sounds commonly represented by the letters *c*, *g*, and *s* are those heard at the beginning of *cat*, *go*, *so*. The fact that these letters also represent other sounds (*cent*, *gem*, *has*, for example) will be introduced later.

referred to as visual-auditory perception of consonants. The following six procedures are suggested for promoting visual-auditory perception of single consonants in the initial position in words.

1. Write such known words as *by, boat, baby, ball, boy, bake* in a column. As children pronounce the words, ask them to listen carefully to the first sound in each word. When pupils agree that the words all begin with the same sound, ask whether they also look alike at the beginning. Then comment that the words all begin with the *b* sound and that the letter *b* stands for this sound. Write the letter *b* above the words.

Associating initial consonant sounds with letters

Start a second column by writing the capitalized form *By* opposite *by*, and have both forms pronounced. Establish the idea that both forms are the same word, the only difference being that the word *By* begins with a capital letter. After writing *B* above the word *By*, write the capitalized forms of the other "b" words. Conclude by having pupils pronounce and compare the forms of each pair of words. This procedure may be used to promote visual-auditory perception of any consonant letter.

2. Write the letters *b, t,* and *r* on the board. Then display a picture of something beginning with the *b* sound, a ball, for example. Ask children to point to the letter on the board that stands for the first sound in the name of the picture. Continue with pictures of other objects, a top, a turtle; a balloon, a boat; a ring, a rooster, for example.

3. Write the letters *b, f, l,* and *s.* Pronounce *beaver,* and ask a child to point to the letter that stands for the sound he hears at the beginning of the word. Continue with such words as *fun, lamp, sit, better, little, silly.*

4. Write the letter *b* and under it in a column such known words as *bunny, bang, go, dig,* and *bump.* Ask a pupil to draw a line under the words that begin with the letter *b.* Then have the words pronounced and ask children to think

of and pronounce other words that begin with a *b* sound. Use this procedure with other consonant letters.

5. If youngsters have learned to write, they can write the letter that represents the initial sound in the name of a pictured object. For example, you might give each child a page that contains such pictured objects as a rake, a nut, a rope, a nail, a ring, and a nest, leaving room in front of each object for a child to write the letter that represents the first sound in the name of the object.

6. Write a sentence like "I like my new t_____," and have children guess what the last word might be (*toy, top,* etc.). Change the initial consonant to *d* and then to *h*, and have children supply words that complete the sentence.

When children can associate appropriate sounds with several single consonant letters, they are ready to begin using consonant substitution (see pages 78-80).

As children acquire ability to associate sound with single consonant letters in the initial position in words, they should also have developmental training in visual-auditory perception of final consonants.

1. Write *top* and *not*, pronounce them, and call attention to the position of the letter *t* and to the sound that it represents **Associating** in each word. Then pronounce a list of words that begin **final consonant** or end with the sound of *t* and that are spelled with the **sounds** letter *t*. When children decide that a word begins with the **with letters** sound of *t*, list it under the word *top*, but if they decide that it ends with the sound of *t*, write it under *not*. Have pupils pronounce each word and point to the letter *t*. Use similar procedures to develop visual-auditory perception of other single consonant letters in the final position in words.

2. Write the letters *p, m, n, d*. Pronounce the word *man* and ask a pupil to point to the letter that stands for the sound he hears at the end of the word. Continue with such words as *cup, red, in, am, plan, hop, spin, feed*.

As soon as children can associate consonant sounds with letters, two major phonetic understandings should be introduced: (1) consonant letters may be "silent" in words; that is, every consonant letter in a word may not represent a sound; (2) some consonant letters (notably *s, c,* and *g*) represent more than one sound. The next group of procedures is designed to develop both of these understandings.

1. Write the word *let* and have it pronounced. Ask pupils what sound they hear at the beginning of the word. Then pronounce *tail* and ask pupils where they hear the *l* sound in this word. Write *tail* and call attention to the letter *l*. Next write *call* and have it pronounced. Ask pupils how many *l*'s they see in this word and how many *l* sounds they hear. Repeat with *fell, will, doll, Bill, all.* Comment that two *l*'s stand for the same sound as one *l*. (Children may refer to the second *l* as a silent letter.) Continue with such pairs of words as *beg, egg; had, add; fur, purr; this, miss; if, off,* leading pupils to observe that two like consonant letters at the end of a word stand for a single sound.

2. Write the words *book* and *back* and have them pronounced. What sound do pupils hear at the end of *book?* at the end of *back?* What letter stands for this sound in *book?* How many consonant letters represent this sound in *back?* Then write such known words as *stick, duck, sack, brick* and have them pronounced. Develop the idea that the letters *ck* represent the *k* sound. (Children may refer to the letter *c* as a silent letter.)

3. Write such groups of known words as *know, knew, knife,* and *wren, write, wrist.* After pupils pronounce the first group, ask what sound each word begins with. With what letter does each word begin? Does the letter *k* represent a *k* sound? Bring out that in words that begin with the letters *kn* the *k* is a silent letter. Use similar procedures with the words *wren, write, wrist* to bring out that in words that begin with the letters *wr* the *w* is a silent letter.

A consonant letter may not represent a sound in a printed word

4. To strengthen the understanding that consonant letters may be silent in words, write such pairs of known words as *shelf* and *calf*, *milk* and *talk*, *cold* and *could* and have them pronounced. In which word in each pair does the letter *l* stand for a sound? In which is the letter *l* silent? Use similar procedures with the letter *b* and such pairs of words as *grab* and *lamb*, *web* and *climb*, *tub* and *crumb*.

5. To call attention to the voiced and unvoiced sounds that the letter *s* may stand for, write the words *this, yes, bus, gifts, books,* and *boats* in a column on the board. As children pronounce the words, ask them to listen for the sound that the letter *s* stands for in each word. Remind pupils that this sound is called the *s* sound and is heard at the beginning of such words as *see, say,* and *sat.* Then write the words *is, has, his, boys, runs, bells* in another column and have them pronounced. Ask whether the letter *s* in these words stands for the same sound that it does in the words in the first column. When children agree that it does not, comment that the letter *s* in these words stands for the *z* sound and that this sound is represented by the letter *z* at the beginning of such words as *zoo* and *zero.* Conclude by writing *was, us, talks, pigs, pets, goes, bees, mouse, noise, nose, horse.* As pupils pronounce them, ask whether the letter *s* stands for the *s* sound or for the *z* sound.

A consonant letter may stand for more than one sound

6. Write such known words as *cat, come,* and *cut* and have them pronounced. Ask children what sound the letter *c* stands for in each of these words (the *k* sound). Use similar procedures with such known words as *city, center,* and *cent,* leading pupils to note that the letter *c* stands for the *s* sound in these words. Conclude by writing such known words as *fence, nice, place, once, picnic, fancy, second, magic.* As each is pronounced, ask whether the letter *c* stands for the *k* or for the *s* sound.

7. Use known words like *get, gem, giant, large, big, change, forget, magic, together* and procedures similar to those in

the preceding exercise to develop the concept that the letter *g* may stand for the *g* sound or for the *j* sound.

Consonant substitution

As noted earlier, a child can learn to use consonant substitution to attack unfamiliar printed words as soon as he can (1) call up from memory the form of a known word from his basic stock of sight words, (2) note the similarity in form between a known word and an unfamiliar printed word, (3) associate sounds with a few consonant letters, (4) blend an initial consonant sound (and later, a final consonant sound) with the remaining phonemes in a word. At this level of growth, a child uses a known word as a basis for analyzing an unknown word.

The following procedures are suggested for promoting the use of consonant substitution in attacking new words.

1. Write in a column on the board the words *book, can, toy, pet, he, no, now, talk, say, run.* Then write the word *get* and ask children to find a word in the column of words that looks like *get* except for the first letter. Have *pet* and *get* pronounced, and lead pupils to note that they sound alike except at the beginning. Continue with the following words: *look, walk, day, boy, me, so, how, fun.*

    Substituting initial consonants in words and blending sounds into word wholes

    Next, write the word *pet* on the board. Explain that you are going to change the first letter of the word *pet* to make a new word. Erase the *p* and substitute *b.* Have the word *bet* pronounced. Interchange these initial consonants several times so that pupils are aware of the substitution technique. Continue substituting *b* for the initial consonant in such words as *me, call, my, tell, run, jump, sat.*

2. Write such known words as *way, fast, man* on the board. As pupils pronounce the first word, ask whether they can think of a word that looks and sounds like *way* except at the beginning. When such a word as *day, may,* or *say* is mentioned, erase the *w* in *way* and substitute the initial con-

sonant of each word that pupils suggest. Continue with
fast and *man*.

3. Write a known word, *make*, for example, and ask children
to tell how to change this word to the word *take* and to the
word *bake*. Then write a sentence containing an unknown
word that is like a known word except for the initial consonant, for example, "I saw a boat on the *lake*." Ask children to read the sentence.

4. The procedure suggested in this exercise should be used
often to provide practice in consonant substitution and rapid
blending of sounds. By substitution of initial consonants,
change known words to such unknown words as those indicated in parentheses and note pupils' ability to attack the
new words: *now* (*how*); *cat* (*rat, sat*); *sack* (*pack, tack*);
bang (*sang, rang*); *boat* (*goat*); *car* (*far*); *get* (*set, wet*);
could (*would*); *hen* (*ten, den*); *time* (*dime*); *well* (*sell*).

5. To provide practice in using consonant substitution to attack new words in context, write such sentences as those
below in which the italicized words are new. Note whether
pupils can use initial consonant substitution to attack each
new word. Whenever children attack unfamiliar words in
context, emphasize the importance of noting whether the
word they have identified makes sense in the sentence.

The kitten was *fat*.   The toy *fell* on the floor.
The *men* were working.   Please *dust* the table.

6. Write sentences in which a known word that may serve as
a basis for consonant substitution is used preceding an unknown word. For example, in the following sentences, the
italicized words are unknown. The known words *take, fun,
Jack,* and *soon* serve as a basis for consonant substitution.

Jack said, "I will take the *rake* and work in the yard. It
will be fun."
But the *sun* was hot, and soon Jack was tired.
"My *back* hurts," he thought. "I think it must be *noon*."

If a child has difficulty in analyzing any of the new words, ask him to find another word that looks like the new word except for the first letter. Write the known word and by substituting consonants change it to the new word.

7. To introduce final consonant substitution, use procedures similar to those suggested for initial consonant substitution. For example, the fourth procedure on page 79 may be used with such words as *him* (*hit, hid, hip*); *but* (*bun, bus*); *pet* (*peg, pen*); *can* (*cat, cab, cap*).

Substituting final consonants in words

8. To give practice in using both initial and final consonant substitution, write the known word *not* and have it pronounced. Erase the *n* in *not* and substitute an *h*. Have the word *hot* pronounced. Change *hot* to *hop* and continue substituting initial or final consonants to make the words *top, pop, pot,* and *dot*. Continue similarly with *sit* (*hit, hip, lip, tip, tin*); *but* (*hut, hug, bug, bus, bun*); *pan* (*pat, pad, sad, lad, lap, nap, cap, can, man, mad, had, hat*).

Two-letter consonant symbols and consonant blends

Children who have learned to associate sounds with single consonant letters should readily learn to associate sounds with two-letter consonant symbols and with consonant blends. They learn that the two-letter consonant symbols (*ch, sh, th,* and *ng*) stand for single sounds. They also learn that two or more consonant sounds may be blended as in the words *blue, tree, stream,* and that the consonants *l, r,* and *s* are common "blenders." If pupils can use consonant substitution to attack an unfamiliar word that is like a known word except for a single consonant letter, they can use the same method to analyze a word that looks like a known word except for a consonant blend or a two-letter consonant symbol.

Associating sound with two-letter consonant symbols and blending sounds into word wholes

1. To develop awareness of two-letter consonant symbols that represent one consonant sound, write the known word *child* and have it pronounced. Point to the letters *ch* and explain

that these two letters usually stand for one consonant sound
—the sound heard at the beginning of *child*. Then pronounce such known words as *chicken, much, which, chair,*
and ask whether pupils hear the *ch* sound at the beginning
or at the end of each word. Write each word and underline
the letters *ch*. Use similar procedures with such known words
as *she, shall, push, rush, should, splash* to introduce the
two-letter consonant symbol *sh*.

2. To promote visual-auditory perception of the two-letter consonant symbol *ng*, write such known words as *sing, long,
bang*. As each word is pronounced, ask pupils to listen
carefully to the sound heard at the end. Then point to the
letters *ng* in each word and explain that these two letters
stand for this sound. To give pupils practice in attacking
new words that end in the letters *ng*, write the known word
wish and have it pronounced. Then erase the letters *sh* and
substitute the letters *ng*. Have pupils pronounce the word
wing. Continue with *sun* (*sung*) and *sat* (*sang*).

You may also wish to call attention to the fact that the
consonant sound heard at the end of *sing, bang,* and *sung*
is also heard in words like *thank, think,* and *chunk*, even
though the words are not spelled "thangk," "thingk," and
"chungk."

3. To call attention to the two sounds (voiced and unvoiced)
that the two-letter consonant symbol *th* usually represents,
write the words *thing* and *these* on the board. Ask children
to pronounce the words. Then ask whether they can hear
the difference between the consonant sound that the letters
th represent at the beginning of the word *thing* and the consonant sound that these same letters represent at the beginning of the word *these*. Continue with these pairs of words:
third, then; thump, that. Explain that the letters *th* usually
stand for these two sounds—the sound heard at the beginning of *thing, third, thump* and the sound heard at the
beginning of *these, then, that*.

Next, pronounce *thumb* and ask whether the first sound in this word is like the first sound in *thing* or in *these*. When pupils respond *thing*, write *thumb* under the word *thing*. Continue with the words *thought, them, than, think, they, thick, thank*.

Conclude by pronouncing such known words as the following and having children tell whether they hear a *th* sound at the beginning, in the middle, or at the end of each word: *thimble, south, weather, both, this, together, mouth, teeth, there, bath, bathe*. Then write the words.

4. To give practice in using consonant substitution to identify new words containing two-letter consonant symbols, write sentences like those shown below. The italicized words are new words. Do not write the words in parentheses. They are examples of known words that pupils may use as a basis for consonant substitution.

We played on the *shore*. (more)
It began to *thaw* last night. (saw)
We had to *chop* wood. (hop)
Did the bee *sting* you? (stick)

The next procedures are suggested for promoting the ability to identify consonant blends in words. For the most part, these procedures are based on *l* blends but they may be used to introduce any two- or three-letter consonant blend.

1. Write the known word *pay* and have it pronounced. What consonant sound do pupils hear at the beginning of *pay?* Then change the word *pay* to *play* and have *play* pronounced. What consonant sounds do pupils hear at the beginning of *play?* Have *play* pronounced again and lead pupils to note that the two sounds represented by the letters *pl* are spoken almost as one sound. Explain that we call these two sounds a blend. To emphasize that the sound represented by *l* is a "blender," write known words like *blue, clean, fly, glad, slow* and have them pronounced.

Associating sound with consonant blends and blending sounds into word wholes

2. Write the known word *jump* and have it pronounced. Change it to *plump* and have the new word pronounced. Continue with *cow* (*plow*); *hop* (*plop*); *hat* (*flat*).

3. Pronounce such words as *cloud, black, flame, glue,* and *sleep.* With what two letters do pupils think each word begins? As children respond, write each word.

4. When *l, r,* and *s* have been presented as "blenders," write sentences like those shown below. Note pupils' ability to use consonant substitution as a means of identifying each italicized word, which should be one that children have not yet encountered in reading.

> He *slid* down the hill on his *sled.*
> The *score* was 2 to 1 when Joe *struck* out.
> I will *fry* this *slice* of meat.

5. When children know enough words that begin with the letters *tw, sw, qu,* and *wh* (*twin, swim, queen, why*), lead them to note that these letters also represent blends. (The letter *q* is followed by *u* in English spelling, and the letters *qu* represent the sounds [kw] as in *quit.* The letters *wh* generally represent a blend of the sounds that the letter *h* and the letter *w* usually represent [hw] as in the words *why* [hwī] and wheel [hwēl].)[1] Use procedures similar to those given in the preceding exercises and such words as *twin, twig, twist, twelve; swim, sweep, swing, swish; quack, queen, quit, quick, queer; what, wheat, when, where.*

Combining phonetic analysis with context clues

Procedures have been suggested for developing skill in using consonant substitution to attack new words in sentences. Here a child combines phonetic analysis with the use of context clues. However, for thorough mastery of consonant substitution or of any other word-attack skill,

[1]In some standard regional pronunciations no distinction is made between the initial sounds in such words as *which* and *witch; whale* and *wail.*

a child must have many opportunities to apply the skill independently while he is reading interesting content.

In fact, the most valuable way to develop a child's initiative in using word analysis is to expect him to unlock new words on his own as he reads. Of course, if a child asks what a word is while reading a story, you should tell him the word so that he can go on with his reading. You will want to help him analyze the unfamiliar word for himself after the story has been discussed. Suppose a child who has learned to use consonant substitution has asked for help with the word *sold*. You might write *sold* on the board, reminding him that he asked for help with this word. Then ask him if he can think of a word that looks like *sold* except for the first letter. When he mentions a word like *cold*, write it, change the initial consonant to *s*, and ask him to pronounce *sold*. Then have him read from the book the sentence in which the word *sold* occurred.

Using roots and endings in structural analysis

During the first stage of progress as children learn to associate consonant sounds with consonant letters and to use consonant substitution, they should also learn to identify structural elements as meaningful parts of words (roots in compounds and in inflected forms, and simple inflectional endings). As pupils do so, they develop the understandings that (1) endings may be added to a root word, (2) root words may be joined to form a compound, (3) a root retains its meaning in compound or inflected forms.

Identifying root words and inflectional endings

Before children are expected to use structural analysis as one method of analyzing printed words, attention should be focused on the way inflected forms are used in speaking.

The first three procedures provide readiness for structural analysis. The remaining procedures in this section are suggested for helping children analyze a word that is like a known word except for the ending -s, -es, -'s, -ed, or -ing.

1. Show or give pupils pictures of various objects that may be classified into groups. In discussing and classifying the objects, children will be led naturally to use singular and plural forms of nouns like *toy* and *animal* as they say, "That is a toy. It goes with the other toys." "That is an animal. It belongs with the other animals."

   Preparing orally for structural analysis

2. To focus attention on the use of spoken words that end in -*ing*, show pictures in which children are engaged in some activity. Ask pupils to tell what the children are doing (running, jumping, etc.).

3. Ask children to recall past activities. As they tell "what happened this morning," for example, they will likely use past tenses of verbs ending in -*ed* (walked, played, etc.).

4. As soon as children can recognize in print such root words and inflected forms as *car* and *cars; boat* and *boats; jump* and *jumps,* you will want to begin establishing the idea of what a root word is and what an ending is. Write the word *car* and have it pronounced. Explain that you will add an ending to this word; then add *s* and have *cars* pronounced. To bring out the relationship in meaning, have *car* and *cars* used in oral sentences. Continue with *boat, boats; jump, jumps.* Explain that we call words like *car, boat,* and *jump* to which endings may be added root words.

   Identifying roots and the inflectional endings -s and -es

5. Write *cat, cats, dog, dogs* on the board. Place the word cards for *one, two, three, four, a, the* on the chalk ledge. Ask a child to select a card to be placed in front of each word on the board. Then distribute word cards for *pony, horses, hen, eggs, barn, chickens, cat, pigs.* Have a child select a card from the ledge that may be correctly placed in front of the one that he holds. Give each child an opportunity to engage in this exercise.

6. Write such sentences as "You have one box. I have three boxes." Ask children to read the two sentences and to tell what ending is added to the root word *box* to make a word meaning "more than one box." Then write such sentences as "Mother put the dishes on the table. Mother put the dish on the table," and ask children to tell which sentence means that Mother put more than one dish on the table.
7. Write on the board such sentences as "I *wish* I had a pony. Bill *wishes* he had a pony." After pupils have read the sentences, point to the word *wishes* in the second sentence and ask children what ending is added to the root word *wish*. Ask whether adding the ending *-es* to *wish* makes a word meaning "more than one wish" in this sentence. Comment that we say "I wish," but "He wishes" or "Bill wishes."

    Continue by writing such known words as *pushes*, *splashes*, *potatoes*, and *bushes*. Ask pupils to identify the root word in each. Then use each inflected form in an oral sentence and ask whether or not adding the ending *-es* makes a new word that means "more than one _____." For example, you might say, "The rain *splashes* against the window." "These *bushes* have berries on them." (This procedure may also be used with the ending *-s*.)
8. Write two pairs of sentences like the following, underlining the italicized words (the underlined words should be inflected forms that can be used as either nouns or verbs).

        He *walks* to school.   I'll give you three *guesses*.
        I swept the *walks*.   Joe always *guesses* right.

As children read each pair of sentences, ask in which sentence the underlined word means "more than one _____." What is the root word in each underlined word? What ending has been added to the root word? Then write the inflected forms *walks*, *guesses*, *bats*, *watches* on the board. When these words are not in sentences, can pupils tell whether the words mean "more than one _____"? Lead children to note that the only way to tell whether a word to which the ending -s or -es has been added means "more than one _____," is to see or hear that word used in a sentence.

9. Write the inflected forms *churches, knocks, foxes, pulls, catches, hands, mixes.* Ask children to use each word in a sentence and to tell whether the word means "more than one _____."

10. Write the words *looks* and *walks* and have them pronounced.

Identifying roots and the inflectional endings -ed and -ing

Ask a child to find and frame the root words and to tell what ending was added to make *looks* and *walks.* Have children use the root words and their inflected forms in oral sentences. Continue similarly with the known inflected forms *looked* and *walked.*

Then write on the board sentences like those given below. The sentences should contain known roots to which the ending -ed is added. (The inflected forms should be those that pupils have not yet encountered in reading.) Notice children's ability to attack the inflected forms in context. Have pupils underline the root word in each.

Tim thanked me for the candy.   We laughed at the clown.
I asked Mother for a cookie.   It snowed last night.

11. Write the inflected forms *wanted* and *painted* and ask a child to frame the root in each. Continue with *splashed, bumped,* and *rained, played.* Have children pronounce the inflected forms and lead them to note that the ending -ed is not always pronounced the same. Explain that -ed sometimes sounds as it does in *wanted,* sometimes as it does in *splashed,* and sometimes as it does in *rained.*

12. Write the root word *walk* and have it pronounced. Add the ending -ing and have the inflected form *walking* pronounced. Have pupils use *walk* and *walking* in oral sentences. Continue similarly with the root words *work, go, eat, hurry,* and *paint.* Conclude by writing such inflected forms of known words as *galloping, trying, seeing.* After children have iden-

tified the root word and ending in each, have the inflected forms used in oral sentences.

13. Present an exercise like the following. Ask children to select the word that completes each sentence and then to read the sentence aloud.

The boys were _____.
    plays   played   playing

The man was _____ the car.
    pushes   pushing   pushed

Father _____ the car yesterday.
    washes   washed   washing

14. Write the sentence "Here is Ann's toy," and have it read. Ask pupils to whom the toy belongs. Then ask someone to point to the word that tells whose toy it is. Continue similarly with "Here is Bob's dog." Explain that when we want to show that something belongs to someone, Ann, for example, we write *Ann* (write the word) and add this mark (') and the letter *s*. Continue similarly with *Bob* and *Bob's*. Tell children that the mark is called an apostrophe.

Identifying roots and the inflectional ending -'s

15. Write pairs of sentences like those given below, one pair at a time. Have the first pair read silently and then ask such questions as "What does Tom see? To whom does the boat belong? Can you point to the word that tells whose boat it is?" Continue with the other sentences.

Guess what Tom can see.
Tom can see Bill's boat.

What can Mother see?
She can see Jane's doll.

16. Write sentences that contain known root words to which the endings -s, -es, -'s, -ed, -ing are added. As children read each sentence, point to the inflected form and ask what the

word is. If anyone has difficulty, cover the ending and ask, "What is this word?" indicating the root word. Then ask what the entire word is. Comment, "Yes, that is the word *think* with the ending *-ing* added to make *thinking*."

Identifying contractions

Children have learned that an apostrophe indicates possession. Since they are likely to encounter contractions in reading, they should understand that an apostrophe does not always indicate possession. The following exercises build understanding of contractions in which one letter is omitted.

1. Write *don't* on the board and have it pronounced. Then write the words *do not* and explain that the word *don't* means the same thing as the words *do not*. *Don't* is a shorter way of saying *do not*. An apostrophe is used to show that a letter has been left out of *do not*.

   Next, write a sentence containing a contraction, for example, "*Let's* play ball after school." When children have read the sentence, ask what two words the contraction *let's* stands for. Write *let us* above *let's* and have pupils compare the two ways of saying the same thing. Continue similarly with such contractions as *isn't, haven't, didn't, weren't*.

2. Write such groups of words as the following:

hasn't	*let's*	*I'm*
had not	let it	I was
has not	let his	I am
has no	let us	I have

Point to *hasn't*, have it pronounced, and ask someone to underline the two words below *hasn't* that mean the same thing as *hasn't*. Continue similarly with the other groups. (Similar procedures may be used later to call attention to contractions in which two or more letters are omitted— *she'll, I've, he'd*, etc.)

Identifying roots in compounds

The next procedures are suggested for developing ability to attack compounds made up of two known root words.

1. Write the known roots *rain* and *coat* and have them read. Comment that when these two root words are put together, they make a long word, and write *raincoat*. Tell children that we call this kind of word a compound. To introduce the concept that a compound is a word composed of root words that combine their meanings to make a new word, comment that a raincoat is a coat a person wears to protect him from rain.

   Then write sentences containing compounds made of two known root words (see those given below). As children read each sentence, ask what the root words are in each compound and what the compound means.

   > I rang the *doorbell.*
   > Father made a *doghouse* for Sandy.
   > We ran *downhill.*

2. Write on the board such sentences as "A house for a doll is called a _____." Ask children to read the sentence silently and to tell what one word goes in the blank. Write the word *dollhouse* in the blank. Continue with sentences containing such compounds as *sailboat, boathouse, mailbox.*

Combining structural and phonetic analysis

When pupils can identify the inflectional endings *-s, -'s, -es, -ing,* and *-ed* (structural analysis) and can use consonant substitution (phonetic analysis), they are ready to learn how to combine the two types of analysis to identify in context an inflected form of an unfamiliar root word that can be attacked through consonant substitution.

The next group of procedures is suggested for helping children see how they can attack many unfamiliar printed words by combining structural and phonetic analysis at a simple level.

1. Write an inflected form made up of an unknown root word (that can be attacked by using consonant substitution) plus

Attacking inflected forms of unknown roots

a known inflectional ending, *cooked*, for example, and ask pupils what ending they see on the word. Then cover the *-ed* and note whether pupils can readily identify the root *cook*. If they have difficulty, point to *cook* and ask whether they can think of a word that looks like this word except at the beginning. When a known word like *book* is mentioned, write it, erase the letter *b* and substitute the letter *c*. Then suggest that pupils try saying the new word. After *cook* is pronounced, add the ending *-ed* to it and have *cooked* pronounced. Then have *cooked* used in an oral sentence.

Use similar procedures with the inflected form *coaches*, this time encouraging pupils to use final consonant substitution to identify the root word *coach* (from *coat*).

2. Write sentences containing inflected forms of unknown root words that pupils can identify by using consonant substitution. Note children's ability to attack the new words independently. If anyone has difficulty, help him analyze the word as suggested in the preceding exercise. Sentences like those given below may be used. (Do not write the words in parentheses, they are examples of known words that pupils may use as a basis for consonant substitution.)

> Mother was *mending* my coat. (send)
> Her hat *matches* her dress. (catch)
> We *chained* our dog to the fence. (rain)
> This is *Nick's* dog. (pick)

The purpose of the procedures given up to this point has been to develop skills and understandings that enable children to analyze simple types of words. In phonetic analysis pupils have learned to associate consonant sounds with letters and to use consonant substitution as a method of attacking unfamiliar one-syllable words in context. In structural analysis children have acquired understanding of root words and simple inflectional endings as units of meaning. They have learned to identify in context inflected forms of root words to which known endings have been added and contracted and compound forms of known root words. Pupils who have mastered these skills and understandings should be able to analyze four general types of words when they encounter them in reading:

Types of words that can be attacked through consonant substitution and simple structural analysis

1. A word like a known word except for one consonant letter, a two-letter consonant symbol, or a consonant blend at the beginning or end of the word (*bat, chat, slat, cast,* or *cash* from the known word *cat,* for example)

2. A known word to which the inflectional ending *-s, -'s, -es, -ed,* or *-ing* has been added with no change in the spelling of the root (*bells, laughed, playing,* for example)

3. A contracted or compound form of two known words (*don't, playground,* for example)

4. An inflected form of an unknown word, if the root word is like a known word except for one consonant letter (or a two-letter consonant symbol or a blend) at the beginning or end of the word (*called,* for example, from *ball*)

A child analyzes the first type of word by using phonetic analysis, the next two types of words by using structural analysis. With the fourth type of word he must combine structural and phonetic analysis.

Children who have learned to analyze these types of words are ready for new steps in word analysis. In phonetic analysis they are ready to learn how to determine vowel sounds in one-syllable words. In structural analysis they are ready to learn how to identify suffixes and additional inflectional endings as meaningful parts of words.

Using vowels in phonetic analysis

Children must first learn to identify vowel sounds in words and to associate these sounds with letters of the alphabet if they are to develop competence in using vowels in phonetic analysis. As children learn to associate sounds with one or two vowel letters, two fundamental understandings should become apparent: (1) each vowel letter is used to represent more than one vowel sound, for example, the letter *i* in *fit*, *fine*, and *fir;* (2) the same vowel sound may be represented by different letters or combinations of letters in the spelling of words, for example, the vowel sound in *fine* and *my* and in *sail* and *say*.

When children understand that the relationship between vowel sounds and letters is far more variable than between consonant sounds and letters, they are ready to learn to use visual clues to help them determine which vowel sound to try first in unfamiliar one-syllable words.

Associating different vowel sounds with a letter

This first group of procedures promotes ability to associate vowel sounds with the letter *i* (and *y*) and introduces the two concepts of variability stated above. At the same time, they give valuable practice in blending vowel and consonant sounds into word wholes. The general procedures suggested for the letter *i* should be used to help children associate long, short, and *r*-controlled vowel sounds with the other vowel letters (*a, e, o,* and *u*).

1. Write "I like apples" on the board and have the sentence read. Call attention to the first word in the sentence, note

The letter i stands for more than one vowel sound

that it has only one letter in it, and recall that the name of the letter is *I*. Ask whether pupils can hear the sound that the letter *i* stands for in the next word in the sentence. (Write a capital letter *I* and a small *i*.) Have the word *like* pronounced again and point to the letter *i* in it.

In a column to the left, write the known words *find, side, white, high, ice.* As pupils pronounce each one, underline the letter *i.* Then explain that the sound that the letter *i* stands for in these words is often called the long *i* sound. Use similar procedures and the known words *is, in, if, did, milk, fish* to call attention to the short *i* sound.

2. To give practice in discriminating between the long and short *i* sounds, write such known words as *right, him, five, ride, it, sit, fine, big, time, pig.* As pupils pronounce each, ask whether they hear the long or the short *i* sound.

3. To call attention to another sound that the letter *i* stands for, write three columns of known words, for example, (1) *pig, pin, limp, hit;* (2) *line, light, time, kind;* (3) *bird, first, shirt, girl.* As pupils pronounce the words in the first column, ask what vowel sound they hear in each (short *i*). Repeat with the long *i* sound in the second column. Next, explain that the letter *i* sometimes stands for another sound. Pronounce each word in the third column and point to the letter *i* in each. Then ask pupils what letter comes after the *i* in each of these words. Explain that when the letter *i* is followed by *r* in the spelling of a word, the *i* usually stands for the vowel sound that is heard in *bird.*

Conclude by writing such known words as *dirt, hide, thin, life, circus, hid, thirst, kind.* As pupils pronounce each word, ask whether the letter *i* stands for the long *i* sound, the short *i* sound, or the sound of *i* followed by *r.*

4. Pronounce the word *my* and ask pupils what sound they hear at the end of the word (long *i*). Then write the word

Vowel sounds that may be represented by the letter i or y

my and ask children to pronounce it and to tell what letter stands for the long *i* sound. Comment that the letter *y* often stands for a long *i* sound. Then write such known words as *fly, cry, why, by.* As pupils say each word, ask them which *i* sound they hear and what letter stands for it.

Next, comment that the letter *y* sometimes stands for another *i* sound. Write the known words *hurry, baby, happy, pony, story.* As pupils pronounce each word, under-line the letter *y*. Point out that in these words the letter *y* stands for the short *i* sound.[1] Conclude by writing such known words as *try, party, very, sky, candy, hungry, sly.* As youngsters pronounce each one, ask whether the letter *y* stands for a long or short *i* sound.

5. Write such pairs of known words as *why, white; it, funny; miss, many; try, time.* Lead pupils to compare the *i* sounds heard in each pair of words and the letters that stand for the sounds. Point out that generally the letter *i* stands for an *i* sound at the beginning or middle of a word and the letter *y* stands for an *i* sound at the end of a word.

6. To give practice in associating vowel and consonant sounds with letters and in blending the sounds into words, write **Blending consonant and vowel sounds** a word containing a short *i* sound that pupils have not en-countered in reading, *drip*, for example. Tell pupils that the letter *i* in this word stands for the short *i* sound and ask them to pronounce the word. Continue with new words like *swift, rich,* and *ship.*

Next, write the new word *child* and explain that the letter *i* stands for the long *i* sound. Have pupils pronounce the word. Then write *shy* and tell pupils that the letter *y* stands for the long *i* sound. Have *shy* pronounced. Con-tinue similarly with the new words *blind, wild,* and *dry.*

As children learn to associate vowel sounds with the letters *a, e, o, u* and with combinations of vowel letters,[2] they will be strengthening the understandings that (1) a vowel let-ter stands for more than one sound and (2) the same vowel

[1] In normal conversation the sound that final *y* represents in an unstressed syllable is not exactly a short *i* sound but something in between a short *i* and a long *e* sound. Some dictionaries mark this sound short *i*, others long *e*. In this book the sound is called short *i*.

[2] The vowel sounds that children learn to identify at this stage of progress are those heard at the beginning of these words: *at, age, air, are, end, eat, earn, it, ice, odd, oak, or, oil, out, up, use* and in the middle of *put* and of *rule.*

sound may be represented by different letters or combinations of letters. For example, as soon as pupils have learned to associate with the letter *a* the sounds heard in the words *at, ate, car*, they should learn that the letter *a* followed by *i* or *y* usually stands for the long *a* sound. Gradually they note and use other visual clues to vowel sounds.

Noting visual clues to vowel sounds (a̲ and i̲)

When children can identify the vowel sounds heard in *it, ice, bird, at, ate, car* and can associate these sounds with the letters *i, y*, or *a*, they are ready to note visual clues that will help them decide which of these vowel sounds to try first in an unfamiliar word.

1. To develop an awareness of two vowel letters together as a visual clue to vowel sound, write such known words as *ran, rain, stand, stay, catch, train*. As each word is pronounced, ask whether pupils hear a long or a short *a* sound.

Then write such known words as *paint, tail, wait, sail*. Ask pupils to pronounce each word and to tell what vowel sound they hear in it (long *a*). What letter do pupils see

Two vowel letters together (ai̲ or ay̲)

after the letter *a* in each of these words? Do they hear an *i* sound? Have the words pronounced again and ask, "When you see the letter *a* followed by *i* in the spelling of a word, which *a* sound will you try first?" Use similar procedures and the known words *day, play, stay, pay* to develop the understanding that the letter *a* followed by *y* at the end of a word usually stands for the long *a* sound.

Conclude by writing sentences that contain such unknown words as *plain, braid, gray, clay* and note pupils' ability to attack these words. If any pupil has difficulty, call attention again to the visual clue to vowel sound (the letter *a* followed by *i* or *y*) in each word.

2. To extend awareness of the effect of the *r* sound upon the preceding vowel sound, write such known words as *bird, third, first* and have them pronounced. Recall with pupils

that when the letter *i* is followed by *r*, it usually stands for the sound heard in these words. Then write such known words as *car*, *far*, *park*. Have the words pronounced and ask children to listen to the sound that the letter *a* stands for in these words. Ask pupils what letter comes after the letter *a* in each of the words. Have the words pronounced again and ask, "When you see the letter *a* followed by the letter *r* in a word, which *a* sound will you try first?"

One vowel letter (i or a) followed by r

Conclude by writing such unknown words as *skirt*, *card*, *squirt*, and *sharp* in sentences. Point to the word *skirt* in the first sentence and ask pupils to tell what letter they see that helps them know which sound to try first for the letter *i*. Then have the sentence read aloud. Continue similarly with the other words. Lead pupils to conclude that the letter *r* following the letter *i* or *a* is a "sign" that will help them determine which *i* or *a* sound to try first in a new word.

3. To further develop ability to use visual clues to vowel sound, write the words *wait*, *way*, *bark*, and review the understanding that before we decide what sound the letter *a* stands for, we must notice what letter comes after *a*. Then write the known words *ball*, *small*, *salt*. Ask pupils to pronounce the words and to listen carefully to the sound that *a* stands for in each. Through questioning, bring out that it is neither the long, the short, nor the *r*-controlled *a* sound. Next ask what letter pupils see after the letter *a* in each of these words. Then write such known words as *saw*, *fawn*, and *caw* and repeat the procedure. Lead pupils to conclude that the letter *l* or *w* following the letter *a* is a clue that will help them know which *a* sound to try first.

The letter a followed by the letter l or w

4. Procedures like this and the next one should be used frequently to give children practice under guidance in applying what they have learned about visual clues to vowel sound. Write directions containing such unknown words as *chalk*, *arm*, *bark*, *yawn*, *whirl*—"Bring me some chalk," for example, and "Raise your right arm." After underlining each

unknown word, point to it and ask someone to tell what letter he sees in it that will help him know what sound to try first for the letter *a* or *i*. Then ask him to do what the sentence tells him to do. Through discussion, review the idea that when we see the letter *a* or *i* in a word, we should look beyond it to see what letter follows, since this letter may help us know which *a* or *i* sound to try first in the word.

The visual clue usually follows the vowel letter

5. Write incomplete sentences like the following, and for each ask pupils to choose from two unknown words the one that completes the meaning of the sentence.

> I knew the cookies were in the _____. jay jar
> She _____ the papers on the table. laid lard
> He got up at _____ to go fishing. dart dawn

Extending understanding of vowels

When children have learned to associate the vowel sounds heard in *me, met,* and *her* with the letter *e,* they are ready to extend their understanding of the effect of *r* on vowel sounds and of two vowel letters together as a visual clue to vowel sound. In addition they will learn to use other visual clues to vowel sound in printed words.

1. This exercise reviews the sounds that the letters *i* (or *y*), *a,* and *e* represent and promotes understanding of what a vowel is. Begin by writing such known words as *it, ice, at, ate, me, met* and ask what sound the letter *i, a,* or *e* stands for in each word. Then comment that what we have called long and short sounds are vowel sounds and that the letters that stand for long and short sounds are called vowel letters. Next, review the understanding that vowel letters also stand for other vowel sounds by writing such known words as *bird, car, call,* and *her* and having them pronounced.

Initial understandings of what a vowel is

In conclusion, call attention again to the words *bird* and *her.* Ask pupils to listen carefully to the vowel sound as they say each word. Do they hear the same vowel sound in each? When pupils agree that they do, comment that the letter *e* followed by *r* often stands for the vowel sound heard in *bird*, *first*, and *third*.

2. This procedure checks auditory perception of vowels and promotes the understanding that vowels are phonemes.

Vowel sounds are important to meaning

Pupils note that changing one vowel sound affects meaning. They also gain practice in rapid blending of sounds.

Say the sentences "Mother has a pan in her hand," and "Mother has a pain in her hand." Ask whether the sentences mean the same thing. Which words are different in the sentences? What vowel sound do pupils hear in the word *pan?* in the word *pain?* Continue with the same sentence and the words *pin* and *pen*. Lead pupils to note that changing one vowel sound changes meaning.

Next, write *like*, have it pronounced, and ask what vowel sound pupils hear. Under *like*, write *lick*, have it pronounced and the vowel sound identified. Continue with *lack*, *lake*, and *leak*. Have the words pronounced again. Bring out that changing one vowel sound changes meaning.

Generalizing about visual clues

When children have developed some understanding of vowels and of how vowel sounds are indicated in the spelling of words, they are ready to generalize about patterns of visual clues that they find in words. The following procedures stress the forming of generalizations or principles that serve as visual clues to vowel sounds.

1. To introduce the understanding that the position of a single vowel letter in a word is a clue to vowel sound, write such known words as the following in columns: (1) *am, ask, at, end, egg, elf, if, in, is;* (2) *back, fast, can, let, best, red, did, fix, him;* (3) *be, me, she, he, my, cry, fly, try.*

As each word in the first column is pronounced, ask what vowel sound is heard in it. Have the list of words pronounced again and lead pupils to observe that all the words contain a short vowel sound. Then ask where the vowel letter occurs in each word. In like manner, lead pupils to note that in each word in the second column the vowel letter stands for a short sound and is in the middle of the word. Then ask whether children would try a long or a short vowel sound in a new word if the only vowel letter were at the beginning or in the middle of the word.

Have the words in the third column pronounced and ask whether the vowel letter in each stands for a long or a short vowel sound. Where does the vowel letter occur in all these words? What kind of a vowel sound would pupils try first in a new word containing one vowel letter at the end?

Briefly review the three groups of words and lead children to generalize in their own words that *if there is only one vowel letter in a word, it usually stands for a short vowel sound unless it comes at the end of the word.*

2. To give practice in using the position of a single vowel letter as a visual clue to vowel sound and in blending sounds into word wholes, write sentences containing words that pupils have not yet encountered in reading—*pill, task, pink, sly, hi, ant, elk, ink,* for example—and note pupils' ability to attack the words. If anyone has difficulty, point to the new word in the sentence and ask, "How many vowel letters do you see in this word? Where is this vowel letter? Would you expect the vowel letter to stand for a long or a short sound? Why?"

3. To review the effect of *r* following a single vowel letter, write such pairs of known words as *had* and *hard, ten* and *term, will* and *whirl.* Ask pupils to pronounce the first pair of words. What vowel letter do they see in each word? What vowel sound do they hear in *had?* Why would they expect to hear that vowel sound? What vowel sound do they hear in *hard?* Why would they expect to hear that vowel sound? Continue similarly with the other pairs of words. Lead pupils to generalize in their own words that

if the vowel letter in a word is followed by r, *the vowel letter usually stands for an* r-*controlled vowel sound rather
than a short vowel sound.*

4. This exercise extends the understanding that two vowel let-

Two vowel
letters together
as a clue
to vowel sound

ters together are a visual clue to vowel sound. Write the
known word *met* on the board. Have it pronounced and
ask pupils what vowel letter they see in *met* and what vowel
sound they hear. Why would they expect to hear a short
vowel sound? To the right of *met,* write the known word
meat. Have *meat* pronounced and ask pupils how many
vowel letters they see. What are they? How many vowel
sounds do they hear? What vowel sound is it (long *e*)?
Does the letter *a* in *meat* stand for an *a* sound? Continue
with *best* and *beast, bet* and *beet, ran* and *rain, pan* and
pain, step and *steep, fed* and *feed, pin* and *pie, pat* and *pay.*

To help pupils generalize that *if there are two vowel
letters together in a word, the first usually stands for a
long vowel sound and the second is silent,* have the words
meat, beast, beet, rain, pain, steep, feed, pie, and *pay*
pronounced again. Ask, "When you see two vowel letters
together in a word would you try a short or a long vowel
sound? Which of the two letters stands for the long sound?"

5. Write such sentences as those given below and note pupils'
ability to attack the italicized words, which should be words
that children have not yet encountered in reading.

A *stray* dog came to our house.
Mother said she had a *treat* for us.
That boat can *speed* over the water.
I lost my *key.*
We had *hail* and *sleet* last night.

6. This exercise stresses the importance of using meaning clues
as a check on visual clues to vowel sound by pointing out
that the letters *ea* may stand for several vowel sounds.
Write on the board such groups of known words as (1) *leaf,*

squeak, meat, eat; (2) *head, bread, dead, spread;* (3) *bear, learn, heart.* Have the first group of words pronounced and ask pupils what vowel sound they hear in each word. Would they expect to hear this vowel sound? Why? Then ask pupils to pronounce each word in the second group and to tell what vowel letters they see and what vowel sound they hear (short *e*). Explain that when we see the letters *ea* in a word, we usually try the long *e* sound first. If this sound doesn't make a word that fits in the sentence, we must try another sound.

Next, have the words in the third group pronounced. Lead pupils to note that the vowel sound is different in each. Develop the idea that when the letters *ea* are followed by *r* in a word, they may stand for any of these three sounds.

In conclusion, ask pupils to read sentences containing such new words as *reach, pearls, dread,* and *pear,* and note their ability to pronounce the new words.

7. To introduce final *e* as a visual clue to vowel sound, write such known words as *ate, bake, game, late, take, like, nice, fire, ride, time, side.* As pupils pronounce each word, ask what vowel letters they see and what vowel sound they hear. Which vowel letter stands for this sound? Does the final *e* stand for a vowel sound? Next write such pairs of known words as *hat, hate; hid, hide.* Have *hat* and *hate* pronounced and ask what vowel sound pupils hear in *hat.* Why would they expect to hear a short *a* sound? What vowel sound do pupils hear in *hate?* What vowel letter do they see at the end of *hate?* Continue with the other pairs of words, leading pupils to generalize that *if there are only two vowel letters in a word, one of which is final* e *preceded by a consonant letter, the first vowel letter usually stands for a long sound and the final* e *is silent.*

In conclusion, write sentences containing such new words as *cape, chime, hire, wade, ripe,* and note pupils' ability to attack the new words.

Final e as
a visual clue
to vowel sound

8. To provide practice in attacking new words in context, write sentences like those that are given below. Note whether pupils use visual clues to vowel sound and context clues as a means of analyzing each italicized word.

> There is a *lake east* of town.
> *Ferns* grow well in the *shade.*
> The farmer went to *search* for the *lame* horse.
> There is a *wire* fence around our *lawn.*
> He will *wear* a *mask* on Halloween.

9. When pupils have learned to identify the short, long, and r-controlled vowel sounds that the letter *o* represents (*not, no, north*), write these groups of known words: (1) *got, go, no, nod;* (2) *load, coat, roam, soap;* (3) *rope, wrote, rode, home;* (4) *horn, short, form, cord.* Have pupils check to see whether the clues they have used on the basis of the letters *i, a,* and *e* (the position of a single vowel letter in a word, two vowel letters together, final *e,* the letter *r* following a vowel letter) help them determine which vowel sound to try first when they see the letter *o* in a word. Then provide opportunity for children to attack such new words as *porch, throat, note, rock* in context.

Generalizations are checked as new vowels are introduced

10. When children have learned to identify the short, long, and r-controlled vowel sounds that the letter *u* represents (*up, use, fur*), write such groups of known words as (1) *bug, shut, dust;* (2) *cube, fuse, cute;* (3) *burn, hurt, turn* and have them pronounced. Again have pupils check to see whether visual clues (the position of a single vowel letter in a word, final *e,* the letter *r* following a vowel letter) help them determine which vowel sound to try first when they see the letter *u* in an unfamiliar printed word. Then write sentences containing such new words as *blur, clump, fumes,* and note pupils' ability to attack them.

11. Use such known words as *full, put, pull, push* and *Ruth, rule, duke, tune* in sentences to illustrate two more vowel

sounds that the letter *u* may represent.[1] Then reëmphasize the importance of using meaning clues to check visual clues to vowel sound.

The next two exercises extend children's use of visual clues to vowel sound by familiarizing them with additional clues. The first exercise modifies the understanding that final *e* is a clue to a long vowel sound. The second exercise modifies the understanding that a single vowel letter in the middle of a word is a clue to a short vowel sound.

1. This exercise promotes the understanding that a single vowel letter followed by two consonant letters and a final *e* usually represents a short vowel sound. Write such known words as *ate, these, time, use* in a column on the board and have them pronounced. Ask pupils what vowel sound they hear in each word and why they would expect to hear that vowel sound. Then write such known words as *dance, fence, since, pulse* in a second column to the right of the first column of words. Have the second column of words pronounced and ask pupils what vowel sound they hear in each word. Call attention to the single consonant letter following the first vowel letter in each word in the first column of words and to the two consonant letters following the first vowel letter in each word in the second column. Bring out that *a single vowel letter followed by two consonant letters and a final* e *usually represents a short vowel sound;* whereas a single vowel letter followed by one consonant letter and a final *e* usually represents a long vowel sound. Write sentences containing new words like *rinse, rice, trade, badge, fudge, huge, fringe* and note pupils' ability to attack them.

2. To call attention to some common spellings that are clues to long vowel sounds, write the following words in three columns: *cold, hold, gold, fold; high, fight, might, light;*

Generalizations are modified or extended in light of additional spelling patterns

---

[1] The long *u* sound may be heard in such words as *duke* and *tune*. You will want to present these words as your class says them.

find, mind, bind, kind. As pupils pronounce the words in each column, ask them what vowel sound they hear. Call attention to the spellings of the words and bring out that the letter *o* followed by *ld* and the letter *i* followed by *gh* or *nd* usually stand for long vowel sounds.

Visual-auditory perception of diphthongs

When pupils can use visual clues to identify long, short, and *r*-controlled vowel sounds in words, they should learn to associate the diphthongs heard in *boy* and in *out* with the letters that represent them.

The letters oi and oy represent the same sound

1. When pupils can identify the sound of the diphthong heard in *boy*, they should associate the sound with the letters *oi* and *oy*. The sound and letters should be presented in groups of known words so that pupils can see that the letters *oi* and *oy* are used to represent the same sound. By comparing such words as *my, mine; fly, fine; boy, boil; toy, toil; joy, join*, pupils should recall the generalization that the letter *y* is usually used to represent an *i* sound at the end of a word and should note that *oy* is used to represent the *oi* sound at the end of a word.

The letters ou and ow represent the same sound

2. This exercise helps pupils associate the diphthong heard in *house* with the letters *ou* and *ow*. Write such known words as *loud, sound, mouth* and *clown, town, cow* and lead pupils to note that the letters *ou* and *ow* may stand for the same vowel sound. Then write sentences like the following, and note pupils' ability to recognize the italicized words:

A pig's nose is called a *snout.*
A *crowd* of boys watched the game.
I need a *pound* of *brown* sugar.

Strengthening concepts of variability

As pupils associate vowel sounds with letters, they constantly strengthen the concepts that the same letter or letters may represent different sounds and that different letters may represent the same sound. The next group of procedures reviews known vowel sounds and their common spellings and introduces additional spellings for the sounds.

1. When children have learned to associate the diphthong heard in the words *crowd* and *down* with the letters *ow*, they should then contrast the vowel sound in such words as *blow*, *grow*, *know* with that in *cow*, *now*, and *how*. Thus the concept is developed that the only way to determine the sound that the letters *ow* stand for in an unfamiliar printed word is to try both sounds and decide which sound makes a word that fits the context. Pupils should have ample opportunity to combine meaning clues and phonetic analysis in attacking new words like those that are italicized in the sentences below.

> We sometimes say that an *owl* looks wise.
> Ted wanted to *row* the boat.
> She put the apples in a *bowl*.
> Animals often *prowl* at night.

The same letter or letters may represent different vowel sounds

2. Pupils should learn to associate the vowel sounds in *good* and *soon* with the letters *oo*. By contrasting the vowel sound heard in such known words as *book*, *stood*, *foot* with that heard in *too*, *school*, *food*, pupils can readily see that they must use meaning clues to determine which sound the letters *oo* stand for. Children should have many opportunities to analyze in context such words as *spoon*, *brook*, *tool*, *loop*, and *hook*.

3. Write such groups of known words as (1) *burn, hurt, turn;* (2) *bird, first, third;* (3) *her, term, fern* and have them pronounced. Ask whether children hear the same vowel sound in all these words. When children agree that the vowel sound is the same, call attention to the spelling. What vowel letter do they see in each word in the first group? What letter follows the letter *u?* Continue similarly with the other two groups. Lead children to generalize

Different letters may represent the same vowel sound

that the letters *u*, *i*, and *e* when followed by *r* usually stand for the same vowel sound.

4. As children compare the vowel sound in the words *full*, *put*, *push* with that in *wood*, *book*, *stood* and the vowel sound in *Ruth*, *rule*, *tune* with that in *food*, *pool*, *room*, bring out that these two vowel sounds are commonly associated with the letters *oo* as well as with the letter *u*.

5. Write such known words as *noon* and *rule* and have them pronounced. Then write *blew* and *flew* and have them pronounced. Lead pupils to note that the vowel sound in *noon*, *rule*, *blew*, *flew* is the same and that the letters *ew* as well as *oo* and *u* may represent this sound.

6. To review the sound that the letter *a* usually represents when it is followed by the letter *w* or *l*, write the known words *straw*, *caw*, *walk*, *tall* and have them pronounced. Then write *cause* and have it pronounced. Lead pupils to compare the vowel sound in *cause* with that in *straw*, *caw*, etc. Bring out that the letter *a* followed by *u* may stand for the same vowel sound that *a* followed by *w* or *l* does.

Using endings and suffixes in structural analysis

As children learn to identify vowel sounds in printed words, they should also be learning to identify additional inflectional endings and suffixes as meaningful parts of words. At the same time, pupils should note that in spite of spelling changes, a root retains one of its meanings in an inflected or derived form. The procedures given in this section are designed to help children identify (1) the inflectional endings *-en* and *-er*, *-est* (of comparison); (2) the suffixes *-er* (of agent), *-y*, *-ly;* (3) root words in inflected or derived forms in which a change in spelling occurs (final consonant doubled, final *y* changed to *i*, final *e* dropped in the root before an ending or suffix).

Identifying new inflectional endings (-en, -er, -est)

The following procedures strengthen understanding of the way in which structural elements function in words and emphasize the root word as a meaning unit in inflected forms. The endings -en and -er, -est (of comparison) are introduced.

1. Write the known words *fall* and *fallen* and have them pronounced. Ask someone to underline the root word *fall* in *fallen* and to tell what is added to *fall* to make *fallen*. Then have each word used in an oral sentence. Repeat with *eat* and *eaten*.[1]

   Identifying the ending -en

2. Write the word *long* and have it pronounced. Then add -er and have the word *longer* pronounced. Repeat with *longest*.

   Identifying the endings -er and -est

   To call attention to the meaning of -er and -est, draw three lines of varying lengths on the board and label them *first*, *second*, and *third*. Have pupils read the following sentences and fill in the blanks after studying the lines on the board.

   The _____ line is the longest of all.
   The _____ line is shorter than the second.
   The _____ line is the shortest of all.

   Then write such words as *loud, louder, loudest; tall, taller, tallest*. Have each pronounced, and either write sentences to illustrate the use of the various forms or have pupils use the words orally in sentences.

3. Write sentences that contain -er or -est forms of known roots, *warmer, smallest, sooner*, for example, and ask children to read each sentence. Point to the inflected form and ask, "What is this word?" If a child has difficulty, ask, "Do you see an ending on the word? What is the ending?"

---

[1]Although -en is used as an inflectional ending in this exercise, it is also a common suffix. At this level, children should have no difficulty in recognizing either the form or meaning of such derived forms of known roots as *sharpen, frighten*, and *golden*, in which -en is a suffix.

Cover the ending and ask, "What word do you see now?" When he has identified the root word, ask him to pronounce the entire word. Point out that this is the root word *warm*, for example, with the ending *-er* added to make *warmer*.

4. Write the words *cold, colder, coldest* and such sentences as "Father says that it is much _____ than it was yesterday" and "This is the _____ weather we have had this year." Ask pupils to use the appropriate form of *cold* in the blank as they read each sentence.

Identifying suffixes as meaning units

As soon as pupils have learned to associate long and short vowel sounds with the letters *i* and *y*, they should learn to recognize the suffixes *-y* and *-ly* as meaning units. They should also learn to identify the suffix *-er* (of agent).

1. To develop ability to recognize derivatives formed by adding *-y* to known root words, write *rust* and have it pronounced. Add *-y* to make the derivative *rusty* and have it pronounced. To bring out the meaning of the derivative *rusty*, ask several pupils to use it in a sentence. Continue with the following:

The suffixes -y and -ly as structural elements

| bump | (bumpy) | rain | (rainy) | sleep | (sleepy) |
| dust | (dusty) | trick | (tricky) | sand | (sandy) |

Next, underline the root word in each derived form and comment that we call the *-y* that is added to these root words a suffix. Conclude by writing sentences like the following, which contain derived forms of known roots to which the suffix *-y* has been added. Have the sentences read and note pupils' ability to attack the italicized words.

One *windy* day John raked leaves until he was tired.
Then he sat down on a *grassy* spot and said, "I like *snowy* days better than *windy* days."

2. Write such known words as *cloud, rock, mist, squeak,* and have them used in oral sentences. Then add the suffix *-y* to

each root and have the derived forms used in oral sentences. Ask children to tell what each derived form means.

3. To introduce the suffix -ly, write the known words *friend* and *friendly* on the board and have children use each in an oral sentence. Ask a pupil to underline the root word *friend* in *friendly* and to tell what was added to *friend* to make *friendly*. Continue with such words as *sudden, suddenly; slow, slowly; quick, quickly*. Comment that -ly is a suffix that is added to the ends of words to make new words.[1]

4. Write the incomplete sentence "The baby was sleeping _____," and the words *quiet* and *quietly* to the right of the sentence. Ask pupils to read the sentence and to tell which of the two words might be used in place of the blank. Continue with the sentence "We take a _____ newspaper," and the words *week* and *weekly*.

5. Write on the board sentences containing derived forms of known root words, *softly, tightly, soapy, silky*, for example. Underline the derivatives. When pupils have read each sentence, point to the underlined word and ask what root word pupils see in it and what suffix has been added to this root word.

6. To promote ability to recognize the form and meaning of derivatives made by adding -er (of agent) to a root word, write the word *farm* and have it pronounced. Then ask, "What do you call a man who farms?" When pupils suggest *farmer*, add -er to the word on the board and have it pronounced. Explain that we can often make a word that tells what we call a person who does something by adding the suffix -er to the word that tells what he does. Continue with the derivatives *builder, helper, owner, singer, camper*. To test understanding of the meaning of the suffix -er, have pupils use the derived forms in sentences.

Identifying the form and meaning of the suffix -er

[1]Obviously, at this level, no attention need be called to the fact that the suffix -ly has two functions—that of making adjectives from nouns (*friendly*) and that of making adverbs from adjectives (*suddenly*).

7. Ask pupils to read and supply the missing word in such sentences as "A teacher is a man or woman who _____." "A hunter is a man who _____." "A worker is a person who _____."

8. Explain that a word formed by the addition of the suffix -*er* does not always mean "a person who _____." Ask what the word *cleaner* means in the phrase "a vacuum cleaner"; what *sprayer* means in the phrase "a paint sprayer." Then write such derived forms as *bumper, toaster, heater,* and *locker,* and ask children to use each in a sentence.

Recognizing changes in spelling before affixes

The procedures in this section are designed to develop the understanding that a root word retains its meaning in an inflected or derived form even though a spelling change occurs before the ending or suffix (the final consonant of the root may double as in *muddy;* the final *y* may change to *i* as in *earliest;* the final *e* may be dropped as in *hoping*). This understanding can be developed when pupils recognize in print many inflected or derived forms like *dropping, sunny, cried, carrier, baking, lacy* and know the meaning of the affixes involved.

The first two procedures are suggested for developing ability to recognize inflected and derived forms of known roots in which the final consonant letter is doubled before an ending or suffix.

1. To review the understanding that two like consonant letters represent one consonant sound, write such known words as *tell, add, miss* and have each pronounced. For the word *tell,* ask how many *l*'s pupils see and how many *l* sounds they hear. Continue with *add* and *miss.*

Next, write the known words *drop, dropped, dropping* on the board and have the root word *drop* pronounced. Then point to *dropped,* have it pronounced, and underline the root *drop* in it. Ask children what else besides the ending -ed is added to the root word *drop* to make *dropped*.

Final consonant
letter doubled
before
an ending
or suffix
How many *p* sounds do children hear in *dropped?* Continue with *dropping*. Explain that (1) often the final consonant letter of a root word is doubled before an ending or a suffix, (2) although we see two like consonant letters, we hear only one consonant sound. Continue similarly with the root *swim* and its derived form *swimmer*.

Conclude by writing the words *getting, sunned, runner, hopped, shutter, fattest,* and *foggy*. As each inflected or derived form is pronounced, ask a pupil to underline the root word to which an ending or suffix has been added and to use the inflected or derived form in an oral sentence.

2. Write sentences containing inflected and derived forms of known roots in which the final consonant is doubled before the ending or the suffix (see the sentences given below). Ask pupils to read each sentence and to tell what the root word is in each italicized form.

> It was a *sunny* summer day.
> Tim was *cutting* the grass.
> Father was *digging* in the garden.
> Mother said, "It's the *hottest* day of the year. Let's go *swimming*."

The next three procedures are designed to promote ability to identify inflected and derived forms of known root words in which the final *y* is changed to *i* before an affix.

1. Write the word *cry* and have it pronounced. Then say the word *cried* and write it on the board. Recall with pupils that

Final y
changed to i
before
an ending
or suffix
the letter *i* and the letter *y* may stand for the same sounds. Next ask, "What did I do to the root word *cry* before adding -*ed?*" Similarly, compare the root word *carry* and its derived form *carrier*. Bring out that changing the letter *y* to *i* does not change the sound of the root word.

Write such sentences as "I *hurried* to school" and "I *dried* the dishes," underlining the italicized words. As children read each sentence, point to the underlined word and ask them to tell what was done to the root word before an ending was added.

2. Write the word *baby* and say, "I am going to change this root word to make it mean more than one baby." Change the *y* to *i* and add *-es*. Repeat with *penny* and *pennies*. Then write such sentences as "There were two *families* of birds in our yard." "The boys like to ride their *ponies*." "Tell us some *stories*." As children read each sentence, point to the italicized word and ask what the root word is. Write the root word after the sentence (for example, *family*).

The above procedures may be used to illustrate the changing of *y* to *i* before the endings *-er* and *-est* and before the suffix *-ly* as in *busier*, *busiest*, and *busily*.

3. To call attention to the fact that two affixes may be added to a root word, write the word *sun*. Ask pupils to pronounce the word and to use it in a sentence. Then write *sunny*

Recognizing changes in spelling before two affixes

under *sun;* have *sunny* pronounced and used in a sentence. Ask pupils to tell what suffix was added to the root word *sun* to make *sunny* and what change occurred in the root *sun* when the suffix was added. Then comment that you will add something to *sunny* to make another word. Write *sunniest* under *sunny*, and have *sunniest* pronounced and used in a sentence. Ask pupils what was added to *sunny* to make *sunniest* and what change occurred in *sunny* before the ending was added. To bring out that both *sunny* and *sunniest* come from the same root word, underline the root *sun* in each form. Continue with *mud*, *muddy*, and *muddiest*.

The following procedures are suggested for helping children develop ability to attack inflected and derived forms of known words in which final *e* is dropped before an ending or a suffix,

1. Write the known word *make* and ask pupils to pronounce it. Erase the final *e* and add *-ing*, calling attention to the drop-

ping of *e*. Have children pronounce the known word *making*. Direct attention to the fact that dropping the final *e* does not change the sound of the root word by asking such questions as "What is the root word in *making*? [Write *make* after *making*.] How many vowel letters do you see in *make*? What vowel sound do you hear? Does dropping the silent *e* before *-ing* change the sound of the root word?"

Final *e* dropped before an ending or suffix

List such known words as *liking, hiding, taking*. Point to the word *liking* and have it pronounced. What ending do pupils see on this word? What is the root word? Then write the root word (*like*) and the ending (*-ing*) after the word *liking* to emphasize that final *e* is dropped before the ending *-ing*. Repeat with the other words in the list.

2. Write the endings *-ed, -en, -er, -est* and remind pupils that these endings are often added to words. Then write such known words as *liked, taken, later, latest*. Using the general procedures suggested in the preceding exercise, develop the concept that although final *e* is dropped before the endings *-ed, -en, -er, -est*, the vowel sound in the root remains long. Use similar procedures with the suffix *-er* and the derived forms *baker, racer, writer, driver* and with the suffix *-y* and the derived forms *lacy, bony,* and *nosy*.

3. Write such pairs of known words as *hopping, hoping; chatted, hated*. Lead pupils to note that in the first word of each pair there are two like consonant letters before the ending, that the root word ends in a single consonant letter, and that the vowel sound in the root is short. Lead pupils to note that in the second word in each pair there is only one consonant letter before the ending, that the root word ends in final *e*, and that the vowel sound in the root is long.

Changes in spelling give clues to vowel sound in root words

4. Write such known words as *hotter, biting, sitting, safest, biggest, smiled, miner, swimmer*. Ask pupils to write each root word to which an ending or suffix has been added. Have them tell whether the vowel sound is long or short in each root and why they would expect that vowel sound.

Combining structural and phonetic analysis

Pupils should learn to combine structural and phonetic analysis in order to analyze inflected or derived forms of unfamiliar one-syllable root words in which there are clues to vowel sound (*droning, winner, sprawled, shyly*). To do so, children must be able to (1) identify a known ending or suffix, (2) recognize any change in the spelling of the root before an ending or suffix, (3) apply visual clues to vowel sound in the root word. The following procedures promote ability to combine phonetic and structural analysis in attacking inflected or derived forms of unknown root words and compounds in which one root is unknown.

1. Write on the board a sentence containing an inflected form of an unknown root word, for example, "Jane *slammed* the door." Point to the word *slammed* and ask pupils what ending they see on the word. Then ask, "What do you see just before the ending? What vowel sound will you try first in the root word? Why? What is the root word? What was done to the root word *slam* before the ending was added?" Then ask children to pronounce the word *slammed* and to read the sentence aloud.

   Attacking inflected and derived forms of unknown roots

2. Write *winner* and ask a child to underline the root word. When *win* is underlined, ask, "What vowel sound will you try first in this root word? Why?" Have pupils pronounce the root *win* and its derivative *winner*. Have *winner* used in an oral sentence. Continue similarly with the words *stirring, porches, flatly, begged, yawning,* and *speaking.*

   Write sentences like the following containing inflected forms of unknown root words: "The frogs were *croaking.*" "Ben *grabbed* the lines and *yelled* to the pony." Have the sentences read, noting pupils' ability to identify the new words.

3. Write *tamest* and ask, "What ending do you see on this word? How many consonant letters are there just before the

ending? Do you think the root word ends in *e?* Why? What vowel sound will you try first in the root word?" Have *tamest* pronounced and used in an oral sentence. Continue in like manner with such derived forms as *glider, diver, trader, voter.*

4. Write sentences like those given below and check pupils' ability to attack the italicized words.

> Father was *spading* the garden.
> The dog's ears *flopped* as he ran.
> We heard the *droning* sound of the airplanes.
> The *hiker* stopped to eat his lunch.
> The man *sprawled* in his chair.
> We take the *daily* paper.
> The birds were *chirping.*

5. To help pupils attack one unknown root in a compound (*beam* in *sunbeam*, for example), write the new word *beam.*

Attacking compounds— one known, one unknown root Ask what vowel sound children will try first in this word. Why? Have *beam* pronounced. Next write the compound *sunbeam.* What two words do pupils see in it? What does *sunbeam* mean? Recall that a word made up of two root words that combine their meanings is called a compound. Continue similarly with the new root word *bone* in the compound *wishbone.*

Next, write the words *loaded, hailstone, bobbing,* and *toothbrush.* Ask pupils to pronounce each word and to tell whether it is made up of a root word and an ending or whether it is a compound word. Then write sentences like those given below. Note pupils' ability to attack the unknown root words (*pitch, base, chip, tea, wreck, slice, faint*).

> Tom is *pitcher* on our *baseball* team.
> I *chipped* my mother's best *teapot.*
> The men were *shipwrecked.*
> She was *slicing* the bread.
> The sound of the motor grew *fainter.*

Summary

This chapter has covered the first stage of progress in phonetic and structural analysis (see the charts on pages 39 and 55). The goals of the procedures have been to develop (1) phonetic skills and understandings that enable children to analyze independently one-syllable root words and (2) structural skills and understandings that enable children to analyze many inflected, derived, and compound forms.

In phonetic analysis children have learned to identify consonant and vowel sounds in words and to associate these sounds with letters of the alphabet. They have learned to use visual clues to vowel sound that help them know which vowel sound to try first in an unfamiliar printed word.

In structural analysis children have learned to identify inflectional endings (-s, -'s, -es, -ing, -ed, -en, -er, -est) and suffixes (-y, -ly, -er) as meaningful parts of words and to identify the root word as a meaning unit in inflected or derived forms, including those in which the final consonant is doubled, the final y is changed to i, or the final e is dropped before an ending or suffix.

By the end of the first stage of progress in word analysis, a child should be able to attack in context the seven general types of words listed below in addition to those already listed on page 92.

Skills and understandings developed at the first stage of progress

Types of words that can be analyzed

1. One-syllable words in which there are visual clues to the vowel sound (for example, position of single vowel letter in *it, hem, fly, he;* the letter *r* following a single vowel letter in *car, her, fir, horn;* final *e* in *stake, hike, tone, use;* two vowel letters together in *gain, deep, moan*)

2. One-syllable words in which the vowel sound is represented by the letters *oo, ow, ou, oi,* and *oy* (*soot, tool, flow, gown, hound, spoil, joy,* for example)

3. Inflected forms of known roots to which the endings -*en* and -*er*, -*est* (of comparison) have been added (*eaten, longer, longest,* for example)

4. Derived forms of known roots to which the suffixes -*y*, -*ly*, and -*er* (of agent) have been added (*snowy, sadly, farmer,* for example)

5. Inflected and derived forms of known roots in which the final consonant is doubled, final *y* is changed to *i*, or final *e* is dropped before an ending or suffix (*sunny, tried, hoping,* for example)

6. Inflected or derived forms of unknown one-syllable roots that can be analyzed phonetically to which a known ending or suffix has been added; including those root words in which the final consonant is doubled, the final *y* is changed to *i*, or the final *e* is dropped before the ending or suffix (*neatly, slimmest, fried, slimy,* for example)

7. Compounds of one known root and a one-syllable root that can be attacked phonetically (*workbench,* for example)

To attack the first two types of words listed, a child uses phonetic analysis. He uses structural analysis to attack the next three types of words. With the sixth and seventh types listed, he must combine structural and phonetic analysis.

When children have acquired the skills and understandings presented in this chapter, they are ready for the second stage of progress in word analysis. In phonetic analysis children will learn to apply visual clues to vowel sound, together with their knowledge of consonants, to the accented syllable in two-syllable words. They will also learn to use visual clues to syllabication and to accent. In structural analysis pupils will become familiar with prefixes, with additional suffixes, and with the understanding that suffixes have a grammatical function. Procedures for helping pupils analyze two-syllable root words and additional kinds of inflected and derived forms are given in the next chapter.

Chapter five | Word analysis at the second stage of progress

Developing ability to attack two-syllable words

The procedures given in this chapter are designed to develop skills and understandings that will help children attack two-syllable root words with or without inflectional endings, suffixes, or prefixes. The development of these skills and understandings characterizes the second stage of progress in both phonetic and structural analysis (see the charts, pages 39 and 55).

Using syllabication in phonetic analysis

Children are now ready to learn to identify syllables and accent and to determine syllabic divisions in printed words. They can then apply visual clues to vowel sound to the accented syllable and the understanding that accent affects vowel sounds to the total word. The procedures suggested in this section are designed to help a child (1) hear syllables and accent, (2) note how accent affects vowel sound, (3) use visual clues to syllabication, (4) apply visual clues to vowel sound in the accented syllable, (5) blend the syllables into a word whole.

Auditory perception of syllables and accent

The next group of procedures develops ability to hear syllables and accent and promotes understanding of the syllable as a unit of pronunciation.

1. Write such known words as *I, me, go, not, jam* on the board. As pupils pronounce each word, ask what vowel letter they see and what vowel sound they hear in each. Develop the idea that there is at least one vowel letter and one vowel sound in each word in our language.

   Then write the words *hate, rain, sweet, please* and have pupils tell how many vowel letters they see and how many vowel sounds they hear in each.

   Next, comment that in some words we hear one vowel sound; in many others we hear two vowel sounds. Then write the known words *part* and *party,* and say, "Listen carefully as I pronounce these two words. In the first word you will hear one vowel sound, in the second word two vowel sounds." As you pronounce the words, pat out the syllables —one pat for the first word and two pats for the second. Pat a little harder for the accented syllable than for the unaccented syllable in the two-syllable word. Continue with *fan, fancy; sand, sandwich; win, window.* Then have pupils pronounce the words and pat out the syllables. (This type of kinesthetic response promotes children's ability to hear syllables and develops an awareness of accent.)

2. Write the known word *lady,* pronounce it, and ask children to tell how many vowel sounds they hear in it. What are these two vowel sounds? Repeat with the words *yellow, funny, planning, childish.*

   A syllable is a part of a word in which a vowel sound is heard

   Explain that a word or a part of a word in which we hear one vowel sound is called a syllable. Review the first list of words in the preceding exercise (*I, me, go,* etc.) and develop the idea that these are one-syllable words. Have pupils pronounce the second list of words (*hate, rain,* etc.)

again and develop the idea that since we hear only one vowel sound in each, these are also one-syllable words. Review such two-syllable words as *party*, *lady*, *sandwich*, asking pupils to pronounce each word and to tell how many vowel sounds they hear. Develop the idea that if we hear two vowel sounds in a word, that word has two syllables.

3. This exercise helps children identify accent and develops the understanding that in a two-syllable word one of the syllables is accented more than the other. Tell children to listen carefully as you say a word that has two syllables. Then pronounce *lady*, accenting the first syllable. Say *lady* again, accenting the second syllable. Ask pupils which pronunciation sounds right. Do the same with each of the following words: *sandwich*, *planning*, *fancy*, *window*. Then pronounce all the words again, accenting the second syllable in each. Ask children why they think these pronunciations sound funny. (Pupils will probably say that the second syllable sounds too loud.) Explain that when we say a two-syllable word, we say one syllable more loudly or forcefully than the other and that this loudness or force is called accent. Then have pupils pronounce the words and tell which syllable is accented in each.

In a word of more than one syllable, one of the syllables is accented more than the other (or others)

Use similar procedures with two-syllable words like *command*, *suppose*, *mistake*, *connect*, *machine*, which are accented on the second syllable.

4. Write such known words as *holly*, *basement*, *empty*, *behave*, *baggage*, *selfish*, *cunning*, *parade*, *hundred*, *merry*, *manage*, *today*. Ask pupils to pat out the syllables as they say these words, patting a little harder for the accented syllables. Since every fourth word has the accent on the second syllable, a rhythmic pattern emerges.

5. This exercise provides readiness for the understanding of the way in which accent affects vowel sounds. Begin by writing such known words as *silent*, *become*, *suppose*, *polite*, *shadow*, *secret*, *penny*. As children pronounce each

word, ask how many syllables they hear and which syllable is accented. Then pronounce each word again, first accenting the correct syllable, *si'lent, be come'*, and then deliberately accenting the wrong syllable, *si lent', be'come*. Lead children to note that unless we accent a word correctly it is hard to recognize it.

6. To promote ability to recognize the schwa sound, the soft unstressed vowel sound commonly heard in unaccented
<small>Identifying the schwa sound</small> syllables,[1] write the known words *ago, aloud*, and *along* on the board and pronounce them. Then ask pupils to pronounce each word and to tell which syllable is accented. Point to the letter *a* and lead pupils to observe that the letter *a* stands for the same sound in each word. Explain that this soft unstressed vowel sound is called the schwa sound and that the schwa sound is commonly heard in unaccented syllables.

Use the same procedures with the known words *sofa, panda, soda, zebra*, in which the schwa sound is heard in the last syllable.

7. To help pupils note that any vowel letter may stand for the schwa sound, write the following words and pronounce them: *gallop, suppose, linen, circus, peril, salad, focus, command*. For each word ask pupils (1) how many syllables they hear, (2) which syllable is accented, (3) what vowel sound they hear in the unaccented syllable, (4) what letter stands for the schwa sound.

8. To help children discriminate between vowel sounds in unaccented syllables and to promote understanding that not all unaccented syllables contain the schwa sound, pronounce the following words: *bronco, April, picnic, unite, alone, rescue, antique, away*. As you say each word, have pupils identify (1) the number of syllables, (2) the accented syllable, (3) the vowel sound in the accented syllable. Then

[1]The symbol for this sound is ə.

pronounce each word again and ask what vowel sound is heard in the unaccented syllable (the schwa sound is heard in the unaccented syllables of *April, alone,* and *away*).

Visual-auditory perception of syllables

The next group of procedures strengthens children's awareness of the syllable as a pronunciation unit and introduces the syllable as a visual unit.

1. To introduce syllables as visual units, write such known words as *appear, school, straight, picture, whisper, proud, strange, candle* and have them pronounced. Ask pupils how many syllables they hear in each word. As children respond, write the one-syllable words in a column and the two-syllable words in another column, dividing the two-syllable words into syllables (*ap pear, pic ture, whis per, can dle*). Explain that we can show how words are divided into syllables by leaving a small space between the syllables.

2. Write the lists of known words suggested below, leaving a small space between the syllables. (Children should see and pronounce each word as a whole, not as two words.)

at	can dy, lad der, ap ple, ba by, a cross
ate	ta ble, ham mer, pa per, a pron, a part
all	au tumn, al ways, a loud, aw ful, sand wich
ago	at tend, hap py, a head, a bout, la zy
arm	gar den, a round, par ty, bar gain, car rot
her	pur ple, cir cus, car ry, hur ry, cher ry

Have a pupil pronounce the word *at*. Then have him pronounce the next word in the first line (*can dy*) and ask pupils to tell whether or not the vowel sound in the first syllable sounds like the vowel sound in *at*. When pupils agree that the vowel sound is similar in both words, ask the pupil who is pronouncing the words to underline the syllable *can* in *candy*. Continue in the same way with the other words in the line, underlining only those syllables in which a short *a* sound is heard. Follow the same general procedures with the words in the other lists.

3. Write *rab bit* and have it pronounced. Ask pupils to tell how many syllables the word has and which syllable is accented. Then have them tell whether the vowel sound in the accented syllable is long or short. Continue with such words as *re main, mid dle, let ter, de cide, fan cy, ex act.*

4. Write in a column on the board the words *fun ny, ug ly, ti ny, naugh ty, hap py.* Ask pupils to pronounce each word and to tell which syllable is accented. Then have them say the words again and tell what vowel sound they hear in the unaccented syllable (short *i*).

Visual clues to vowel sound in accented syllables

As soon as a child has learned to hear syllables and has seen them as parts of word wholes, he is ready for the understanding that visual clues to vowel sound in one-syllable words also apply to accented syllables in longer words.

1. Write such known words as *set, rock, silk, no, by, cut.* As children pronounce each one, discuss the visual clue to vowel sound. Pupils should apply the generalization that a single vowel letter usually represents a short sound unless it comes at the end of the word.

Position as a clue to vowel sound in accented syllables

Next, write such words as the following, leaving a small space between syllables (do not put in accent marks until children tell you which syllable is accented):

si′ lent	sil′ ver
la′ dy	lad′ der
ho′ ly	hol′ ly
se′ cret	sec′ tion

Ask pupils to read each word in the first column and to tell which syllable is accented. Explain what an accent mark is, and mark the accented syllables. Then ask what vowel sound (long *i*, etc.) pupils hear in the accented syllables

and why they would expect to hear a long vowel sound.
Lead them to observe that in each word the vowel letter is
at the end of the syllable. Repeat with the second column,
leading pupils to note that in each word the vowel sound
in the accented syllable is short and the vowel letter in the
accented syllable is in the middle of the syllable.

2. Write an unknown word, *vel′vet*, for example, showing
syllables and accent. Ask pupils whether they think the
vowel letter in the first syllable will stand for a long or a
short vowel sound and why. Then write the sentence "The
dress was made of *velvet*" and ask pupils to read it. Use
the same procedure with such words as the following:

si′ ren	We heard the fire *siren*.
rib′ bon	She had a blue *ribbon* in her hair.
hu′ mor	He has a good sense of *humor*.

3. To review the understanding that two vowel letters together
in a word are a clue to a long vowel sound, write such words
as *pail, eat, sweet, feel, rain*. Have pupils pronounce each
word and tell what vowel letters they see and what vowel
sound they hear. Why would they expect to hear that sound?
Next, write such words as the following in two columns,
showing syllable divisions only:

Two vowel letters together as a clue to vowel sound in accented syllables

bea′ ver	bet′ ter
rea′ son	res′ cue
tai′ lor	tab′ let
dain′ ty	dan′ dy

As pupils identify the accented syllable in each word in the
first column, write in the accent mark. What vowel sound
do pupils hear in each accented syllable? Why would they
expect to hear a long vowel sound? Lead pupils to note
that in each word there are two vowel letters together in
the accented syllable. Repeat with the second column, leading pupils to observe that in each word the vowel sound in

the accented syllable is short and the vowel letter in the accented syllable does not come at the end of the syllable.

4. To extend the understanding that visual clues to vowel sound apply to accented syllables as well as to one-syllable words, write the known words *ate, ride, home, use* and review final *e* as a visual clue to a long vowel sound.

Final e or r as a clue to vowel sound in accented syllables

Then write the words shown below (without the accent marks). As pupils pronounce each one, ask which syllable is accented (write in the accent mark). Have children identify the vowel sound in the accented syllable and ask why they would expect to hear that sound.

pa rade′	sup pose′
ex plode′	sur prise′
ex cuse′	de cide′

Use similar procedures with the known words *car, her, bird, fort, hurt; gar′den, de part′, cer′tain, des sert′, thir′ty, or′der, re port′, tur′tle* to introduce *r* as a clue to vowel sound in an accented syllable.

Visual clues to syllabication and vowel sound

When children have learned that visual clues to vowel sound apply to accented syllables within words, they are ready to learn how to divide printed words into syllables so that they can analyze unfamiliar two-syllable words in context.

The next six procedures help children make three basic generalizations that aid in determining syllabic divisions and vowel sounds in printed words of two syllables:

If the first vowel letter in a word is followed by two consonant letters, the first syllable usually ends with the first of the two consonants. (*lad der, slen der*)

If the first vowel letter (or letters) in a word is followed by a single consonant letter, that consonant usually begins the second syllable. (*la dy, sea son*)

If a word ends in *le* preceded by a consonant letter, that consonant usually begins the last syllable. (*la dle, peb ble*)

1. Write such known words as *winter, enter, after, jolly, cab-bage, sister, curtain.* As pupils pronounce the word *winter,* ask which syllable is accented and whether the vowel sound in the accented syllable is long or short. Then ask whether pupils think the first syllable in *winter* is *wi* or *win.* Why? (If the first syllable were *wi,* we would likely hear a long *i* sound in *winter.*) Divide the word into syllables (*win ter*). Continue similarly with the remaining words (*en ter, af ter, jol ly, cab bage, sis ter, cur tain*). Call attention to the words that are divided into syllables and ask, "If you see two consonant letters after the first vowel letter in a new word, with what letter do you think the first syllable will end?"

Two consonant letters following the first vowel letter

2. To check pupils' ability to attack two-syllable words in context, write the following sentences:

One day Sue tried to put a *collar* on her pet bird.
But the bird would *flutter* its wings.
Then it would *scamper* away across the *carpet.*

When pupils have read each sentence silently, ask where the first syllable in the italicized word ends and what vowel sound they tried in the first syllable and why. Note whether pupils have difficulty or distort accent in deriving the un-known words. If, for example, a child says (kol är') instead of (kol' ər) for *collar,* ask whether that sounds like a word he knows; then suggest that he think of the meaning of the word in the sentence and try accenting the word on the other syllable.

3. Write on the board pairs of known words, for example, *happy, paper.* After pupils pronounce *happy,* ask them to tell (1) which syllable is accented, (2) what vowel sound they hear in the accented syllable, (3) whether the first

vowel letter is followed by one or two consonant letters, (4) where they would expect the first syllable to end. Divide *happy* into syllables (*hap py*). Use similar procedures with

One consonant letter following the first vowel letter

paper, leading pupils to note that the vowel sound is long and therefore the first syllable is probably *pa* (write *pa per*). Continue with pairs of known words like *mustard, music; motto, moment; tinder, tiny*. In conclusion, call attention to the words *pa per, mu sic, mo ment, ti ny*, which have been divided into syllables. Ask, "If you see one consonant letter after the first vowel in a word, where do you think the first syllable will end?"

Remind children that when they attack a word they must always check to see whether the word sounds like a word they know, since visual clues to syllabication may not always work. To illustrate, write the name *Robert*. Ask children whether they think the first syllable is *Ro* or *Rob*. Then ask them to pronounce *Robert*.

4. Write sentences containing such unknown words as those that are italicized in the sentences below. Ask pupils to read each sentence. If any pupil has difficulty with a new word, help him divide it into syllables and ask him to pronounce the first syllable and then the whole word. Then ask, "Does that sound like a word you know? Does it fit into the sentence?" For example, if anyone has difficulty recognizing the word *model* because he has divided it *mo del*, suggest that he divide it into syllables another way, *mod el*. Make sure that pupils understand that visual clues to syllabication help them know which syllabic division to try first in a printed word, but that they may have to try another syllabic division to get the correct pronunciation.

> The *pilot* climbed into the plane.
> Jack builds *model* airplanes.
> That bar of iron is *solid*.
> Betty sang a *solo*.
> Dan was a *major* in the army.

5. Write such known words as *table, maple, rifle, bugle.* As pupils pronounce each word, ask them what vowel sound they hear in the first syllable. Where would they expect the first syllable to end? Divide the words into syllables (*ta ble, ma ple, ri fle, bu gle*). Next write such known words as *candle, middle, giggle, mumble* and have them pronounced. Ask pupils whether they think the first syllable in *candle* is *ca* or *can.* Why? Divide the word into syllables (*can dle*). Continue with *mid dle, gig gle, mum ble.* Call attention to the words that are divided into syllables and lead children to note that if a word ends in *le* preceded by a consonant letter, that consonant goes with *le* to form a syllable.

The letters le preceded by a consonant letter

Next, write such known words as *eagle, purple, steeple, able* and have pupils divide the words into syllables. Then have children note the visual clue to vowel sound in the accented syllable of each word and identify the vowel sound.

Conclude by writing sentences like the following in which unknown words are italicized. Have pupils read each sentence and note their ability to identify the words.

This make-believe story is a *fable.*
A package is sometimes called a *bundle.*
We heard the *rumble* of thunder before the storm.

6. This exercise reviews the visual clues to syllabication that have been presented and provides opportunity for pupils to use these clues as they attack new words in context.

Applying visual clues to syllabication and to vowel sound in new words

Write such known words as *stumble, curtain, reason, hollow, stupid.* Ask pupils to tell where they think the first syllable ends in each word and why. Have each word pronounced and discuss the visual clue that aids in determining the vowel sound in the accented syllable.

Next, write sentences like those on the next page, underlining the italicized words, which should be words that pupils have not yet encountered in reading. As pupils read each sentence, discuss (1) where the first syllable ends in each of the underlined words, (2) which syllable is accented, (3) what sound of the vowel in the accented syllable pupils tried first and why.

> Before Christmas Tom took a *tumble* and hurt his *elbow*.
> Sally put *bacon* in the *skillet*.
> When it began to *sizzle*, it burned her.
> Mother lost her *thimble* and *needle*.
> She laughed and said, "This has been a *hectic* day. What a way to start the Christmas *season*."

The effect of accent on vowel sound

The next group of procedures strengthens understanding of the way accent affects vowel sounds in syllables.

1. Write the following known words in two columns, showing syllabic divisions but not accent marks:

Visual clues to vowel sound usually apply only in accented syllables

de ny′	ti′ ny
ap ply′	fan′ cy
re ply′	hur′ ry

Have the words in both columns pronounced, ask which syllable is accented in each word, and mark the accented syllable. Lead pupils to note that in all the words the letter *y* comes at the end of a syllable. Then ask what vowel sound the letter *y* represents in every word in the first column (long *i*). Does the letter *y* stand for a long *i* sound in the words in the second column? Does the letter *y* represent a long *i* sound when it comes at the end of an accented or at the end of an unaccented syllable? Lead pupils to generalize in their own words that a visual clue to vowel sound usually applies only in accented syllables.

2. Write such pairs of known words as *ap ple, ap peal; a pron, a lone*, dividing the words into syllables. As each pair of words is pronounced, ask which syllable is accented in each word. Mark the accents. Then ask what vowel sound pupils hear in the first syllable of each word. Why do

pupils think that the letter *a* stands for a short *a* sound in the first syllable of *apple* but not in the first syllable of *appeal?* Why do they think that the letter *a* stands for a long *a* sound in the first syllable of *apron* but not in the first syllable of *alone?* Emphasize again that a visual clue to vowel sound usually applies only in an accented syllable.

3. Write the words *moun tain, com plain, mo ment, fas ten, les son, sup pose,* leaving a small space between the syllables in each word. As pupils pronounce each word, ask which syllable is accented. (If any children have difficulty in hearing the accented syllable in a word, pronounce the word for them, deliberately accenting and giving full value to the vowel sound in the wrong syllable.) When pupils decide which syllable is accented in each of the words, mark the accented syllable. Then lead children to note again that visual clues to vowel sound apply to accented syllables only. In the words *mountain* and *complain,* for example, the same two vowel letters occur together in the second syllable, but only in the accented syllable *plain* do the letters *ai* stand for a long *a* sound. Have the words pronounced again and lead pupils to note that in the unaccented syllable in each of these words the schwa sound is heard.

Additional visual clues to syllabication

After children have had experience in using the visual clues to syllabication given on pages 126-127, they should become aware of the following visual clues:

When the first vowel element in a word is followed by a consonant blend, the blend often begins the second syllable. (*a pron, cy clone*)

When the first vowel element is followed by a two-letter consonant symbol (*sh, th, ch*), this symbol is not usually broken when the word is divided into syllables and may go with either syllable. (*duch ess, e ther*)

When the first vowel element is followed by the letter *v*, *v* may go with the vowel that precedes or follows it to form a syllable. (*e ven, sev en*)

The letters *ck* go with the preceding vowel to form a syllable. (*sock et, pick le*)

1. To introduce additional visual clues to syllabication, use such known words as the following and procedures similar to those given on pages 127-128:

    Consonant blends—*se cret, pro gram, a pron, cy clone*
    Two-letter consonant symbols—*wheth er, e ther; ush er, a shamed; Rich ard, a chieve*
    Vowel followed by *v*—*clev er, fe ver, gra vy, grav el*
    Vowel followed by *ck*—*tick et, buck le, jack et*

2. To check pupils' ability to use the preceding visual clues to syllabication in attacking unknown words in context, write such sentences as the following, underlining the italicized words. As pupils read each sentence, ask how they identified each underlined word.

    We saw many fire *hydrants* in the city.
    The cold wind made me *shiver*.
    Mother went to a *fashion* show.
    The sign said "*Private*."
    Tim has a new *method* for adding numbers.
    We saw a *cobra* and a *python* in the zoo.
    My brother plays *tackle* on the football team.

Using prefixes and suffixes in structural analysis

At the beginning of the second stage of progress in structural analysis, children identify common prefixes and extend their knowledge of suffixes. As they learn how these structural elements function in words, they strengthen the understanding that root words retain their meaning in inflected and derived forms and that prefixes, suffixes, and inflectional endings are meaningful parts of words. The procedures that follow should be used when they will prove most helpful to young readers. The prefixes and suffixes mentioned will not all be taught at any one time or in any given sequence. Each of these structural elements should be introduced at a time when children know several words in which the affix occurs and at a time when they will be encountering new words that contain the affix.

Identifying prefixes as meaning units

The next group of procedures presents prefixes as meaningful parts of words. The same general procedures suggested for presenting the prefix *un-* may be used for presenting other prefixes (*dis-* and *im-*, for example).

1. To introduce the prefix *un-* as a meaningful part of a word, write the sentence "Tim was not happy" and have it read.

Identifying a prefix as a visual unit and a meaning unit Then write "Tim was unhappy" and have this sentence read. Ask whether the two sentences mean the same thing. When pupils agree that the meaning is the same, ask what means "not" in the second sentence. Next, write such known derivatives as *unlucky, untrue, unwise*, and ask what *un-* means in each. Have each derived form used in a sentence.

Then write such known derivatives as *unlock, untie*, and *unwrap* and have each used in a sentence. Ask pupils whether *un-* means "not" in these words. What does it mean? Bring out that *un-* may mean "the opposite of" as well as "not" and explain that a syllable like *un-* that is added to the beginning of a word is called a prefix.

2. Write such words as *willing* and *unwilling* and such sentences as "The boys were lazy. They were _____ to do their share of the work." Ask pupils to read the sentences and to tell which word completes the meaning.

3. Write such known words as the following on the board: *unsold, uninvited, unwashed, unloaded, unspoken, unfinished, uncovered, undressed, uncertain.* Say a sentence like "Tommy took off his clothes and went to bed." Ask pupils which word listed on the board means the same thing as "took off his clothes." Use similar procedures with the italicized word or phrase in each of the following sentences:

> At the end of the day my work was *not done.*
> The men *took everything out of* the truck.
> The children were *not sure* about the date of the party.
> The *dirty* dishes were left on the table.
> Mother *took the cover off* the baby.

4. When pupils have become familiar with several prefixes, write an exercise like the following, using known prefixes and root words:

un-, im-, dis-

_____agree	fail to agree
_____ripe	not ripe
_____polite	not polite
_____real	not real

Call attention to the prefixes at the top of the exercise. Have pupils pronounce the word *agree* and ask them to tell which of the prefixes they would add to *agree* to make the word mean "fail to agree." Write *dis-* in the blank before the word. Continue with the other words.

Extending knowledge of suffixes

The same general procedures suggested for presenting the suffix *-less* may be used for presenting such suffixes as *-ish,* *-ful,* and *-ness.*

1. To help children recognize derivatives formed by adding the suffix *-less,* write the sentence "Mr. Brown had no home" and have it read. Then change *had no home* to *was home-*

less and lead pupils to note that the meaning of the sentence
has not changed. Next have pupils use such derived forms
as *friendless, toothless, fearless* in oral sentences. Ask what
each derived form means. Lead pupils to generalize that
the suffix *-less* usually means "without" or "having no."

Identifying the form and meaning of additional suffixes

2. Ask pupils to read and supply the missing word in such
sentences as "A sleeveless sweater is a sweater without
_____," "A cloudless sky is a sky without _____," "A
childless person is a person who has no _____."

3. Use such words as *cheerful, childish,* and *kindness* (derived
forms of known roots) in sentences to introduce the suffixes
-ful, -ish, and *-ness.* For example, write the sentence "Tom
is cheerful" and have pupils identify the root word and the
suffix in *cheerful.* Next have the sentence read and ask
pupils to tell what the sentence means without using the
word *cheerful.*

Combining structural and phonetic analysis

Up to this point, children have learned to identify prefixes as meaningful parts of words and have extended their
knowledge of suffixes. They have learned to use visual
clues to syllabication and have developed two understandings about accent: (1) in a word of more than one syllable,
one syllable is stressed more than another; (2) accent affects
vowel sounds; for example, visual clues to vowel sound
usually apply only to accented syllables. The procedures
that follow develop the understanding that endings and
suffixes are usually unaccented and provide practice in
attacking two-syllable root words in inflected, derived, and
compound forms.

The understanding that the accent usually falls on or
within the root word in a derived or inflected form is introduced in the first group of exercises.

1. Write such known words as *boxes, bigger, confessing, whirling, tempted, enchanted, cheaper, objecting, tested, smallest, hidden, duller, freshest, fallen.* Point to the word *boxes* and ask a pupil to tell what ending he sees on the word (*-es*). What is the root word? Then have him pronounce *boxes* and ask how many syllables he hears and which syllable is accented. Place an accent mark after the syllable *box.* Continue in the same way with the other words in the list. Then ask pupils whether the ending is accented in any of these words. Where does the accent fall in each word? Lead children to generalize that when an ending forms a separate syllable in a word, that syllable is usually unaccented—the accent falls on or within the root word.

Endings that form syllables are usually unaccented

Next, write in another column such known words as *ripen, wiser, widest, blazing, exciting, preparing, practicing.* Discuss each word, following the general procedure suggested in the preceding paragraph, and write the accent mark in the appropriate place (*rip'en, wis'er, wid'est, blaz'ing,* etc.). Lead pupils to note that in each of these words (1) the ending is preceded by a single consonant letter; (2) the final *e* in the root word is dropped before the ending; (3) dropping the final *e* does not change the sound of the root word; and (4) the accent falls on or within the root word.

Then write the words *grasped, whirled, scraped, flagged, mailed,* and have the ending identified in each. As pupils pronounce each word, ask whether it has one or two syllables. Point up the idea that an ending does not always form a separate syllable.

2. Write on the board sentences containing unknown words, "Tom *bragged* about how well he could swim," "The teacher was *grading* our papers," for example. Have pupils read each sentence. Then point to the unknown word and have it pronounced. Ask how many syllables it has and (if the ending forms a syllable) which syllable is accented.

3. Write the known suffixes -y, -ly, -ful, -ish, -ness, -less. Remind pupils that we often add one or more of these suffixes to a word to make a new word. Illustrate by writing the following groups of words: *breeze, breezy; busy, busily; fool, foolish, foolishness; care, careful, careless, carefully; plenty, plentiful; fuss, fussy, fussiness.* Have pupils pronounce the words in each group. As they pronounce each derivative, ask them to tell which syllable is accented. Place an accent mark after the accented syllable. Then ask where the accent falls in all these words. Lead pupils to generalize that when one or more suffixes are added to a word to make another word, the accent falls on or within the root word.

Suffixes are usually unaccented

The next procedures check ability to combine structural and phonetic analysis to attack unfamiliar two-syllable roots in inflected, derived, or compound forms.

1. Write on the board a word containing an unknown two-syllable root, *amusing*, for example. Ask pupils to tell what ending they see on the word and with what letter they think the root word ends. Write *amuse* after the inflected form. Then ask pupils to pronounce the root word and the inflected form. If children have difficulty, ask them how many syllables they think *amuse* has and where they think the first syllable ends. Which syllable is accented? What vowel sound would they try first in the accented syllable? Why?

Attacking derived and inflected forms of unknown two-syllable roots

Next, write sentences containing such unknown words as *enclosed, cradled, exploring, favored, whimpered, stammering, referring, proclaiming.* Check pupils' ability to use visual clues to syllabication and vowel sound in attacking each new root word.

2. Write, "I liked the coziness of the room." Point to the new word *coziness* and ask a pupil what suffix he sees at the end of it. Cover the suffix and ask him with what letter he thinks the root word ends. Write *cozy*. Note whether pupils use visual clues to syllabication and to vowel sound in attacking

cozy. Then ask them to pronounce the whole word *coziness.* Ask pupils to read the sentence and to tell what the sentence means without using the word *coziness.*

3. Give children copies of sentences containing underlined inflected or derived forms of new words that can be attacked by combining structural and phonetic analysis, for example, "The cruel king was *merciless,*" "The boy's *surliness* cost him many friends," "The noise was *confusing.*" Ask pupils to read each sentence, to write after it the root word and suffix or ending that make up the underlined word, and to draw a line under the accented syllable in the root word. What clue to vowel sound do pupils see in each accented syllable?

Extending skill in attacking parts of compounds

When pupils have learned to attack unfamiliar two-syllable root words, they should be able to apply this ability to roots in compounds. The final procedure is suggested for helping children attack compounds in which a two-syllable root is a word they have not yet encountered in reading. By applying visual clues to syllabication and to vowel sound in the unknown root, pupils can derive the pronunciation and hence the meaning of the total form.

4. Write sentences containing such compounds as *motorboat, passageway, lumberyard, battlefield* (*boat, way, yard,* and *field* should be known words). Point to *motorboat* in the first sentence, and ask pupils to identify the word that forms the second part of the compound. Cover the root *boat,* and ask where the first syllable probably ends in the word forming the first part of the compound. Suggest next that pupils use visual clues to vowel sound and try accenting each syllable, if necessary, to figure out the pronunciation of this two-syllable word. Have the word *motor* pronounced and then have the compound pronounced. Ask what the word *motorboat* means and have the sentence read aloud. Note whether children can analyze the compounds in the other

sentences independently. If anyone has trouble, repeat the procedure given for the compound *motorboat.*

The procedures given thus far in this chapter have been designed to help children analyze two-syllable root words with or without affixes. In phonetic analysis children have learned to identify syllables as units of pronunciation and to hear accent. They have also learned to use visual clues to syllabication and to apply visual clues to vowel sound in accented syllables. In structural analysis pupils have learned to identify prefixes as meaningful parts of words and have learned many new suffixes. Children who have mastered these skills and understandings should be able to identify in context four general types of words in addition to those discussed in Chapter Four:

Types of words that can be analyzed

1. Two-syllable root words in which there are visual clues to syllabic divisions and to vowel sound in the accented syllable (*pup pet, pu pil, pur ple,* for example)

2. Derived forms of known words to which the prefixes *un-, im-, dis-* or the suffixes *-less, -ness, -ish, -ful* have been added (*unexpected, impossible, penniless, loneliness,* for example)

3. Inflected and derived forms of unknown two-syllable roots (that can be attacked phonetically) to which known affixes have been added (*slumbering, successful, uncommon, disrespectfully,* for example)

4. Compounds made up of one known root and one unknown two-syllable root that can be attacked phonetically (*gingerbread, motorboat, needlework,* for example)

To attack the first type of word a child uses phonetic analysis; to attack the second type he uses structural analysis. With the third and fourth types of words he must combine structural and phonetic analysis.

Up to this point in phonetic analysis pupils have had to try accenting first one syllable and then the other in an unfamiliar two-syllable word to arrive at its pronunciation. Now they are ready to note clues in the spellings of two-syllable words that aid in determining accented syllables. In structural analysis children are ready to acquire understanding of the grammatical function of suffixes and to learn the meaning of additional prefixes and suffixes.

Using accent in phonetic analysis

The procedures in phonetic analysis in the remainder of this chapter are designed to increase pupils' understanding of accent. As pupils progress, they will generalize about clues to accent in many two-syllable root words and in inflected and derived forms of two-syllable roots. They will also develop understanding of the way accent is sometimes determined by meaning (*per′mit, per mit′; con′tract, con tract′*) and will learn to identify secondary accent.

Noting visual clues to accent

The visual clues to accent that pupils learn to apply to two-syllable root words are listed below and on the next page. These clues are extensions of visual clues to vowel sound and to syllabication, and the last two clues combine phonetic and structural analysis.

Two like consonant letters following the first vowel letter (*cannon, furrow*) are a clue to an accented first syllable and to a short vowel sound in that syllable except when the vowel sound is controlled by *r*.

The letters *ck* following a single vowel letter (*nickel, jacket*) are a clue to an accented first syllable and to a short vowel sound in that syllable.

A final syllable ending in *le* preceded by a consonant letter (*ramble, eagle*) is usually unaccented.

Final *e* or two vowel letters together in the last syllable (*parade, complain*) are a clue to an accented final syllable and to a long vowel sound in that syllable.

Two like consonant letters before an ending or a suffix (*regretted, propeller, forbidden, referring*) are a clue to an accented final syllable in the root word and to a short vowel sound in that syllable (except when the vowel sound is controlled by *r*).

A single consonant letter following a single vowel letter before an ending or a suffix that begins with a vowel (*competing, refusal*) may be a clue either to a dropped final *e* and to a long vowel sound in an accented second syllable of the root or to an unaccented final syllable of the root (*trumpeter, traveling*).

The next group of procedures is suggested to introduce visual clues to accent and to vowel sound.

1. To introduce two like consonant letters following the first vowel letter as a clue to an accented first syllable, write known two-syllable words like the following in two columns:

Two like consonant letters following the first vowel letter		
	cannon	hurry
	lesson	porridge
	kitten	stirrup
	hollow	burrow
	supper	horrid

Have the words pronounced. Then ask how many syllables pupils hear in each and which syllable is accented. Lead pupils to note the clue to accent in the spelling of these words by asking these questions: "What follows the first vowel letter in all these words [two like consonant letters]? If you see two like consonant letters after the first vowel letter in a two-syllable word, which syllable will you try accenting first? If the two like consonant letters are *r*, what vowel sound will you try first in the accented syllable? Why? If the two consonant letters are not *r*, will you try a long or a short vowel sound first? Why?"

Next, write sentences containing two-syllable words that pupils have not yet encountered in reading (see the italicized words in the sentences given below). The new words should contain the visual clue to accent that has just been presented. Note pupils' ability to attack the new words.

I like to play *tennis*.
We could not cross the *torrent* of muddy water.
The building had many stone *pillars* around it.
Mother said not to leave *rubbish* in the *attic*.

2. To introduce the letters *ck* as a clue to an accented first syllable and to a short vowel sound in that syllable, write such known words as *pocket, nickel, tickle, package* and have them pronounced. Ask pupils how many syllables each word has and which syllable is accented. Then lead pupils to note the clue to accent in these words by asking, "What two letters follow the first vowel letter in each of these words? When you see the letters *ck* after the first vowel letter in a two-syllable word, which syllable will you try accenting first? Will you try a long or a short vowel sound in the accented syllable? Why?"

The letters ck following the first vowel letter

In conclusion, write such sentences as the following and note pupils' ability to attack the italicized words:

We painted the *picket* fence.
Mary tore a hole in her *stocking*.
Tom cut the weeds with a *sickle*.
The story was about a *rocket* ship.

3. To bring out that a final syllable ending in *le* preceded by a consonant letter is unaccented, write such known words as *battle, maple, marble, eagle, simple* and have them pro-

nounced. Ask pupils which syllable is accented in each word. Is the last syllable accented in any of the words? If pupils see a two-syllable word ending in a consonant letter followed by the letters *le*, which syllable will they try accenting first? Then have pupils pronounce each word again and tell what vowel sound they hear in the accented syllable and why they would expect to hear that vowel sound.

A final syllable ending in a consonant and le

To conclude, write such sentences as the following and note pupils' ability to attack the italicized words:

Mother told me to *gargle* with salt water.
I like *noodle* soup.
The boy was *idle* all day.
Damp wood is hard to *kindle*.
Mother bought a *ladle* at the sale.

4. To introduce final *e* or two vowel letters together in the final syllable of a two-syllable root as a clue to an accented final syllable, write the following words:

Final e or two vowel letters together in the second syllable

parade	obtain
provide	indeed
mistake	complain
complete	conceal

Ask pupils how many syllables they hear in each word and which syllable is accented. Do pupils hear a short or a long vowel sound in each accented syllable? What clue to a long vowel sound do they see in the words in the first column? in the words in the second column? If pupils see a final *e* or two vowel letters together in the second syllable of a two-syllable word, which syllable will they try accenting first? What vowel sound will they try first in that syllable?

Next, introduce the understanding that final *e* following *c*, *g*, or *v* is not necessarily a clue to accent or to a long vowel sound. Following *c* or *g*, it is merely a clue to the "soft" sound of *c* or *g*, and it always follows *v* at the end of

English words. To help pupils arrive at this generalization, write the following known words and use the same general procedures suggested in the preceding exercises:

oblige	savage
advice	notice
behave	native

Conclude by writing the sentences given below. As pupils read each sentence, note their ability to apply visual clues to accent and vowel sound in the italicized words.

The sign read "*Proceed* slowly."
The enemy tried to *invade* England but did not *succeed.*
The *captives* did not *survive* the cold weather.
The *surface* of the road was uneven.

5. Recall that two like consonant letters are a clue to accent and to vowel sound in two-syllable root words like *cannon, supper, kitten.* Then comment that a doubled consonant letter before an ending or suffix is also a clue to accent and to vowel sound. To illustrate, write the known words *forgetting, admitted, beginner, preferring.* Ask which syllable is accented in the root word of each. Is the vowel sound in that syllable long, short, or *r*-controlled? Then call attention to the doubled consonant before the ending or suffix; bring out that two like consonant letters before an ending or a suffix are a clue to an accented final syllable in the root word and to a short vowel sound in that syllable except when the vowel sound is controlled by *r*.

Two like consonant letters before an ending or suffix

Conclude by writing the words *permitted, occurring, excelling, regretted, forbidden.* Ask which syllable pupils would accent, what vowel sound they would try first in the accented syllable, and why.

6. To call attention to a single consonant letter before an ending or a suffix as a clue to accent and to vowel sound, write groups of known words like those on the next page:

completing	carpeting
promoting	piloting
refused	focused
securing	murmuring

As children pronounce each word in the first column, ask which syllable is accented in the root word, what vowel sound they hear in that syllable, and why they would expect to hear that sound (root ends in *e*). Bring out that in these words the single consonant letter before the ending is a clue to a dropped final *e* in the root word. Next, call attention to the single consonant letter before the endings in the second group of words and ask, "Is this single consonant letter a clue to a dropped final *e* in the root?" Have each word pronounced, and ask pupils to tell which syllable is accented in the root word.

One consonant letter preceded by a single vowel letter before an ending or suffix

Continue by having the words pronounced again, this time in pairs (*completing, carpeting,* etc.). Lead the class to note that a single consonant letter before an ending or a suffix is not a clue to a short vowel sound in an accented final syllable of a root word. Then help pupils generalize that a single consonant letter following a single vowel letter before an ending or a suffix is either a clue to (1) an accented final syllable in the root word and to a long vowel sound in that syllable or (2) an unaccented final syllable in the root word.

7. To strengthen understanding of the clues to accent presented in the two preceding exercises, write such words as *regretted, carpeted, competed.* Point to *regretted* and ask, "If you had never seen this word before, how would you try pronouncing it? Why?" Then point to *carpeted* and to *competed* and ask whether pupils would try pronouncing these words with a short vowel sound in the second syllable of the root, (kär pet′id) and (kəm pet′id). Why not? How would pupils try pronouncing these words? Why? Continue similarly with the words *allotted, devoted,* and *pivoted.*

8. To check pupils' ability to use the visual clues to accent they have learned, write sentences containing unfamiliar words to which pupils can apply the clues. Note whether children can attack the unfamiliar words as they read the sentences. Sentences like the following in which the unfamiliar words are italicized may be used:

> The *blizzard compelled* us to stay indoors.
> Because of a broken *propeller*, our flight was *canceled*.
> I can hang by my knees from a *trapeze*.
> The man was *accused* of *committing* a crime.
> The *remote* island had its own laws and *justice*.
> We should *acquaint* ourselves with *traffic* laws.
> One *bucket* of water was *ample* for our needs.

Noting accent patterns

During fourth grade when most children are introduced to glossaries and dictionaries, they become acquainted with secondary accent and with the mark that indicates it in pronunciations. The next group of procedures introduces secondary accent and two common accent patterns in root words of two syllables and in compounds. At the next stage of progress pupils will learn other patterns of accent that will help them pronounce multisyllabic words.

1. This exercise presents a common pattern of accent in compound words—a primary accent on or within the first word and a secondary accent on or within the second word. Write the following compounds (the syllabic divisions and accent marks are shown for your convenience only):

Accent in compounds

> railroad   (rail′ road′)
> houseboat   (house′ boat′)
> bedtime   (bed′ time′)
> countryside   (coun′ try side′)
> waterfall   (wa′ ter fall′)
> thunderbolt   (thun′ der bolt′)

Have children pronounce each compound, identify its roots, and use the compound in a sentence. Then have each compound pronounced again and ask which root is accented more strongly than the other root. Write the syllabication of each compound after the word and mark the accents.

Explain that some words have two accents and that one of these accents is not stressed as much as the other. This lighter accent is called a secondary accent (write the term). Explain that the stronger accent is called a primary accent. Call pupils' attention to the two marks used to indicate primary and secondary accent. Then have children pronounce the compounds again and listen to the accents. Bring out that a common pattern of accent in compounds is a primary accent on or within the first word and a secondary accent on or within the second word.

2. If pupils have difficulty hearing accent in compound words, you might use this technique. Ask pupils to listen carefully as you say two sentences and to tell you what each sentence means. Say the following sentences:

> Mary was homesick.
> Mary was home sick.

In the first sentence there is a primary accent on *home* and a secondary accent on *sick*. This accent pattern indicates a compound word that means "longing for home." In the second sentence the word *sick* carries a stronger accent than it does in the compound word. The difference in accent signals a phrase or two words that mean "ill at home." As you say the sentences, pupils should readily grasp the meaning of each. Lead them to note that accent indicates a difference in meaning between a compound word like *homesick* and the two separate words *home sick*. Continue similarly with the following compounds and sentences:

> Bob said he saw a horsefly.
> Bob said he saw a horse fly.

I saw a bluebird.
I saw a blue bird.

Mr. Jones has a greenhouse.
Mr. Jones has a green house.

Noun-verb accent

The pronunciation of many words (*permit,* for example) depends upon their meaning in a given context. If the word *permit* is used to refer to a thing (noun use), it is pronounced (pèr'mit). When it means "let; allow" (verb use), the accent shifts to the second syllable and it is pronounced (pər mit'). In such words as *permit, record, contest,* accent indicates meaning—usually an accent on the first syllable indicates noun meaning; an accent on the second syllable indicates verb meaning. The following exercises present this pattern of noun-verb accent.

1. Write *object* on the board and ask children to pronounce it. Some will probably accent the word on the first syllable (ob'jikt) and others on the second syllable (əb jekt'). Comment that we cannot tell how to pronounce a word like this unless it is used in a sentence. To illustrate, write two sentences like the following:

   The *object* was hidden by the tall grass.
   I *object* to music when I am studying.

   Have the first sentence read and ask pupils what the word *object* means. Which syllable is accented? Continue similarly with the second sentence. Lead pupils to note that there are two pronunciations for *object.* When it means "thing," it is accented on the first syllable; when it means "be opposed," it is accented on the second. The pronunciation of this word can only be determined by its use in context. Use similar procedures with *permit* and *annex.*

2. As soon as pupils have a knowledge of grammatical terminology, you will want to point out that in such words as *object* and *permit* the accent usually falls on the first syllable

when the word is used as a noun and on the second syllable when the word is used as a verb. To illustrate, write such pairs of sentences as the following on the board:

> We keep a *record* of all the cattle on our ranch.
> We *record* the number of cattle in each herd.

> We bought a *present* for Miss Brown.
> We will *present* it to her on Monday.

Have each pair of sentences read and the accented syllable identified in each italicized word. How is the word used when the first syllable is accented (noun)? when the second syllable is accented (verb)? Lead pupils to generalize that the accent usually falls on the first syllable when the word is used as a noun and on the second syllable when the word is used as a verb. Continue similarly with the words *combat, project, digest, escort* in pairs of sentences.

3. Write the words and incomplete sentences given below on the board. Ask children to read each pair of sentences aloud and to use the word printed above the sentences in the blanks. With each sentence ask children to tell which syllable of the word they accented and why.

convict

The _____ escaped from prison.
The jury will _____ the prisoner.

rebels

Many _____ fought against the government.
Joe _____ against homework.

contest

Tom said he could _____ my right to be on the team.
I wanted to enter the _____.

refuse

We cleaned the _____ from our basement.
They _____ to work on holidays.

Using affixes in structural analysis

Up to this point in structural analysis, children have acquired a basic knowledge of roots, inflectional endings, suffixes, and prefixes as units of meaning. As pupils progress in reading, they should be learning new affixes. They should also learn that in addition to being meaning units suffixes have a grammatical function.

Identifying new affixes as meaning units

The next group of procedures introduces the prefixes *re-* and *fore-* and the suffixes *-ward* and *-or*.

1. To introduce the prefix *re-* as a meaningful part of a word, write such sentences as the following on the board, underlining the italicized words:

> I had to *repack* my bag three times before I could shut it.
> I didn't know how to *repay* the stranger for his kindness.

After pupils have read each sentence, have them identify the root and the prefix in the underlined word. Use the first sentence to illustrate that the prefix *re-* sometimes means "again," the second sentence to point out that *re-* sometimes means "back."

Then write the words *uncooked* and *recooked* in sentences. Have pupils identify the prefix in each word and contrast the meanings of the words. Continue with *unwritten* and *rewritten*.

2. To introduce the prefix *fore-* as a meaningful part of a word, write the derived form *forehead* and ask, "Is your forehead in the front or back of your head? What prefix is added to the word *head* to make a new word meaning 'the front part of the head'?" Next write the derivative *forenoon* and ask, "When we speak of the forenoon, do we mean the part of the day coming before or after noon?" Help pupils generalize that *fore-* means "in front" or "before."

To conclude, write such derived forms as *forefeet, forepaws,* and *foreground* in sentences and have pupils discuss their meanings.

3. To introduce the suffix *-ward,* write the derived form *backward* and ask, "If you fall backward do you fall toward the front or toward the back? What was added to the root *back* to make the new word *backward?*" Underline the suffix *-ward* and lead children to understand that it means "toward" or "in the direction of." Then write such derived forms as *upward, eastward, downward, seaward* in sentences and have children discuss their meanings.

4. Before introducing the suffix *-or,* you might use such words as *teach, teacher; freeze, freezer* in sentences to recall that the suffix *-er* is often added to a word to make another word meaning "a person or thing that _____." Then write such sentences as the following, underlining the italicized words:

Bob will *sail* his boat in the race.
He is a good *sailor.*

She will *visit* us next summer.
We enjoy having her for a *visitor.*

Copper wire will *conduct* electricity.
Copper wire is a *conductor* of electricity.

As each pair of sentences is read, ask (1) which of the underlined words is the root word, (2) what suffix is added to the root to make a new word, and (3) what the new word means. Lead pupils to note that the suffix *-or* has the same meaning and pronunciation as the suffix *-er,* the only difference being the spelling.

Conclude by writing such derived forms as *inventor, reporter, actor, eraser, harvester, refrigerator, composer, reflector.* Have pupils identify the root and suffix in each and use each in a sentence.

Recognizing the grammatical function of suffixes

Awareness that suffixes have a grammatical function promotes facility in using and interpreting language. As pupils observe the difference in usage between root words and their derived forms (*sad, sadly; teach, teacher; bright, brightness*, for example), they acquire functional understandings of grammar without necessarily being introduced to grammatical terminology. From this point on in structural analysis, as new suffixes are introduced, children's attention will be called to the grammatical function of the suffix as well as to its lexical meaning.

The next two procedures introduce the understanding that, in addition to being meaningful parts of words, suffixes have a grammatical function.

1. Write the following pairs of sentences. Review the meaning of the suffix *-er* and its variant *-or* by asking what the derived form means in the second sentence of each pair.

> Mr. Brown will *farm* that land next year.
> He is a good *farmer*.
>
> Jim will *act* in that play.
> He is a well-known *actor*.

Next, bring out that the root word *farm* tells what Mr. Brown will do and that *farmer* tells what we call a person who does that. *Act* tells what Jim will do and *actor* tells what we call a person who does that. Help pupils generalize that when we add the suffix *-er* or *-or* to a word that expresses an action (verb), we make a new word that tells what we call the person or thing that performs the action (noun). (If your pupils are familiar with the parts of speech, you will of course use such terms as *noun* and *verb*.)

2. Write the groups of sentences that are given on the next page, and use procedures similar to those in the preceding exercise. Use the italicized words in the first column to

help children generalize that when we add the suffix -*y*, -*ly*, or -*less* to a word that names a person or a thing (noun), we make a new word that describes someone or something (adjective). Use the italicized words in the second column to help children generalize that when we add -*ly* to a root word that describes something or someone (adjective), we make a new word that tells "how" or "in what manner" something is done (adverb).

The *wind* blew.	She spoke in a *soft* voice.
It was a *windy* day.	She spoke *softly*.
Tom is my *friend*.	Jane gave *correct* answers to
He is a *friendly* person.	the questions.
Tom asked the *friendless*	She answered the questions
boy to join our club.	*correctly*.

Summary

This chapter has covered the second stage of progress in phonetic and structural analysis (see the charts on pages 39 and 55). The goals of the procedures have been to develop skills and understandings that enable boys and girls to analyze independently two-syllable root words with or without affixes.

Skills and understandings developed at the second stage of progress

In phonetic analysis children have learned to use visual clues to syllabication and to accent as aids in determining the pronunciation of an unfamiliar two-syllable word. They have also become acquainted with simple patterns of accent. In structural analysis children have learned to identify prefixes as meaningful parts of words and have noted that suffixes have a grammatical function.

By the end of the second stage of progress, pupils should be able to use word analysis to identify in context four types of words (in addition to those on page 139):

Types
of words
that can be
analyzed

1. Two-syllable root words in which there are visual clues to accent (for example, two like consonant letters following the first vowel letter in words like *attic* and *stirrup*)

2. Inflected or derived forms of two-syllable roots in which there are visual clues to accent (a doubled final consonant, for example, before an ending or a suffix as in *omitting*, *conferred*, and *propeller*)

3. Derived forms of known words to which the prefixes *re-* and *fore-* or the suffixes *-ward* and *-or* have been added (*reconsidered*, *forewarn*, *eastward*, *inspector*, for example)

4. Derived forms of unknown words like *combine*, *allotted*, *feeble*, *stubborn* that contain visual clues to accent to which known affixes have been added (*recombine*, *unallotted*, *feebleness*, *stubbornly*, for example)

To identify unfamiliar words of the first type, pupils use phonetic analysis; for the third type, they use structural analysis. For the second and fourth types of words, readers use a combination of phonetic and structural analysis.

When boys and girls have acquired the skills and understandings presented in this chapter, they are ready for the third stage of progress in word analysis. To arrive at the pronunciation of multisyllabic words, pupils will learn to (1) identify patterns of accent, (2) note shifting accent in derivatives, (3) use suffixes as clues to primary accent. As pupils learn many new affixes in structural analysis, they will (1) group affixes as to meaning and function, (2) strengthen their understanding of root words, (3) use position of words in sentences and word endings as clues to meaning. Procedures for helping pupils acquire these skills and understandings are given in the next chapter.

Chapter six | Word analysis at the third stage of progress

During the preceding stage of progress in word analysis, boys and girls learned to attack unfamiliar printed forms of two-syllable root words with or without known affixes. In the third stage of progress, which is covered in this chapter, pupils develop phonetic and structural understandings that help them figure out the pronunciation and meaning of multisyllabic words when they encounter them in print (see the charts on pages 39 and 55). Of course these longer words must be in a pupil's oral vocabulary. If they are not, he will need to consult a dictionary.

Using accent in multisyllabic words

At the third stage of progress in phonetic analysis, pupils are first introduced to common patterns of accent in words of three or more syllables. Awareness of these patterns, coupled with previous knowledge of the way in which accent affects vowel sounds, helps readers attack multisyllabic words. Many of these longer words are derived forms of known roots; and as pupils progress, they learn that in many instances a root word does not retain its original pronunciation in a derived form. Accent often shifts to another syllable with resulting changes in vowel sounds (*mo'ment, mo men'tous; rem'e dy, re me'di al; com pare', com'pa ra ble*).

Patterns of accent in multisyllabic words

If pupils are to attack multisyllabic words successfully, they must increase their understanding of accent. At this level of growth, pupils note patterns of accent[1] in multisyllabic words and learn to use these patterns to help them pronounce words of three or more syllables. The following procedures are suggested for developing ability to identify accent in multisyllabic words.

1. Write known words of three or more syllables in two lists on the board (see below). The words in the first list should be accented on the first syllable, those in the second list on the second syllable.

The first or the second syllable is accented in multisyllabic words

accident	opossum
confident	determine
carpenter	parenthesis
passenger	ridiculous
eligible	intelligent

Have the words pronounced and ask how many syllables pupils hear in each. Lead them to note that each word has more than two syllables. Then comment that there is a pattern of accent in longer words that helps a reader decide how to accent these words. To illustrate, have pupils pronounce the words in the first list again and tell which syl-

[1]See the footnote on page 49.

lable is accented (the first). Continue with the words in the second list (the second syllable is accented in each). After pronouncing these words, do children notice a pattern of accent that would apply to words of three or more syllables? Explain that these words illustrate a common pattern of English accent—*words of three or more syllables are accented on either the first or the second syllable.*

Use known words like the following for additional practice in hearing this pattern of accent: *hospital, melody, Africa, lavender, principle, capable, taffeta, ornament, moccasin, vitamin; thermometer, magnificent, department, molasses, democracy, America, experiment, extravagant, arithmetic, apprentice.*

2. Once pupils understand that in multisyllabic words the first or second syllable is accented, they are ready for the generalization that the accent on the first or second syllable may be a secondary accent.

To begin, recall that some words (*home'sick', rail'-road'*, for example) have two accents and that one of these accents is not stressed as much as the other. This lighter accent is called a secondary accent and the stronger accent is called a primary accent. Dictionaries and glossaries use two kinds of marks to show these accents. Have children turn to a glossary or dictionary and find words containing both primary and secondary accent marks. Have them note the two kinds of marks used. Suggest that they pronounce the words and listen for the accented syllables. Then you might pronounce some words and ask pupils to tell which syllables are accented in each.

Auditory perception of secondary accent

Next, write these two groups of words on the board, showing accented syllables:

al' li ga' tor   op' por tu' ni ty
su' per vi' sor   o' ver come'
ter' ri to' ry   un' der take'
nec' es sar' y   in' ter rupt'

Lead the class to note that in the first group of words the first accent is a primary accent and the second accent is a secondary accent. In the second group of words the first accent is a secondary accent and the second accent is a primary accent. Then have each group of words pronounced, making sure that children can hear the difference between the two accented syllables in each word.

3. Write the following groups of words on the board, showing accented syllables:

cel' e bra' tion	re spon' si bil' i ty
con' ti nen' tal	de ter' mi na' tion
en' ter tain'	en cy' clo pe' di a
in' tro duce'	ap pen' di ci' tis

As pupils pronounce the words in each group, tell them to listen carefully to the accents. Then ask whether there is an accent on the first or second syllable in each word. What kind of an accent? Bring out that in each word there is an accent on the first or second syllable and that this accent is a secondary accent.

The accent on the first or second syllable may be a secondary accent

Next, write these words on the board, showing syllable division but not accent marks:

in' vi ta' tion	in' de pen' dence	e lec' tro mag' net
ap' pre hen' sive	au' di tor' i um	an tic' i pa' tion

Ask children to pronounce each word and to tell which syllable is accented with a secondary accent and which syllable carries a primary accent. Lead pupils to generalize in their own words that the accent on the first or second syllable in a long word may be a secondary accent.

4. After pupils develop the understanding that there is an accent on the first or second syllable in multisyllabic words and acquire skill in hearing primary and secondary accent, they are ready to note a common pattern of accent. This exercise presents this pattern of accent—*a secondary accent*

on the first or second syllable followed by one unstressed
There is *syllable before the primary accent.*
usually one
unaccented
syllable
between the
secondary and
primary accent

Write such words as the following (in addition to those used in the third exercise), showing accented syllables:

sat′ is fac′ tion	a ris′ to crat′ ic
hip′ po pot′ a mus	ex am′ i na′ tion
u′ ni ver′ sal	o rig′ i nal′ i ty

Ask children to look at each word and to pronounce it. Note whether they can hear a pattern of accent in these words. Lead pupils to point out that there is a secondary accent on the first or second syllable followed by one unstressed syllable before the primary accent. Comment that this pattern of accent is a very common one.

For additional practice in hearing this common pattern of accent, use the words *volunteer, recommend, individual, Mississippi, manufacture, apparatus, extravaganza, communication, superiority, evaporation.*

5. To check pupils' ability to apply understandings of syllabic division, vowel sound, and accent to unfamiliar multisyllabic words in context, write such sentences as the following, underlining the italicized words:

We visited a very old *cathedral* in *Portugal.*
Tom knows how to play the *accordion.*
My *ancestors* came from France.
Phosphorus shines in the dark; we say it is *luminous.*
The *peninsula* of Norway and Sweden is often called *Scandinavia.*

Suggest that pupils pronounce each underlined word to themselves, determine the accented syllable or syllables. and decide what vowel sound they would expect to hear in the accented syllables. Ask pupils to read each sentence aloud. As they do so, note their ability to pronounce the underlined words.

As children develop awareness of accent in longer words, they will notice other patterns of accent. For example, there are words like *superintendent* and *representation* in which two unstressed syllables occur between the syllable that carries a secondary accent and the syllable that carries a primary accent (*su'per in tend'ent, rep're sen ta'tion*). Pupils will notice, too, a pattern of accent in words like *alligator* and *secretary* in which the primary accent occurs first, an unaccented syllable next, and then the secondary accent (*al'li ga'tor, sec're tar'y*). The accent pattern introduced in the fourth exercise (a secondary accent on the first or second syllable, one unstressed syllable, a primary accent) is emphasized in this section because it is a common one and assumes importance later when suffixes are introduced as clues to primary accent.

Other patterns of accent

Shifting accent in derived forms

As pupils learned to identify patterns of accent in multisyllabic words, they may have noticed that many of these longer words are derivatives (*ridiculous, celebration, satisfaction, continental, anticipation*, etc.). As stated in Chapter Three (page 51), from this point on in phonetic analysis, the understandings that are developed help pupils pronounce derivatives.

The procedures in this section call attention to the fact that in many derivatives the root word does not retain its original pronunciation. The primary accent may shift to another syllable, often with resulting changes in vowel sound (*mo'ment, mo men'tous; re side', res'i dent; sym'bol, sym bol'ic*, for example). This understanding, coupled with knowledge of patterns of accent in multisyllabic words, prepares boys and girls for the next step in phonetic analysis— that of using suffixes as clues to accent (pages 186-192).

1. Write the root word *moment* and its derived form *momentous,* and have the words pronounced. Ask pupils where

the accent falls in the root and then write it in (*mo'ment*). Do the same with the derivative (*mo men'tous*). Continue similarly with such root words and derivatives as those given below (the accent marks should not be written in until pupils identify the accented syllables).

sym' bol	sym bol' ic	cour' age	cou ra' geous
or' i gin	o rig' i nal	pho' to graph	pho tog' ra pher
com' e dy	co me' di an	med' i cine	me dic'i nal
ex cel'	ex' cel lent	com pare'	com' pa ra ble
ad mire'	ad' mi ra ble	har' mo ny	har mo' ni ous

Have each root and its derived form pronounced again and lead pupils to note that in these pairs of words the shift in accent affects vowel sound. For example, in the second syllable of *moment* the schwa sound is heard. When the accent shifts to the second syllable in *momentous*, a short vowel sound is heard in that syllable. Next, recall with pupils the understanding that in our language words are accented on the first or second syllable. Then lead the class to note that this generalization applies to both the roots and derivatives on the board, even though the root accent shifts to another syllable in the derived forms.

Shifting primary accent in derivatives changes pronunciation of root words

2. Write the root *ornament*, have it pronounced, and ask pupils which syllable is accented. Write in the accent mark (*or'na ment*). Then write the derived form *ornamental*, have it pronounced, and ask pupils how many accented syllables they hear in this word. On which syllable does the primary accent fall? the secondary accent? Next, write in the two accent marks (*or'na men'tal*). Lead the class to note that the primary accent in the root word has shifted to another syllable in the derived form. Ask whether this shift in accent has affected vowel sound. How? Continue similarly with the following root words and their derived forms (write in the accent marks after pupils have identified the accented syllables):

pop' u lar	pop' u lar' i ty
sen' ti ment	sen' ti men' tal
op pose'	op' po si' tion
sym' pa thy	sym' pa thet' ic
ex hib' it	ex' hi bi' tion
sep' a rate	sep' a ra' tion
ad van' tage	ad' van ta' geous
con' ti nent	con' ti nen' tal

Recall with the class that a common pattern of accent in multisyllabic words is a secondary accent, an unaccented syllable, and then a primary accent. Have the derived forms pronounced again, and lead pupils to note that this pattern of accent applies in all of them.

Using affixes and roots in structural analysis

At the third stage of progress in structural analysis, pupils learn increasing numbers of prefixes and suffixes and are encouraged to classify them as to meaning or function. For example, attention is called to a number of prefixes that carry a "negative" meaning and to groups of suffixes that form nouns. Much emphasis is also given to the understanding that roots are core meaning units in derived and inflected forms in spite of changes in spelling or pronunciation.

Identifying prefixes in terms of meaning

The next procedures introduce new prefixes and strengthen the concept that prefixes affect word and sentence meaning.

1. To introduce the prefix *under-*, write such known words as *underfoot, underwater, underfed, undersell,* and *undersized* in sentences. Ask what prefix has been added to these words and have pupils tell what each word means. Since at this level most children are using dictionaries, suggest that pupils find the entry *under-* in their dictionaries and read the defi-

nitions. Suggest, too, that they note in their dictionaries other derivatives formed with *under-*.

To introduce the prefixes *over-, out-, trans-, semi-,* and *sub-,* use similar procedures and such words as *overcharge, oversleep, overtime, overflow; outdoors, outburst, outrun, outlaw; transatlantic, transcontinental, transplant; semicircle, semiprecious, semitropical; subzero, subhead.*

2. To emphasize prefixes as meaning units, write the sentence "The meat was cooked." Then add the prefix *under-* to *cooked* and discuss how the meaning of the sentence has changed. Continue by adding the prefixes *over-, re-, semi-,* and *un-* to *cooked.* Next, have pupils use *populated* in a sentence. Change *populated* to *unpopulated* and discuss its meaning. Continue by adding the prefixes *over-, under-, re-,* and *semi-* to *populated.* Have pupils use the derived forms in sentences and tell what they mean.

Classifying prefixes with "negative" meanings

As new prefixes with "negative" meanings are introduced, the relationship in meaning should be called to pupils' attention. The following procedures are suggested for classifying "negative" prefixes.

1. Have pupils read the following sentences: "This set of books is complete" and "This set of books is incomplete." Ask whether the sentences mean the same. What prefix in the second sentence changes the meaning? What does the prefix *in-* mean when it is added to the root *complete?* Bring out that a common meaning of *in-* is "not" or "the opposite of." Using similar procedures, have pupils discuss such pairs of words as *regular, irregular; legal, illegal; polite, impolite.* Bring out that the prefixes *ir-, il-,* and *im-* are variants of the prefix *in-* and have the same meaning.

To introduce another "negative" prefix, *non-,* write such words as *nonstop, nonskid, nonbreakable* in sentences (see page 164). Ask what each italicized word means.

> I took a *nonstop* flight to New York.
> We bought *nonskid* tires.
> Plastic bottles are *nonbreakable*.

2. To review the "negative" prefixes that children now know, write the words *unlock, unfair, disconnect, impatient, non-sense, irresponsible*, and *invisible*. Have each derived form used in an oral sentence and ask what it means.
3. Write the prefixes *un-, dis-, in-, im-, il-, ir-, non-* and the sentences given below, underlining the italicized words. Have the first sentence read and call attention to the under-lined words. Then ask pupils to use one of the prefixes to make a word that means the same as the underlined words (*disapproves*). Continue with the remaining sentences.

> Mother *does not approve* of parties on school nights.
> I was *not disturbed* by the noise.
> It is *not lawful* to park on this street.
> His plan was *not practical*.
> My writing is *not legible*.
> This plant is *not poisonous*.
> I *take the cover off* our bird cage every morning.
> A person who is *not responsible* need not apply for the job.
> He showed *lack of respect* for older people.

Noting the grammatical function of new suffixes

The procedures that follow introduce such suffixes as *-ment, -able, -ible, -ous, -al, -ally, -ance, -ence,* and *-ion* and emphasize the understanding that suffixes have a grammat-ical function. Since many suffixes possess little lexical meaning or a lexical meaning that is difficult for pupils to express, an understanding of the grammatical function of suffixes assists readers in getting meaning from sentences. (The way in which you bring out that suffixes have a gram-matical function will of course depend upon your pupils' background of grammar. If they are familiar with parts of speech, you will want to modify these procedures. For example, instead of referring to the word *announcement* as a word that "names something," you will simply call *announcement* a noun.)

1. To introduce the noun-forming suffix *-ment*, write the following pairs of sentences, underlining the italicized words:

Forming nouns
with -ment

They will *announce* the winner on Friday.
We can hardly wait for the *announcement*.

We always *ship* our furniture by truck.
One *shipment* weighed several thousand pounds.

Have the first pair of sentences read, and ask which of the underlined words is the root word and what suffix was added to this root word to make the derived form. Then ask what the derived form means. Next, ask pupils in which sentence the underlined word expresses an action (verb)—names something (noun). Continue similarly with the other pair of sentences. Lead pupils to generalize that when we add *-ment* to a word that expresses an action (verb), we make a new word that names something (noun).

Conclude by writing the words *agree, move, amuse, excite, punish,* and *amaze.* Have *agree* used in a sentence. Then ask pupils whether *-ment* can be added to *agree* to form a new word. What is the new word? Have it used in a sentence. Continue with the remaining words.

2. To introduce the adjective-forming suffix *-able* and its variant *-ible*, write sentences containing such derived forms as *comfortable, packable, readable, breakable; reversible, sensible, digestible, collapsible.* With each example, lead pupils to see that adding the suffix *-able* or *-ible* to a root word makes a word that "describes" or "tells what kind" (adjective). Have each derived form pronounced again, and lead pupils to note that *-able* and *-ible* are pronounced alike. Comment that it may be necessary to consult the dictionary to find out whether to spell this suffix *-able* or *-ible*.

Forming
adjectives
with
-able and -ible

3. To introduce the adjective-forming suffix *-ous,* write the following sentences, underlining the italicized words:

> John liked *humor* in stories.
> John liked *humorous* stories.

Forming adjectives with -ous

Ask children what *humor* means in the first sentence and what *humorous* means in the second sentence. Then ask pupils to think of other phrases or sentences in which they might use the word *humorous.* Lead them to note that when we add *-ous* to the root *humor,* we make a new word that describes (adjective).

Comment that the suffix *-ous* can be added to many words. Pronounce *fame, courage,* and *fury* and see how quickly pupils can come up with the derived forms. Ask them to use each in a sentence and have them observe that the derived form is an adjective. Next, write the derived forms *humorous, famous, courageous,* and *furious.* Ask what change (if any) was made in the root before the suffix *-ous* was added.

Conclude by writing the derived forms *various, nervous, poisonous, joyous, mysterious, outrageous, venomous, murderous, dangerous,* and *envious.* Ask children to write the root words. Suggest that they refer to their dictionaries if they need to check the spelling of any root word.

4. To introduce the suffix *-al,* which may form either adjectives or nouns, write the following sentences, underlining the italicized words:

Forming adjectives or nouns with -al

> Sam enjoyed the *musical* sounds of the waves.
> Joe's *refusal* to eat dinner amused his brother.

Have the first sentence read and the root word and suffix identified in the underlined word. Then ask how the word *musical* is used in the sentence (it describes or tells "what kind" of sounds—adjective). Next, have the second sentence read and the root word and suffix identified in the underlined word. Call attention to the dropped final *e* in the root. Then ask whether the word *refusal* describes something or whether it names something. Help children generalize that adding the suffix *-al* to a word makes a new word that may (1) describe (adjective) or (2) name (noun).

Conclude by writing the following words: *coast, tide, rehearse, survive, tribe, bury, region, continue.* Have *coast* used in a sentence. Then add the suffix *-al* to *coast* and have *coastal* used in a sentence. Continue with *tide* and *rehearse*, noting with pupils any change in the root word when *-al* is added. Then have pupils write sentences in which they use the remaining derived forms. Suggest they use their dictionaries if they need to check the spelling or meaning of any word.

5. This procedure introduces the suffix *-ally* (a variant of *-ly* added to many adjectives ending in *-ic*). To review the suffix *-ly*, write pairs of sentences like those given below, underlining the italicized words; and have the sentences read.

Forming adverbs with -ally

> They were *polite* children.
> Tim spoke *politely* to the stranger.

For each pair ask pupils which underlined word is the root word and what suffix was added to make the derived form. Bring out that the root *polite* "describes" (adjective) and the derived form *politely* tells "how" or "in what manner" (adverb).

Use similar procedures with the following pairs of sentences to bring out that to many descriptive words ending in *-ic* (adjectives) we add the prefix *-ally* to make new words that tell "how" or "in what manner" something is done (adverbs). As pupils read these sentences, note how they pronounce *enthusiastically* (en thü′zi as′tik li) and *energetically* (en′ər jet′ik li). Comment that although the suffixes *-ally* and *-ly* differ in visual form, they are pronounced alike.

He is *enthusiastic* about the plan.
He spoke *enthusiastically* about the plan.

Healthy people are usually *energetic*.
John works and plays *energetically*.

6. To introduce the noun-forming suffixes *-ance* and *-ence*, write the following pairs of sentences:

Bill was told that he would *perform* at the banquet.
His *performance* was first on the program.

Forming nouns with -ance or -ence

An honor such as this does not *occur* every day.
It was not an everyday *occurrence*.

At first Bill was *reluctant* to accept the honor.
But his *reluctance* did not last long.

Everyone was *silent* when Bill appeared.
Afterwards the *silence* was broken by applause.

As pupils read each pair of sentences, ask questions that will lead to these generalizations: (1) by adding the suffix *-ance* or *-ence* to a word that expresses an action (verb), we make a new word that names something (noun); (2) by substituting the suffix *-ance* or *-ence* for the letters *-ant* or *-ent* occurring at the end of a word that describes (adjective), we make a new word that names (noun).

7. To introduce the suffix *-th*, which forms nouns from adjectives, you might begin by reminding pupils that they are familiar with the suffix *-th* that is added to numbers, for example, *fifth, sixth, seventh*. Now they will learn about another suffix that is spelled *-th*. Write the following pairs of sentences, underlining the italicized words:

Forming nouns with -th

The room was too *warm*.
The *warmth* of the room made us sleepy.

My brother is a *strong* man.
His *strength* is amazing.

Have the pairs of sentences read and the suffix -*th* identified. Lead pupils to compare the spelling and pronunciation of *strong* and *strength*. Remind pupils that meaning determines whether a word is formed from a common root. Then lead pupils to point out that adding the suffix -*th* to a root word that describes (adjective) makes a new word that names (noun).

Next, write the following pairs of words on the board: *true, truth; broad, breadth; deep, depth; long, length; wide, width.* Have children use each root and its derived form in oral sentences. Suggest that they use their dictionaries, if they wish, to check meaning.

Conclude by telling children that -*th* is a very old English suffix and that new words have not been formed with this suffix for many years. The suffix -*ness* has taken the place of -*th* in forming new words. Write the sentences "The ill child stayed home" and "Mary's illness kept her at home" and lead pupils to note that -*ness*, like -*th*, added to a word that describes (adjective) makes a new word that names (noun).

8. To introduce the noun-forming suffix -*ion* and its variant -*ation*, write the following pairs of sentences, underlining the italicized words:

Forming nouns with -ion or -ation

We *discussed* ways of raising money.
The *discussion* lasted an hour.

John *informed* me that our holiday would begin on Monday.
This *information* was incorrect.

Have the first pair of sentences read. Ask what the root word is in *discussed* (*discuss*). In the second sentence what suffix was added to the root *discuss?* What does *discussed* mean in the first sentence? How is it used (as a verb)? What does *discussion* mean in the second sentence? How is it used (as a noun)? Continue similarly with the second pair of sentences. Then write other pairs of sentences, using such roots and derived forms as the following: *invent, invention; suggest, suggestion; imagine, imagination; celebrate, celebration.* After pupils have discussed the meaning and function of these words, lead them to generalize in their own words that the suffixes *-ion* and *-ation* make derivatives that are nouns.

9. The procedure suggested in this exercise uses the suffix *-ment* to reinforce the concept that suffixes have a grammatical function. It may be adapted for use with any known suffix. Write the sentence "The clowns amuse the children," and have it read. Then add the suffix *-ment* to *amuse*

Reinforcing the concept that suffixes have a grammatical function and ask whether the word *amusement* makes sense in the sentence. When children agree that it does not, have them use *amusement* in a sentence that means about the same thing as the original sentence, for example, "The clowns provide amusement for the children." Write the sentence that contains the word *amusement* under the sentence that contains the word *amuse* and have both sentences read. Ask pupils why *amusement* doesn't make sense in the first sentence. Bring out that *amuse* is a verb and that when we add *-ment* to *amuse* we make a noun. A noun (*amusement*) cannot be used in a sentence as a verb. Continue similarly with such sentences as "John could not *agree* with Bill" ("John and Bill could not reach an *agreement*"); "Do not *excite* the patient" ("The patient cannot have any *excitement*"); "Many people will *settle* here" ("Many people will form a *settlement* here").

Classifying suffixes by grammatical function

From time to time as new suffixes are introduced, they should be reviewed and discussed in groups according to their grammatical function.

1. To review known noun-forming suffixes, write such derived forms as the following in sentences: *payment, sickness, follower, inventor, growth, appearance, persistence, selec-*

tion, relaxation. After pupils have discussed the meaning and function of each form, comment that the suffixes *-ment, -ness, -er, -or, -th, -ance, -ence, -ion,* and *-ation* are some common noun-forming suffixes.

2. This exercise presents a procedure for grouping suffixes as to grammatical function. To help pupils group suffixes that form nouns, write the following derived forms and incomplete sentence on the board:

teacher	agreement	I like the _____.
inventor	rehearsal	
brightness	celebration	
warmth	performance	

Ask pupils to read each derived form and to identify the root and the suffix. Write the root and suffix after each derived form. Then ask pupils whether they would use the roots or the derived forms to complete the sentence. Why? Next, ask how all the derived forms are alike. Bring out that they all fit into the sentence because they are nouns and that the suffixes *-er, -or, -ness, -th, -ment, -al, -ion, -ance* when added to words make new words that are nouns.

To help pupils group suffixes that form adjectives, use similar procedures with the derived forms and the incomplete sentence given below:

gloomy	sensible	flawless	It was a _____ letter.
humorous	notable	cheerful	
personal	friendly	childish	

Strengthening understanding of the function of a root word

As pupils progress in reading, they are sure to encounter increasing numbers of derivatives. Therefore it is important that they can identify a known root word in a derived form even though the visual form and pronunciation of the root may change in the derivative.

The first two exercises strengthen the understandings that (1) a meaning of a root word is present in derivatives formed from it, (2) a derivative combines the meaning of the root plus that of the suffix or prefix, (3) the grammatical function of a derivative formed by the addition of a suffix is usually different from that of the root.

1. Write the following sentences on the board, underlining the italicized words:

A root word is a core meaning unit in an inflected or a derived form

I *assist* my grandfather after school in his grocery store.
I am Grandfather's *assistant.*
He sometimes calls me his *assistant* clerk.
Grandfather needs my *assistance* in waiting on customers.

When pupils have read the first sentence, ask what the word *assist* means ("help"). Then have the other sentences read and bring out that *assist* is the root word in *assistant* and in *assistance.* Ask whether the meaning of the root ("help") is present in the derived forms *assistant* and *assistance,* and have pupils reword each sentence, using the root meaning ("I am Grandfather's helper," "He sometimes calls me the clerk who helps him," "Grandfather needs my help in waiting on customers").

Next, call attention to the way the underlined words are used in the sentences by asking, "In which of the sentences is the underlined word used as a verb? as a noun? as an adjective?"

2. Write such groups of sentences as the following:

Ann is my friend.
She is a friendly girl.
She will never be friendless.
Her friendliness makes people like her.
Even unfriendly people like Ann.

Have the group of sentences read. Tell children that there are four words in these sentences that are formed from a root word in the first sentence. Ask them what the root word is and what the derived forms are. As pupils respond, underline the root word and the derived forms. Discuss the meaning of the underlined words and have pupils tell how each is used. Continue similarly with the root *educate* and its derived forms *educator, reëducate, uneducated, education, educational.*

3. This exercise extends the understandings that (1) a root word may have more than one meaning, (2) one meaning

Different meanings of a root may be used in its derivatives

of the root word is present in all derivatives formed from it.

Write the following sentences, underlining the italicized words, and have the sentences read:

Miss Lee will *direct* the work of the dramatics club.
Can you *direct* me to the library?
We took the *direct* route to school.

Discuss the meaning of *direct* in each sentence (1. manage; control, 2. tell or show the way, 3. straight).

Next, write the following sentences and have them read. Underline each italicized derivative of *direct*. Have pupils tell which meaning of the root word *direct* occurs in each underlined derived form.

The boat sailed *directly* west.
The play is under Mr. Jones' *direction.*
Unless you follow the *directions* on this package, you may be unable to open it.
My aunt is *director* of the Red Cross in our town.

4. To strengthen understanding of a root word as a unit of meaning, write such sentences as the following on the board and have them read:

The man counted his money.
Then he recounted it.
He did that countless times.
Then he left the country.

Ask pupils which three words are formed from the same root and discuss the meaning of each. Then ask why *country* is not related to the other words. Bring out that the visual form *count* is not a root word in *country* because a meaning of the word *count* is not present in the form. The fact that the pronunciation of the root *count* is not heard in *country* is not an infallible test, since many root words lose their original pronunciation in derived forms—*please* in *pleasant* and in *pleasure*, for example.

Meaning not visual form determines whether words are formed from a common root

Use similar procedures with lists of words like the following:

kindly	famed	painful
unkindly	famous	painless
kindness	famously	painstaking
kindling	famine	painter
skilled	reader	hatching
skillful	reread	unhatched
unskilled	reading	hatcheries
skillet	ready	hatchet

If you discover that some pupils need more work of this type, use similar procedures with such groups of words as these: *flatten, flattest, flattery; furred, furry, furious; rocky, rockier, rocket; needy, needless, needles.*

Rather than try to teach all English affixes by any given level, it is better to stress constantly the understanding that root words are core meaning units in derived forms. This awareness fosters self-confidence and independence in reading on the part of pupils who are daily encountering new derived forms of familiar root words. For example, a pupil who has this understanding and who knows the root words *hero, pursue, advise, title,* and *member* is not likely to be intimidated when he meets the derived forms *heroic, pursuit, advisory, entitle,* and *membership* in context even though he is not familiar with the affixes.

The next two procedures are designed to help pupils infer the meaning of new derived forms of known roots.

1. Write pairs of sentences like those given below. (The first sentence in each pair should contain a known root word, the second a derived form of that root made by the addition of a prefix or a suffix that has not yet been presented.) When each pair of sentences has been read, ask pupils to tell which word in the second sentence is formed from a root word in the first sentence. Then discuss the meaning of the root word and of the derived form.

Inferring the meaning of new derived forms of known roots

> The moon shining on the lake made a beautiful scene.
> There is a scenic drive through the mountains.
>
> I am sure we will reach home before dark.
> An early start will ensure our arriving in time for dinner.
>
> My little brother is just beginning to talk.
> My mother says that I am too talkative.
>
> I am learning how to type.
> My sister is a good typist.

2. Write sentences like those given below, underlining the italicized derived forms (each derived form should be made from a known root word plus a prefix or suffix [or both] that has not yet been presented). When pupils have read each sentence, ask (1) what the root word is in each underlined word and what change, if any, there is in the spelling of the root before the addition of a suffix or ending, (2) what the root word means, (3) what the derived form means.

> The cruel king *enslaved* the people that he conquered.
> *Scarcity* of good water forced the pioneers to move.
> The man in the picture has an unusual *facial* expression.
> After a *momentary* hesitation Ann went on with her talk.

At this stage of progress pupils should have much practice in identifying root words in derived forms in which the pronunciation of the root changes, including those forms in which the spelling of the root changes—*proclaim, proclamation; colony, colonial; divide, division*, for example.

1. Write the following roots and derived forms:

study	admire	divide	admit
studious	admirable	divisible	admission
student	admiration	division	admissible

In spite of changes in spelling and pronunciation a root word retains its meaning

First have the root *study* and its derived forms *studious* and *student* used in oral sentences to bring out the relationship in meaning. Then have the three words pronounced again. How do the pronunciation and spelling of the root change in each derived form? Continue similarly with the other groups of words.

2. Write such roots and derived forms as the following: *nature, natural; collide, collision; office, official; decide, decision; permit, permission.* Have each root and its derived form used in oral sentences, and discuss the meaning of each derivative. Then lead pupils to note how the spelling and pronunciation of each root change in the derivative.

3. Write the derivative *melodious* and ask someone to use it in an oral sentence. What does *melodious* mean? From what root word is it derived? Then ask everyone to pronounce *melody* and *melodious*, and have pupils note the shift in accent and the change in vowel sound in the derivative. Continue similarly with the derived forms *definition, reference, mysterious, industrial, colonial, memorial*.

4. Write the derivatives *provision, satisfaction, explanation, excellence, invasion, exclamation, persuasion*. Point to *provision* and ask someone to use it in an oral sentence. Then ask what the derivative *provision* means and from what root word it is derived. How do the spelling and the pronunciation of the root word *provide* change when the suffix *-ion* is added? Continue similarly with the remaining derived forms.

When pupils have acquired the skills and understandings discussed thus far in this chapter, they should be able to use word analysis to identify the following general types of words in context:

Types of words
that can be
analyzed

1. Words of three or more syllables to which pupils apply understanding of patterns of accent—for example, the first or second syllable is accented in multisyllabic words (*vitamin, industry; intelligent, arithmetic*); the accent on the first or second syllable may be a secondary one (*apparatus, introduce; encyclopedia, appendicitis*)

2. Derived forms of known words that incorporate such prefixes as *in-, ir-, il-, sub-, trans-, semi-, out-, non-* and such suffixes as *-ship, -ment, -able, -ible, -ous, -al, -ion, -ance* (*inconvenient, irregular, illegal, substandard, transatlantic, semicircle, outnumber, nonstop; membership, entertainment, valuable, reversible, humorous, arrival, invention, performance*)

3. Derived forms in which the pronunciation of the root word changes, including those forms in which there is a spelling change in the root (*harmonious, provision, transcontinental, divisor, indivisible, remedial, contribution*)

To attack unfamiliar words of the first type, pupils use phonetic analysis; for words of the second type they use structural analysis, including their knowledge of the grammatical function of suffixes. For words of the third type, pupils must combine phonetic and structural analysis to apply what they have learned about accent—for example, the probability that the root accent will shift in derivatives, the effect of accent on vowel sounds, and patterns of accent. Pupils must also remember that (1) a root retains one of its meanings in any of its derivatives no matter how much its pronunciation and spelling may change, and (2) the total meaning of a derivative combines the meanings of the root and affix (or affixes).

In phonetic analysis, pupils have developed under-standing of common patterns of accent that aid in attacking words of three or more syllables and of the way root accent often shifts in a derivative. Now boys and girls are ready to build upon these understandings as they learn to use such suffixes as *-ion, -ity, -ious,* and *-ical* as visual clues to primary accent.

In structural analysis, pupils will learn the meaning of additional prefixes and suffixes. They will also extend their understanding of the grammatical function of suffixes as they note how the position of words in context, as well as word endings, often furnishes clues to meaning. The suffix *-al,* for example, is added to root words to make adjectives or nouns. It may be added to the word *colony* to make the derived form *colonial.* Whether this derivative means "of or having to do with a colony or colonies" (adjective) or "a person living in a colony" (noun) is largely determined by its position in context as illustrated by these sentences: "The colonial policy of the mother country caused a rebel-lion," "The hero of this story, which is set in India in the 1800's, is a British colonial."

Strengthening ability to attack derivatives

Boys and girls who have mastered the skills and understand-ings of word analysis presented up to this point are reading on an adult level—at least in the area of word attack. That is, they have at their command basic skills of word analysis and understandings of language that enable them to recog-nize in context practically any printed word or meaningful part of a word (root or affix) that is already in their vocabu-laries. The skills and understandings developed in the remainder of this chapter are actually extensions and refine-ments of those taught previously.

Noting meaning and function of new affixes

At this level of growth, pupils become familiar with many new prefixes and suffixes, for example, *mis-, co-, pre-, inter-, super-, ultra-, -ist, -fy, -ize, -ism, -ic, -ity.* They extend to these new affixes the understandings developed at previous levels: (1) prefixes and suffixes are meaningful parts of words; (2) suffixes have a grammatical function. Pupils continue to see relationships in meaning and in grammatical function between groups of suffixes; for example, the suffixes *-ist, -er, -or, -ent, -ant* have the meaning "a person who _____," and the suffixes *-age, -ery, -ism, -er, -or, -ness, -ity* form nouns.

The first seven procedures introduce new prefixes and suffixes as meaningful parts of words. The eighth and ninth procedures emphasize the function of derivatives and strengthen pupils' ability to analyze derivatives that they encounter in reading. The tenth procedure acquaints pupils with word elements from Latin and Greek that are used to form many English words.

1. To introduce the prefix *mis-*, write such pairs of sentences as the following, underlining the italicized words:

Identifying the form and meaning of new prefixes

Dick *interpreted* the timetable for us.
We missed the train because Dick *misinterpreted* the timetable.

Thor was famous for his heroic *deeds*.
Loki was well-known for his *misdeeds*.

As each pair of sentences is read, have the prefix *mis-* identified and discuss the difference in meaning between the two underlined words. Have pupils tell what they think the prefix *mis-* means. Then have them check the meaning of *mis-* in their dictionaries.

Next, ask pupils to think of or find in their dictionaries other words that are made by adding the prefix *mis- (misbehave, misconduct, miscount, misdeal, misdirect, misgov-*

ern, misguide, misinform, misjudge, mislead, misplace, misspell, misunderstand, for example). Have each derived form used in a sentence to bring out its meaning.

This technique of using the root word and the derived form in pairs of sentences that force the meaning of the affix may be used to introduce almost any prefix or suffix as a unit of meaning. After pupils speculate on the meaning of a prefix or suffix, have them verify their surmises by looking up the meaning of the affix in the dictionary. When introducing a new prefix or suffix, be sure that the class works with many derived forms that illustrate the meaning of the affix.

2. To introduce the prefix *in-* meaning "in," "cause to be," etc., review the prefix *in-* (and its variant forms *il-, im-, ir-*) meaning "not." For example, write the following phrases and have pupils discuss the meaning of each:

inaccurate figures	impatient people
illegal parking	irregular shapes

Next, write the words *indoors, infield, inland, insure, imprison, irradiate* and ask whether *in-*, or one of its variant forms (*im-, ir-*), carries a negative meaning in these words. If pupils are not sure, suggest they find each derived form in the dictionary. Comment that these words illustrate that *in-* is often a prefix meaning "in," "into," "within," "on," "make," "cause to be," "toward," etc. Discuss the root word in each and the meaning of the derived form. Have each word used in a sentence.

Then explain that this prefix is sometimes spelled *en-* or *em-*. To illustrate, write *entangle, enforce, enslave, entwine, empower, embankment, embody* and use procedures similar to those suggested in the previous paragraph.

3. This procedure introduces the prefixes *co-, pre-, inter-, super-,* and *ultra-*. Pupils should use their dictionaries to find the meanings of each prefix. To begin, ask what a

copilot is. Then have pupils read the meanings given for the prefix *co-* in their dictionaries. Which definition of *co-* fits the meaning of the prefix in *copilot? co-worker? coauthor? coeducational? coexist?* Suggest that pupils use these words in sentences to bring out the meaning of each.

Then introduce the prefixes *pre-, inter-, super-,* and *ultra-* by using similar procedures with these derivatives:

prehistoric	intersection
prepaid	interurban
precooked	interlace
presuppose	international
supernatural	ultrasonic
supersonic	ultramodern
superman	ultrafashionable
superhuman	ultracritical

If there is doubt about the meaning of any derivative, have pupils refer to the dictionary.

4. This exercise introduces the suffix *-ive* (with its variant form *-ative*) and strengthens the understanding that most suffixes have a grammatical function. Write the following sentences, underlining the italicized words:

Identifying the meaning and function of new suffixes

> The fawn's *protective* coloring and *instinctive* fear of man saved its life.
> Most of us would rather be *productive* than *destructive*.
> The *narrative* and *descriptive* parts of the story were equally interesting.

Ask what each of the underlined words in the first sentence means, suggesting that pupils use their dictionaries if necessary. From what root word does each of the underlined words come? (Write the root above the derived form.) What suffix was added to each root? Then have boys and girls consult the dictionary for the meanings of *-ive*. How is each derived form used in the sentence (as an adjective)?

Use similar procedures with the remaining sentences. When pupils have identified the roots (*produce, destroy, narrate, describe*), lead them to note how the roots change in spelling and pronunciation with the addition of the suffix *-ive*. Can pupils think of other derived forms that come from these same roots? (For example, other words formed from *produce* are *product, production, productivity, unproductive, productively*.) As each derived form is mentioned, have it used in an oral sentence and ask whether it is used as a noun, adjective, or adverb.

To point out that the suffix *-ative* is a variant form of *-ive*, use procedures suggested for the presentation of *-ive* with the italicized words in these phrases:

a *talkative* boy	an *affirmative* answer
an *informative* speech	an *imaginative* tale

Explain that although the suffix *-ive* (or *-ative*) is used to form adjectives, some of these adjectives have also come to be used as nouns. For example, we speak of a person's *executive* ability (adjective) or refer to a person as an *executive* (noun). Other examples are *objective, relative, coöperative, affirmative, representative*. Suggest that pupils try using each in a sentence, first as an adjective, then as a noun. Encourage them to use their dictionaries.

5. After the suffixes *-ian, -ese, -ist, -ent, -ant,* and *-ee* have been introduced, use the following exercise, which groups suffixes that have a common meaning. Write such phrases as the following, underlining the italicized words:

Classifying suffixes in terms of meaning

the *inventor* of the telephone
a *publisher* of children's stories
a treaty between the *Canadians* and the *Japanese*
a *receptionist* in an office
a war *correspondent*
my father's *employee*
an *inhabitant* of Hillside

As pupils read each phrase, have them identify the suffix in the underlined word. What does each phrase mean? Then ask what meaning the underlined derivatives have in common (all mean "a person [or persons] who _____"). What suffixes are used to convey this meaning (*-or, -er, -ian, -ese, -ist, -ent, -ee, -ant*)? How are the derivatives used (as nouns)? Lead pupils to recall (you might also have them consult their dictionaries) that some of these suffixes *-er, -or, -ent,* for example, have other meanings. How can a reader tell that these suffixes in the phrases on the board signify a person (context forces that meaning)?

6. This exercise introduces the noun-forming suffixes *-age, -ery, -ism, -ty* (and its variant *-ity*). Write the following sentences, underlining the italicized words:

Classifying
suffixes
in terms of
function

There was no *shortage* of food during the flood.
Leakage along the levee threatened one town.

The *bravery* of the workers impressed everyone.
A *bakery* sent food to the patrols.

Criticism of his decisions did not prevent the general from doing his duty.
Many acts of *heroism* occurred during the flood that nearly destroyed our town.

We worried about the *safety* of the men at sea.
There are laws against *cruelty* to animals.

The *humidity* is very high today.
We were impressed by the *sincerity* of the speaker.

As each pair of sentences is read, ask pupils to name the suffix in the underlined derivatives. What is the root word of each? What does each derived form mean? How is it used in the sentence (as a noun)? Then ask the class to consult the dictionary for the meanings of the suffixes *-age, -ery, -ism, -ty,* and *-ity.* Lead pupils to note that the definitions given for these suffixes are all noun meanings.

7. To introduce the noun- and adjective-forming suffix *-ary*, write the following sentences and have them read:

> We crossed the *boundary* between the two countries.
> The *statuary* was imported from Italy.
> Mr. Parker was an *honorary* member of the society.
> The book was about an *imaginary* trip around the world.

Ask pupils to tell what suffix is added to each italicized word. What is the root word of each? What does each derived form mean? How are *boundary* and *statuary* used (as nouns)? How are *honorary* and *imaginary* used (as adjectives)? Bring out that the suffix *-ary* may form either nouns or adjectives.

In conclusion, comment that some words ending in *-ary* may be used as both nouns and adjectives. To illustrate, write the following pairs of sentences and discuss how each italicized word is used and what it means in each sentence.

> The *missionary* talked to us about his work.
> *Missionary* work in Africa was explained to us.

> The *military* took control of the government.
> *Military* training is required in some countries.

> My mother belongs to the Women's *Auxiliary* at church.
> The sailboat had an *auxiliary* engine.

8. Use derived forms that pupils have encountered in reading to emphasize the importance of noting meaningful parts of words. For example, suppose that pupils have read a passage in which the phrase "an impenetrable jungle" appears.

Strengthening understanding of the function of derivatives

Ask whether pupils consulted the dictionary for the meaning of *impenetrable*. Or did they note that the word is formed from the root *penetrate* to which the prefix *im-* and the suffix *-able* have been added? Did they blend these meaningful parts to get the total meaning of the derived form? Have pupils tell in their own words what the phrase means. You might emphasize that a derivative enables us to say in one word what otherwise would require several words to express, for example, *impenetrable* instead of "that which cannot be penetrated."

9. Call attention to a page that contains many derivatives in something pupils are reading. Ask them to find and list the derivatives. As pupils compare and discuss their findings, have them identify roots, prefixes, and suffixes in the derived forms and discuss the meaning of the derivatives. If no one has listed a particular derivative, call attention to it and talk over why it should be listed.

10. A familiarity with word elements (*photo-*, *visio*, *bio-*, for example) that are frequently encountered in words can help pupils figure out the meaning of words. Although it is not necessary that pupils know from what language a word element comes, it is important that pupils recognize the word element in words and associate meaning with it.

Recognizing words formed from Latin and Greek word elements

Write or reproduce the following Greek and Latin words and forms along with their meanings. (For purposes of this exercise, you need not discuss the difference between prefixes, combining forms, and words, all of which occur in these lists.)

from Greek	from Latin
auto- self	*bi-* two
bio- life, living things	*calor* heat
geo- earth	*marinus* of the sea
-gram thing written	*mittere* send
-graph thing that writes	*mobilis* movable
hydro- water	*multi-* many
-logy study of	*oleum* oil
-meter measure	*sonus* sound
petro- stone, rock	*sub-* under, below
phone sound, voice	*super-* above
photo- light	*trans-* across, beyond
tele- far, distant	*visio* sight, seeing

Ask the class to study the lists. Then write the word *automobile* and ask pupils to find two word elements in the lists that combine their meanings to make this word (*auto-* and *mobilis*). Can pupils see the relationship in meaning between the forms *auto-* and *mobilis* and our word *automobile*? Continue with *television* (*tele-* and *visio*).

Can pupils think of words that stem partly or completely from the word elements in the above lists (*biology, geology, telegram, telephone, phonograph, hydroplane, biplane, submarine, transmitter, supersonic, calorie, petroleum, biography, autobiography, autograph, geography, marine,* for example)? Discuss the relationship in meaning between the Greek or Latin forms and the words in our language that have been borrowed from them. If there is uncertainty about the meaning of any English word, suggest that pupils consult their dictionaries.

To conclude, write such words as *hydrometer, phonology, autosuggestion, petrology, calorimeter, photometer* and ask pupils to figure out the meaning of each. Then have them refer to the dictionary to check their conjectures.

Using suffixes as clues to primary accent

Because boys and girls are sure to encounter increasing numbers of multisyllabic words as they progress in reading, it is important that they strengthen their understanding of the way accent functions in words. The following exercises present the suffixes *-ion, -ity, -ic, -ical, -ian, -ial, -ious,* and *-ate* as visual clues to primary accent.[1] The primary accent occurs on the syllable preceding the suffixes *-ion, -ity, -ic,*

---

[1]The fact that pupils may not see an English root before these suffixes in all words (in *pedestrian, fastidious,* or *dedicate,* for example) does not affect the usefulness of these suffixes as clues to accent. Nor does it matter if pupils consider that in derivatives like *historian, colonial, mysterious* the suffixes are *-an, -al, -ous* preceded by an *i* that represents a final *y* in the roots, since *-ian, -ial,* and *-ious* are forms of the suffixes *-an, -al,* and *-ous.*

-ical, -ian, -ial, -ious and on the second syllable preceding the suffix *-ate*, for example, *af'fec ta'tion, ab'nor mal'i ty, pho'- to graph'ic, or'a tor'i cal, stat'is ti'cian, sac'ri fi'cial, sur'- rep ti'tious, dif'fer en'ti ate.* Although there are a few exceptions, pupils will find these visual clues to primary accent invaluable in attacking many derivatives. Once pupils know where the primary stress in a word is likely to fall, they should have no trouble handling second-ary stress.

To use these visual clues to accent successfully, pupils should have an understanding of these patterns of accent: (1) an accent (primary or secondary) always occurs on the first or second syllable of English words; (2) a common pattern of accent in longer words is a secondary accent on the first or second syllable, an unaccented syllable, and then the primary accent. (Procedures for developing these un-derstandings are given on pages 156-159.) The suffixes that function as clues to primary accent should also be presented as meaning units.

You will notice that in the following exercises groups of words are given. Grouping words to illustrate patterns of accent develops a feeling for the rhythm of long words and helps pupils generalize for themselves about the way accent functions in words. Of course, the words used in each exercise should be familiar to pupils so that they can pronounce them readily.

1. Write such words as the following in a column on the board: *action, tension, suggestion, vacation, attention, direction, opinion, selection, companion, completion, admission, divi-sion, occasion, explosion, description.* Ask pupils in what way all these words look alike. Bring out that each word ends in the suffix *-ion* and write *-ion* above the column of words. Then have the words pronounced. Ask which syl-lable is accented in all these words. If pupils do not readily respond that the syllable preceding the suffix *-ion* is ac-

-ion as a clue to primary accent

cented, have each word pronounced again and mark the accented syllable (do not erase these words).

Next, write in a second column these words ending in *-ion: introduction, repetition, celebration, aviation, information, execution, exhibition, satisfaction, definition, supervision, administration, determination, examination, imagination.* Have the words pronounced. Ask which syllable receives a primary accent in all these words (the syllable before *-ion*). Mark the primary accent. Then have the words pronounced again, and ask pupils which syllable in each word receives a secondary accent. Mark the secondary accent with a lighter accent mark.

To stress the rhythmic pattern of accent in the derivatives ending in *-ion,* have pupils pronounce the words in both lists again. Bring out that each word has an accent on the first or second syllable and that the words in the second list illustrate a common pattern of accent—a secondary accent on the first or second syllable, an unaccented syllable, and then the primary accent.

Lead pupils to generalize that in every word a primary accent occurs on the syllable preceding the suffix *-ion.* Therefore the suffix *-ion* is a visual clue to primary accent in words. Conclude by asking pupils to think of other words ending in the suffix *-ion.* As words are suggested, write them on the board and ask whether *-ion* is a clue to primary accent in the words.

To present the suffixes *-ity, -ic, -ical, -ian, -ial, -ious* as clues to primary accent use the procedures suggested in this exercise with exercises 2 through 7.

2. Lead pupils to generalize that the suffix *-ity* is a visual clue to primary accent in words—the primary accent usually occurs on the syllable preceding *-ity.*

-ity as a clue to primary accent

First column: *quality, scarcity, density, security, stupidity, hostility, brutality, publicity, solemnity, reality, rapidity, timidity, vitality, mentality, festivity.*

Second column: *opportunity, popularity, curiosity, generosity, masculinity, possibility, technicality, sensitivity, personality, mediocrity, regularity, inferiority, responsibility, originality, desirability.*

3. Lead pupils to generalize that the suffix -*ic* is a visual clue to primary accent in words—the primary accent usually falls on the syllable preceding -*ic*.

-ic as a clue to primary accent

First column: *scenic, cubic, poetic, historic, magnetic, atomic, symbolic, angelic, artistic, heroic, majestic, prophetic, idyllic, hygienic, nomadic.*

Second column: *idiotic, mathematics, scientific, aeronautic, microscopic, sympathetic, energetic, acrobatic, realistic, photogenic, optimistic, automatic, communistic, Napoleonic, artistocratic.*

4. Lead pupils to generalize that the suffix -*ical* is a visual clue to primary accent in words—the primary accent usually falls on the syllable preceding -*ical*.

-ical as a clue to primary accent

First column: *mythical, Biblical, typical, theatrical, electrical, grammatical, historical, methodical, hysterical, political.*

Second column: *biological, geological, alphabetical, astronomical, psychological, biographical, arithmetical, allegorical, egotistical, parenthetical.*

5. Lead pupils to generalize that the suffix -*ian* is a visual clue to primary accent in words—the primary accent usually falls on the syllable preceding -*ian*.

-ian as a clue to primary accent

First column: *Christian, guardian, amphibian, reptilian, musician, barbarian, grammarian, custodian, pedestrian, civilian, historian, Norwegian, librarian, Canadian, magician.*

Second column: *Presbyterian, vegetarian, politician, Scandinavian, Appalachian, Indonesian, humanitarian.*

6. Lead pupils to generalize that the suffix -*ial* is a visual clue to primary accent in words—the primary accent usually falls on the syllable preceding -*ial*.

-ial as a clue to primary accent

First column: *trivial, facial, racial, serial, official, memorial, commercial, bacterial, colonial, industrial, financial, remedial, provincial, centennial, sequential.*

Second column: *beneficial, equatorial, testimonial, confidential, editorial, artificial, secretarial, influential, circumstantial, providential, territorial, dictatorial, controversial, residential.*

7. Lead pupils to generalize that the suffix *-ious* is a visual clue to primary accent in words—the primary accent usually falls on the syllable preceding *-ious.*

-ious as a clue to primary accent

First column: *envious, studious, spacious, amphibious, religious, victorious, laborious, flirtatious, malicious, ambitious, obnoxious, delicious, pretentious, rebellious, notorious, luxurious, harmonious, mysterious, industrious, fictitious.*

Second column: *conscientious, superstitious, avaricious, sacrilegious, sanctimonious, repetitious, ostentatious.*

8. This exercise is designed to help pupils generalize that in words ending in the suffix *-ate* the primary accent usually falls on the third syllable from the end. To begin, write the words *captivate, desperate, infuriate, humiliate, immediate, appreciate* in one column and the words *rehabilitate, intermediate, insubordinate* in another column, and use procedures similar to those given in the first exercise, pages 187-188.

-ate as a clue to primary accent

Next, write these pairs of sentences and have them read aloud:

I will *graduate* in three years.
Bill is a *graduate* of Austin High School.

The man said he could *duplicate* this set of keys.
I wanted to have a *duplicate* set made for my father.

Ask pupils what the words ending in *-ate* mean. How are *graduate* and *duplicate* used in the first sentence of each pair (as verbs)? How is the suffix -*ate* pronounced in these words (āt)? How is *graduate* used in the other sentence (as a noun)? How is *duplicate* used in the other sentence (as an adjective)? How is the suffix -*ate* pronounced in these words (it)? Have the four words pronounced again and ask where the accent falls in each (third syllable from the end). Lead pupils to generalize that (1) the suffix -*ate* at the end of verbs is pronounced (āt), at the end of nouns or adjectives (it); (2) words of three or more syllables ending in -*ate* (regardless of part of speech) contain a primary accent on the third syllable from the end.

To give further practice in using these generalizations, write pairs of sentences using each of the following words, first as a verb, then as a noun or adjective: *associate, appropriate, estimate, alternate.* For each pair, ask what the words ending in -*ate* mean. How does the use of each affect the pronunciation of the suffix -*ate?* Where does the accent fall in each word?

9. To provide practice in using suffixes as clues to accent, write such words as these in groups:

Practice in using suffixes as clues to accent

-ion	-ity	-ic or -ical
veneration	electricity	economic
composition	hospitality	mythological
confusion	nationality	apologetic
-ian	-ial	-ious
Peruvian	ceremonial	suspicious
comedian	celestial	contagious
artesian	torrential	nutritious

As the words in each list are pronounced, ask which syllable (or vowel) receives the heaviest stress, or primary accent, and mark that syllable with a heavy accent. In which words do pupils hear a secondary accent? Where? Why would one expect to hear a secondary accent in these words? How many unaccented syllables occur between the accented ones in each of these words? Then mark the secondary accent and recall that in English (1) some kind of accent falls on the first or second syllable of a multisyllabic word, (2) a common pattern of accent is a secondary accent on the first or second syllable, one unaccented syllable, and then the primary accent.

Call attention to the suffixes above the lists. In words ending in these suffixes, which syllable will most likely receive the primary accent (the syllable before any of the listed suffixes)?

10. Invite pupils to pronounce the tongue twisters given below. They can if they use visual clues to accent. Have pupils check the meaning of any words they do not know.

inimical	unanimity
tragedian	impious
enigmatical	managerial
ignominious	procrastinate

Noting position of words and endings as clues to meaning

At preceding levels of growth, pupils developed the understanding that suffixes, as well as being meaning units, have a grammatical function. For example, adding the suffix -y, -ly, or -less to a noun (snow, friend, home) makes an adjective (snowy, friendly, homeless). Pupils are now ready for the understanding that the position of a word in a sentence, as well as the word ending, is a clue to meaning.

Our purpose is not to teach grammar but rather to use grammar as an additional means of helping pupils understand sentence context. If one does not know whether a word is meant for a noun or a verb, for example, he cannot tell what the sentence means in which the word occurs. What does the headline "Air line demands change" mean? It can mean either that an air line demands a change or that the demands of an air line have changed. The headline is ambiguous because the words demands and change can be either nouns or verbs. However, in sentences there is usually an indication of whether a word is used as a noun, verb, adjective, or adverb. A word may be marked by an ending or a suffix, by the words that are adjacent to it (words like *a, the, quite, rather, many*), and by its position in the sentence.

We can often classify nonsense words if we hear them in well-marked sentences. For example, in the sentence

Position and word ending are clues to meaning and function of a word in a sentence

"The rells vitted the crume," we know that *vitted* is a verb and that *rells* and *crume* are nouns and that some people or things (the *rells*) did something (*vitted*) to someone or something (the *crume*). And again if we hear "She was a rather billiful girl," we know that *billiful* is an adjective. It is clearly marked as such by the suffix *-ful*, by the word *rather*, and by its position in the sentence. And it serves to describe the girl in some way. In "She plays very billifully," *billifully* is clearly marked as an adverb by the *-ly* suffix, by *very,* and by its position after the verb *plays. Billifully* clearly indicates "a manner of playing" in this sentence.

The following exercises focus pupils' attention on word endings and on the position of words in sentences as clues to meaning.

1. Write the sentences given below and have them read. Ask pupils to note where the words ending in *-ly* occur and what they add to the meaning of each sentence.

> The man smiled wryly.
> He walked slowly and wearily.
> Jim shook his head excitedly.

Next, write the incomplete sentence "He moved _____ly." Ask what the word ending in *-ly* will most likely tell. Then have pupils suggest various words ending in *-ly* that might be used to tell how a person moved.

2. Write the following groups of sentences, underlining the italicized words:

We *classify* animals in science.

Some liquids *solidify* at low temperatures.

The filters *purify* the water.

Jane *dramatized* the story.

Spain *colonized* much of the New World.

The flag *symbolizes* our country.

Have the first group of sentences read and ask what suffix is added to each of the underlined words. What is the root word in each? What does each derived form ending in the suffix *-fy* mean? Where does the derivative occur in the sentence? How is it used (as a verb)?

Use similar procedures with the second group of sentences. Then ask how the suffixes *-fy* and *-ize* are alike (both make derived forms that are used as verbs). Have pupils refer to their dictionaries to check the meanings of the suffixes *-fy* and *-ize*. Lead the class to note that the meanings given are verb meanings ("make," "become," "engage in," etc.).

In conclusion, ask how understanding the function of the suffixes *-fy* and *-ize* would help a reader figure out the meaning of the words *simplify, falsify, glorify, equalize, alphabetize, modernize,* providing he knew the roots *simple, false, glory, equal, alphabet,* and *modern.* Have each derived form used in a sentence.

3. Write the following sentences, underlining the italicized words, and have the sentences read:

I found my friend at work in a *cluttered* corner behind some *packing* boxes.

He invented a *musical* instrument.

The *majestic* chords rolled from the *stately* instrument.

The *beautiful* and *melodious* music swelled through the *gloomy* hall.

A burst of *appreciative* applause came from the listeners.

The musician made a *triumphant* bow.

He gave an *excellent* performance.
The evening was very *profitable*.
The train ride from Chicago to Washington seemed *endless*.

Ask how each underlined word is used (to describe a person or thing; as an adjective). Where do most of the underlined words occur in relation to what they describe? Where do they occur in the last two sentences? Have pupils name the suffix added to each underlined word and list the suffixes on the board (*-ed, -ing, -al, -ic, -ly, -ful, -ous, -y, -ive, -ant, -ent, -able, -less*). Comment that these suffixes are some of the most common adjective-forming suffixes in our language.

To illustrate how such suffixes and the position of the words to which they are added may give us a clue to meaning, write such phrases and sentences as the following:

a _____y day
a _____ful person
a _____ous man
We like Sue because she is _____able and _____ly.

Ask how each of the incomplete words will be used. What clues make it easy to predict how each will be used? Then have pupils suggest descriptive words ending in these suffixes that could be used in each phrase or sentence ("a windy day," "a gloomy day," "a snowy day," and so on).

4. Write the following sentences, underlining the italicized words, and have the sentences read:

The *sailor* had a large *collection* of sea shells.
He was a *Canadian* with a *quickness* of hand and great skill and *audacity* in his *occupation*.
There was a grand *defiance* to the sea.
The *roaring* of the wind drowned all other sounds.
An *attendant* pointed to the *wreckage* on the beach.
The *brilliancy* of the sunset dazzled the *watchers*.
The sea was without *movement*.
The secret of man's *existence* seemed about to be revealed.

Have the sentences read and ask how each underlined word is used (to designate a person or thing; as a noun). Lead pupils to note that none of the underlined words is a root word and have them list the suffixes added to these words (*-or, -ion, -ian, -ness, -ity, -ation, -ance, -ing, -ant, -age, -ancy, -er, -ment, -ence*). Explain that these are some of the most common noun-forming suffixes in our language.

5. Pupils may have noticed that the suffix *-ly* when added to words may make either adverbs or adjectives and that *-ing*, *-ant, -ian, -al,* and *-ary,* for example, may form either nouns or adjectives. Remind pupils that the position of words in sentences helps them know whether a word is a noun, adjective, adverb, or verb.

Position can be used to determine grammatical function

To review this understanding, write the following, underlining the italicized words:

The *ghostly* figure drifted *silently* out of sight.
Painting is an *interesting* hobby.
Each *participant* in the contest had an *expectant* look on his face.
The *librarian* arranged a display of *Scandinavian* books.
We saw the *rehearsal* of the *musical* comedy.
Tom's *summary* of the book about a *legendary* hero was interesting.

Have the first sentence read. What suffix is added to each underlined word? Where do the underlined words occur in the sentence? How is *ghostly* used (as an adjective)? How is *silently* used (as an adverb)? Continue similarly with the other sentences.

6. Write the words *beautify, beauty, beautiful, beautifully.* Ask which of the words is the root word and what suffix (or suffixes) has been added to this root to make three derived forms. Then ask pupils to use each word in a sentence. Write each sentence on the board and discuss where the root and its derivatives occur in each sentence,

how they are used (noun, verb, adjective, adverb), and what they mean. Other groups of words you might use are *continuation, continue, continual, continually; stupidity, stupefy, stupid, stupidly; glory, glorify, glorious, gloriously; simply, simple, simplicity, simplify; insistence, insist, insistent, insistently; suspicion, suspect, suspicious, suspiciously; decision, decide, decisive, decisively.*

7. You might conclude this series of exercises with a bit of fun that will reinforce the understanding that word endings and the position of words furnish clues to meaning. Write the following nonsense rhyme for the class to read:

> The toomly bulters stamified a maratant,
> Who lumarized most bightfully.
> He was so trassible and dairitant
> That they fled naftly to their snightity.

Ask pupils what "ideas" they get from reading this nonsensical rhyme even though nearly all the words are not to be found in a dictionary. What helped pupils arrive at the "ideas"?

Summary

Skills and understandings developed at the third stage of progress

This chapter has covered the third stage of progress in phonetic and structural analysis (see the charts on pages 39 and 55). The goals of the procedures have been to develop skills and understandings that enable pupils to attack multisyllabic words that they encounter in their reading.

During this stage of progress in phonetic analysis, boys and girls have acquired mature understandings of the way accent functions in multisyllabic words. They have learned to identify patterns of accent and have noted that root accent often shifts in derivatives. They have also learned to use certain suffixes as clues to primary accent. A knowledge of these clues to accent enables pupils to pronounce many long derivatives, including such tongue twisters as *tragedian, unanimity, ignominious, enigmatical.*

In structural analysis, pupils have learned to recognize as meaningful parts of words increasing numbers of prefixes and suffixes and have classified them as to meaning and function. The understanding has been constantly reinforced that a root word retains one of its basic meanings even though its pronunciation and spelling may change in derived forms. Pupils have also learned to use word endings, coupled with the position of the derivatives in sentences, as clues to meaning.

By the end of the third stage of progress, pupils should be able to use word analysis to identify the following kinds of words when they encounter them in reading (in addition to those mentioned on page 177):

page 177

Types of words that can be analyzed

1. Derivatives formed by the addition of such prefixes as *mis-, in-* (meaning "in," "within," "into," "cause to be," etc.) and its variants *im-, ir-, en-* and *em-, pre-, co-, inter-, super-, ultra-* and such suffixes as *-ist, -ic, -ical, -ty, -ity, -ive, -ian, -ial, -ious, -fy, -ize, -ee, -age, -ery, -ary, -ism, -ate* (*misinterpret, inborn, insure, imprison, irradiate, enforce, empower, premature, copilot, international, superhuman, ultramodern; violinist, melodic, biographical, cruelty, rapidity, protective, musician, commercial, laborious, simplify, symbolize, employee, orphanage, refinery, secondary, criticism, activate*)

2. Derivatives in which the suffixes *-ion, -ic, -ical, -ity, -ian, -ial, -ious, -ate* are clues to primary accent (*exhibition, idiotic, geological, peculiarity, historian, equatorial, censorious, domesticate*)

To analyze the derivatives in the first group, pupils use structural analysis as they apply the understanding that roots, prefixes, and suffixes are units of meaning: Since many of these derivatives contain three or more syllables, to pronounce them, pupils use phonetic analysis as they apply what they have learned about patterns of accent and shifting accent.

To pronounce the derivatives in the second group, pupils use suffixes as visual clues to accent: (1) a primary accent usually falls on the syllable before the suffixes -*ion*, -*ic*, -*ical*, -*ity*, -*ian*, -*ial*, and -*ious;* (2) a primary accent usually falls on the third syllable from the end in multisyllabic words ending in the suffix -*ate* (phonetic analysis). To associate meaning with these derivatives, pupils must identify roots and suffixes as units of meaning (structural analysis).

Pupils who have acquired the skills and understandings developed through the third stage of progress should be able to recognize practically any printed word or meaningful part of a word (root or affix) that is in their vocabularies. For the pronunciation and meaning of totally unfamiliar words, boys and girls, like adults, must use the dictionary. The procedures given in the next chapter are suggested for developing the skills and understandings necessary to successful use of the dictionary.

Chapter seven | The dictionary as an aid to word perception

Printed words are visual symbols for spoken words, and in the early stages of reading it is essential that the printed words children are asked to read be those that are already in their speech. The preceding chapters have been largely concerned with word analysis, which enables a reader to associate a known pronunciation and a known meaning with an unknown printed word. Eventually, however, there comes a time when a child will encounter printed words that he has never used or heard. When this happens, the dictionary becomes an indispensable tool for learning the meaning and pronunciation of unknown words.

To use the dictionary successfully requires a number of skills and understandings that any program designed to promote competence in word perception must assume responsibility for teaching. Three major skills are fundamental to using a dictionary. First of all, a reader must be able to locate the word he wishes to know about. Then he must be able to translate into a spoken word the symbols used to indicate pronunciation. Finally, he must be able to choose the meaning intended by the author and to adapt that meaning to the sentence in which the word is used.

Dictionary skills and understandings

The procedures presented in the remainder of this chapter are designed to teach the following skills and understandings necessary for successful use of the dictionary:

To locate entry words, a child should be able to
—use alphabetical order and general alphabetical position
—use guide words
—identify a root word in an inflected or derived form

To derive the pronunciation of an entry word, he should be able to
—identify consonant and vowel sounds and associate each with the symbol given for it in a pronunciation key
—blend consonant and vowel sounds into pronunciation units or syllables
—recognize the function of visual syllabic divisions and of primary and secondary accent marks
—blend syllables into word wholes with appropriate accent

To derive the meaning of a new word in light of the context in which it appears, he should be able to
—comprehend dictionary definitions
—use illustrative phrases and sentences, pictures and diagrams as aids to meaning
—generalize word meaning from reading several definitions when necessary
—select the meaning (and sometimes the pronunciation) that is appropriate to a given context
—adapt the appropriate definition of a word to fit the context in which it occurs

Building dictionary readiness

Because the skills involved in using a dictionary are many and complex, a sound basic reading program starts early to prepare children for successful use of the dictionary in the middle grades. Beginning at about second grade, lessons that provide readiness for using a dictionary should be an integral part of a program in word perception. The procedures in this section (pages 202-208) are designed to be used with children in the second and third grades. When the dictionary is introduced to pupils in the fourth grade, they should have the skills and understandings developed in this section.

Readiness for locating words in a dictionary

Most children can say the alphabet by the time they come to school or certainly by the end of the first grade. However, being able to rattle off the alphabet and being able to use alphabetical sequence and general alphabetical position are different matters. The first procedures given here are designed to develop the latter ability.

Recognizing and using alphabetical sequence

1. Write the letters *f, d, e, a, c, b, g* and have pupils name each letter. Recall with children that these and other letters are used to stand for sounds in printed words, that there are twenty-six letters in our alphabet. Then ask various pupils to name other letters, writing them on the board as they are named.

    Next, comment that the twenty-six letters arranged in a certain order are called the alphabet. To review the order of the letters, write *a* and ask someone to name the next letter. Then write the letters *a, b, c, d, e, f, g* in one group and have them read in order. Continue with these two groups: *h, i, j, k, l, m, n, o, p* and *q, r, s, t, u, v, w, x, y, z.* Have the entire alphabet read.

2. Write the letters *a, b, c, d, e, f, g* and have them read. Erase the *c* and the *f,* and ask pupils to tell what letter to put in each blank. Then write such known words as the following and have children arrange them in alphabetical order by their first letters: *dance, goat, animal, circus, bear, fence, errand.* This procedure may be used for teaching or reviewing the remainder of the alphabet. The letters

may be presented in two groups: *h, i, j, k, l, m, n, o, p* and *q, r, s, t, u, v, w, x, y, z.*

3. Write such known words as the following: *gate, up, bite, last, quit, rope, cold, zoo, fox, say, vine, each, help, jolly, or, if, no, rest, zipper, keep, apron, pet, will, long, me, old, run, water, please, drink, quack, go, caught, bridge, top, invite, time, jump, miss, you, happy, door, angry, enough, kitten, to, need, uncle, yet, fish, out, many, very, see, do, ago, week* (because few children at this level know words beginning with *x*, none is in the list). Suggest playing a game with these words and explain that one child will find all the words beginning with *a* and pronounce them. Then another child will find and pronounce the words that begin with the next letter of the alphabet, and so on.

4. Write *b, f, h, p, s, w* and ask pupils to tell what letter in the alphabet comes just before each of these letters. Then write *c, j, n, q, s, x* and ask what letter comes after each one of these.

   Write the following words: *deer, meadow, pool, fawn, signal, cane, block, notice, lock, tongue, joy.* Have children pronounce the words and name the letter with which each begins. Then list the words in alphabetical order as pupils tell which comes first, second, third, and so on.

5. To introduce alphabetizing by the second letter in a word, write *add* and *ashes.* Ask, "With what letter does each word begin? Which one would you put first in an alphabetical list? Why?" Lead pupils to note that to alphabetize words that begin with the same letter, we must look beyond the first letter. If the second letters are different, we then alphabetize the words by the second letters. Next, write the following pairs of words and ask which word in each pair would come first in an alphabetical list: *blanket, bowl; coach, cloak; draw, dish; enter, eager; flag, fresh; gun, glue.* As pupils dictate, rearrange the entire list of words in alphabetical order.

Write the words *attic* and *ashamed,* one below the other, and ask which would come first in an alphabetical list and why. Then add the word *alive* to the list and ask which word would come first now and why. As pupils respond, rearrange the words in a new column. Continue with *stuffed, shiver, soldiers; doctor, delighted, dipped; brush, bath, blink; fact, forenoon, fit.*

6. Write the words *sigh, spent, soil, strip* in a column. Ask pupils to tell which of these words would come first in an alphabetical list and why, which would come next, and so on. As pupils dictate, rearrange the words in a second column. Then write the following words in two columns and have pupils arrange the words in each column in alphabetical order: *deal, admire, favorite, dollar, ached, firmly, grinned, coax; peddler, knothole, post, jerk, nod, kind, neat.*

7. This exercise promotes ability to associate letters with their general position in the alphabet. Explain, "We often divide the alphabet into three parts. The first part begins with the letter *a* and ends with *g*. What letters go in between these two?" As pupils name the letters in sequence, write them on the board and above them the label *First Part.* Repeat with the middle part, *h* through *p*, and with the last part, *q* through *z*. Then say the word *dish* and ask children with what letter the word begins and whether this letter is in the first, middle, or last part of the alphabet. Continue with the words *accident, roast, perform, instant, yard, garden, model, hearth, team, lose, enter, understand, quite, office, strike, chief, kettle, finish, zone, brave, wheel, narrow, vegetable, journey.* As additional practice, write the foregoing words. Have a child select the word that begins with *a* and pronounce it. Ask another child to find and pronounce the word beginning with the next letter, and so on.

Recognizing general alphabetical position

Often the word a child wishes to look up in the dictionary occurs in context not as a root word but as an inflected or derived form, *parried* or *smugly*, for example. Since many inflected and derived forms are not main entry words, he must be able to identify the root words in such

Identifying the root word in an inflected or derived form forms in order to locate them in the dictionary. When the child does this, he is applying the understanding that a root retains its meaning in an inflected or derived form. The procedures in structural analysis suggested in Chapters Four and Five for developing ability to identify roots in inflected and derived forms provide readiness for locating words in the dictionary.

Readiness for interpreting dictionary pronunciations

Many phonetic skills and understandings that children should acquire at primary levels provide readiness for learning how to interpret dictionary pronunciations and for using

Phonetic understandings basic to interpreting dictionary pronunciations a pronunciation key. For example, the ability to hear consonant and vowel sounds and to associate them with letters of the alphabet, the ability to hear syllables and accent and to blend syllables into word wholes with proper accent are fundamental to interpreting diacritical marks and other symbols that are used in the dictionary to indicate pronunciations. The fact that the spelling of many entry words looks very different from the series of symbols that show pronunciation—*cough* (kôf), for example—is not likely to confuse the child who has acquired understanding of silent letters in the spellings of words and of the variability of sounds that many letters stand for (*s* as in *see, has,* and *sure; ea* as in *meat, head, break, earn,* for example).

Readiness for using dictionary definitions

When a child begins to use a dictionary to find the meaning of an unfamiliar word, he must apply all the skills in using context clues that he has learned at earlier levels. Basic to his use of the dictionary for word meaning are these two understandings, both of which should be developed in the primary grades: (1) a word may have more than one meaning; (2) meaning must be determined in light of the context in which a word is used.

Procedures like the following when used at second- and third-grade levels provide readiness for deriving word meaning from the dictionary.

1. Write the incomplete sentences given below. Then ask pupils to read each one and to supply the last word orally.

Comprehending
simple
definitions
of meaning

A young bear may be called a _____.
When a boy is grown up, he is called a _____.
When a girl is grown up, she is called a _____.
The part of a building that is below ground is called a _____.

Such things as chairs, tables, and beds are called _____.

2. Write the word *silent* and below it the words *quiet, still,* and *careful*. After pupils have read the words, ask, "Which two of the three words listed below *silent* mean about the same thing as *silent?* What does the other word mean?" Continue similarly with the following:

shy	*scent*	*quickly*	*shout*	*huge*
lazy	odor	rapidly	scream	enormous
timid	money	noisily	yell	narrow
bashful	smell	swiftly	weep	very large

3. Write the following on the board:

Selecting
meaning to
fit context

cross—go from one side to the other

Mother was cross because I came home late.
I told the child not to cross the street.

Have pupils pronounce the italicized word and read the meaning given for it. Then have them read the two sentences silently and tell in which one *cross* has the meaning given in the definition. Discuss the meaning of the word *cross* in the other sentence. Continue with the following:

lean—not fat

I like only lean meat.
He asked us not to lean on the wall.

bank—place for keeping money

John put his savings in the bank.
We sat on the bank of the stream and fished.

orange—a round, juicy fruit

Our school colors are orange and blue.
I ate an orange for breakfast.

4. Write the following:

   cent—penny
   scent—smell

   The _____ of flowers filled the room.
   A piece of gum costs one _____.

Lead pupils to note that the words *cent* and *scent* look different and have different meanings but have the same pronunciation. Then ask which word completes the meaning of each of the sentences. Use similar procedures with these pairs of words: *rode, road; right, write; piece, peace.*

5. Write the following on the board:

   hail—(1) call loudly to, (2) greetings or welcome, (3) rain that has turned to ice

   "Hail to our President!" shouted the people.
   Hail ruined the crops.

   patch—(1) piece to cover a hole, (2) mend, (3) piece of ground

   Mr. Chase cleared a patch near the house for a garden.
   The man put a leather patch on my shoe.

Ask pupils to read the first sentence and to decide which of the three meanings given for the word *hail* fits in that sentence. Repeat with the second sentence. Continue in like manner with the sentences following the word *patch*.

6. Write such words and definitions as the following:

> *notice*—(1) printed sign, (2) see
> *cook*—(1) prepare food by using heat, (2) a person who cooks

After pupils have read the definitions of each word, ask them to use the word in sentences to illustrate each meaning.

7. Present an exercise like the following, underlining the italicized words:

Using a simple definition for a word in context

> One day I saw a *colt* in the field.
> When I walked *toward* him, he *started* to run.
> *Maybe* he was *afraid* of strangers.

away from	of course
young bird	began
in the direction of	perhaps
frightened	young horse

Ask pupils to read the first sentence silently and to tell which word or phrase in the lists below the sentences might be used instead of the underlined word. Continue with the other sentences.

Developing ability to use the dictionary

Let us assume that pupils have acquired the understandings and skills that are essential background for learning how to use the dictionary. The procedures given in the remainder of this chapter are designed to introduce the dictionary and to promote ability to use it as an aid in reading.[1]

[1] The entry words used in these procedures may be found in the *Thorndike-Barnhart Beginning Dictionary* or in the *Thorndike-Barnhart Junior Dictionary* (Chicago: Scott, Foresman and Company, 1959). If another elementary dictionary is being used, you may find it necessary at times to choose other entry words and to adapt the procedures accordingly.

Introducing the dictionary

A child's first experiences with his dictionary should develop the understanding that it is a source for learning the meaning of unknown words. These first experiences should also acquaint him with the general format of the dictionary and build understanding of such terms as *entry word, definition,* and *pronunciation.*

1. A child's introduction to the dictionary should be in a motivated situation. Place a picture of a quay, for example, on the bulletin board. On the board write the question, "Do we have a picture of a quay in our room?" (Any picturable word that is unfamiliar to the class may be used.) When children ask what a quay is (they will probably pronounce it *kwā*), comment, "We have a book that will tell us what a quay [kē] is." Give each child a dictionary and suggest that the class look on page _____ (give the appropriate page number) to see whether they can find the word *quay* in heavy black type. When pupils have read the definition, ask them to point out the picture of a quay on the bulletin board.

2. To introduce the concept that the dictionary has pictures that are aids to meaning, ask, "Do you know what a puffin looks like? [Any animal that the class is likely to be unfamiliar with may be used.] How big is it?" Then tell pupils on which page in the dictionary they can find the answers. Discuss the picture and direct attention to the way in which size is indicated, for example, by the caption below the picture or by relative size of another object in the picture.

3. Tell pupils that the words explained in the dictionary are called *entry words* and are printed in large black type. Write on the board the names of some uncommon animals for which pictures are given in the dictionary that pupils are using (for example, *rhea, marten, pelican*). After each name, write the page number on which the entry word can

be found. Ask pupils to find each entry word, read what the dictionary says about the animal, and look at the picture. Conclude by asking such questions as the following: "Which animals are birds? Which bird looks like an ostrich?"

4. Write such adjectives as *agile, smug, arrogant* with the appropriate page number after each. Ask pupils to read the explanation of meaning (the definition) given for each entry word and then to tell whether they would care to have their friends use that word to describe them.

5. Use one entry to illustrate the idea that the dictionary may do three things to help us understand what a word means: (1) give a definition or explanation of what the word means, (2) give a picture, (3) use the word in a phrase or sentence. Call attention to the pronunciation following the entry word, and explain that the dictionary also shows us how to pronounce words. Conclude by saying something like the following: "The entry word itself shows how the word is spelled. What is the next thing the dictionary tells us about a word [how to pronounce it]? What else can we find out about a word by using the dictionary?" Help children generalize that the dictionary shows the spelling, the pronunciation, and the meaning of words.

Locating entry words

The following procedures (1) extend knowledge of alphabetical order, (2) develop ability to use guide words as aids to locating an entry word, (3) build awareness that inflected and derived forms may not be listed as entry words.

1. Comment that the entry words in the dictionary are arranged in alphabetical order, that unless a person knows the letters of the alphabet in order, he will find it difficult to locate words in the dictionary. Then have pupils write the letters of the alphabet in a column on the left side of a sheet of paper. Ask them to write after each letter a word

Recognizing alphabetical order

beginning with that letter, *a—arm, b—baby,* for example. Suggest that pupils use their dictionaries if they need help in thinking of a word. When all have finished, explain that everyone now has an alphabetical listing of words by their first letters.

2. Tell pupils that John had bought a package of stamps for his collection. Before putting them in his album, he decided to alphabetize the stamps by the names of the countries from which they came. The countries were Norway, France, Argentina, Mexico, Thailand, Portugal, Belgium, Japan, Sweden, Denmark, Italy, Yugoslavia, Greece, Canada, and Ecuador. Ask pupils which country should come first in the list, which should come last. Then suggest that each pupil write the names of the countries in alphabetical order.

3. Figuring out a message in code is fun for children and provides practice in using alphabetical sequence. Write the following messages and note whether pupils can "break" each code on their own. If they cannot, suggest that they write *a* for *b, b* for *c, c* for *d,* and so on, to figure out the first message. For the second, they must reverse the procedure, putting *b* for *a, c* for *b, d* for *c,* and so on (*a* is used for *z*).

> Upnpsspx xf bsf hjwjoh b tvsqsjtf qbsuz gps Upn bu nz ipvtf. Qmfbtf dpnf.   Cjmm

> Sgzmj xnt enq hmuhshmf ld. H'kk ad zs xntq gntrd ax sgqdd n'bknbj.   Chbj

4. To give practice in alphabetizing by the second letter, write the words *aim, are, about,* and *all* in a column on the board. Lead pupils to note that since these words begin with the same letter, they must be arranged alphabetically by the second letter. As pupils dictate, list the words in alphabetical order. Then write the following lists of words, and ask children to copy each list and alphabetize the words in it by second letters.

among	push	this	even
answer	pick	two	egg
alive	pail	top	excuse
ask	place	table	ear
around	pole	turn	elbow

5. Write in a column such words as *glad, glee, gloom, glue,* and lead pupils to note why these words must be alphabetized by the third letter. Then ask pupils to alphabetize the following lists of words:

Christmas	step	day
chop	stay	daughter
chair	store	dark
chin	still	damp
chew	stream	danger

The same procedures may be used for presenting alphabetical sequence by the fourth letter and by the fifth. Use lists of words like the following: *comb, come, comfort, command; character, charge, charm, chart.*

6. Write the following on the board:

1. pack	4. palm	7. past
2. _____	5. _____	8. _____
3. paddle	6. _____	9. pave

pat   pad   paper   park

Ask pupils where the words at the bottom of the exercise should be written in the alphabetical list. As the class dictates, write each word in the appropriate blank.

7. Tell pupils that Ann was making a picture scrapbook for her seven-year-old brother. She decided to label each picture and then to put the pictures in alphabetical order. She cut out pictures of the following: lizard, goat, beaver, chimney, bear, chair, child, beagle, rooster, lemon, goldfish, piano, leopard, gorilla, roof, chipmunk, rose, pigeon, lily,

apron, goose, apple, pie, lion, pig. Ask the class which picture would come first in the scrapbook. Which would come second? Then ask each pupil to write all the words in alphabetical order.

8. To strengthen ability to associate letters with their general position in the alphabet, write the alphabet in three parts, as suggested in the seventh exercise on page 204, and label the parts *First Part, Second Part,* and *Third Part.* Then suggest that pupils look in their dictionaries to see on which pages they find the entry words beginning with the letters in the first part of the alphabet, in the second part, in the third part. Next, write such words as *sly, fortitude, coast, quantity, moccasin, weave,* and ask pupils whether they would find each of these words in the first, middle, or last part of the dictionary.

Using general alphabetical position

9. To provide additional practice in using general alphabetical position, ask pupils to open their dictionaries to entry words beginning with *m*, with *c*, and so on.

10. Have pupils turn to a given page in their dictionaries. Point to the guide word at the left and ask children to notice where this word occurs as an entry on the page. Repeat with the guide word at the right. Lead the class to conclude that the two words at the top of the page are the first and last entry words on that page. Explain that these words are called *guide words*, that they represent the first and the last entry words to be found on a page, and that all the words that come between the guide words in an alphabetical listing are to be found on that page.

Using guide words

Have pupils read the guide words on several pages. Call attention to a few words on each page and point out that these words come in alphabetical order between the guide words.

11. Reproduce or write on the board sample guide words and page numbers for several pages of whatever dictionary children are using, for example:

breadfruit	141	breed
brilliant	143	broil
brunt	145	buff

broad	breathe	brittle
bred	budge	breakfast
bud	bristle	budget
brim	break	brute

Ask pupils to tell on which page (141, 143, or 145) they would find each entry listed below the sample guide words.

Ask on what page pupils would look for the entry word *bribe* and why. Continue with the words *bronco*, *bruin*, *brig*, *briar*, *buffalo*, *brusque*, *brilliance*, *bruise*, *brew*, *brocade*, and *breach*.

12. Explain that although most entries in the dictionary are single words, there are other kinds of main entries. Combinations of words (*shooting star*, *self-important*) and abbreviations (*ans.*, *hr.*), for example, are also main entries and are listed alphabetically. Then write the following on the board. Ask pupils to find each one in their dictionaries and to tell after what entry they found each.

Middle Ages	doz.
daddy-long legs	Dr.
coat of arms	ft.
prairie schooner	no.

13. Write the word *dories* and ask children whether they can find this word as an entry word in their dictionaries. Then ask what the root of the word *dories* probably is. Suggest that pupils look up the meaning of *dory*. Then ask what the word *dories* means. Continue in like manner with the words *muggier*, *jostling*, *deluded*, and *capably*. Lead pupils to generalize in their own words that when they cannot find

Identifying root words as main entries

an inflected or derived form listed as an entry word, they should look for the root word.

14. Write a list of words like *starred, guided, denies, trashy, vaguely* on the board. Ask pupils to copy the words and after each to write the entry word under which they would find the meaning (or meanings) of the root word.

Deriving pronunciations

Obviously, growth in ability to use the dictionary for meaning should parallel growth in using it for pronunciation. Therefore the procedures suggested in this section should be presented to children along with those in the next section (pages 228-241). The procedures listed here for developing skill in using a dictionary for pronunciations are presented in a logical sequence. In general, their purpose is to establish basic understandings that will enable children to use any pronunciation key. At no time should pupils be expected to memorize pronunciation symbols.

Why pronunciations are given in a dictionary

The first group of procedures will help children understand why pronunciation symbols are necessary. They provide a quick review of the following understandings: in the spelling of words (1) a letter of the alphabet (or a combination of letters) may stand for more than one sound; (2) one sound may be represented by various letters (or letter combinations); (3) letters may stand for no sounds.

1. Write the words *dough, through, rough, bough, cough,* and have them pronounced. Lead children to note that it is not always possible to figure out the pronunciation of a word by looking at the spelling. A person who did not know how to pronounce the words given above might assume that they rhyme, since they all end in the letters *ough.* Emphasize the idea that when we do not know how to pronounce a word, we can always turn to our dictionaries.

2. Comment that if each letter of the alphabet stood for only one sound, the dictionary might not need to give the pro-

nunciations of words. To review the understanding that the vowel letters and some consonant letters stand for more than one sound, write the lists of words given below. Have the words in the first list pronounced and lead pupils to note that the letter *a* represents a different sound in each word. Continue similarly with the other lists of words.

a	*e*	*i*	*o*	*u*
hat	end	it	not	up
ate	equal	ice	go	use
all	England	machine	do	rule
arm	café	firm	of	full
any	her	engine	wolf	busy
alone	woolen		or	bury
			lemon	fur
				circus

c	*g*	*s*
car	go	see
cent	giant	has
ocean	rouge	sure
cello		pleasure

3. To review the understanding that one sound may be represented by more than one letter (or combination of letters), write the words *age, bay, break, eight, vein, straight, pain, they*. Ask pupils to pronounce them and to listen to the vowel sound in each. What vowel sound do they hear in all these words (long *a* sound)? Then call attention to the various spellings that represent this sound. Continue similarly with the words *aisle, height, eye, ice, lie, high, buy, sky, rye*, in which a long *i* sound is heard.

Next, write the words *beg, egg, league, ghost, guess* and have them pronounced. Lead pupils to note that each contains the consonant sound commonly referred to as the *g* sound. Then call attention to the different spellings that represent the *g* sound.

4. Review the concept of silent letters in the spellings of words by writing the words *knit, gnat, wren, walk, island, listen, climb, hymn, honest, receipt.* When pupils have pronounced the words, ask them to tell which consonant letter in each word is silent.

Lead the class to generalize on the basis of the preceding exercises that the spelling of many words is not a reliable guide to their pronunciation. Because this is so, the dictionary shows the pronunciation of entry words.

The next group of procedures introduces pronunciation symbols[1] and develops two understandings that are basic to the interpretation of pronunciation symbols: (1) each symbol stands for a sound; (2) the clue to the sound that a given symbol represents is the key word or words in whatever dictionary one is using.

1. Write the word *at* and have it pronounced. Then ask how many sounds pupils hear in the word *at* (two) and how many letters are used in the spelling to represent these sounds

Each symbol stands for one sound

(two). Next, use similar procedures with the word *add*, leading pupils to note that two sounds are heard in this word also but three letters are used in the spelling of the word. Now write after each word its pronunciation as it is given in the dictionary—(at), (ad), and lead pupils to note that in each pronunciation one pronunciation symbol is shown for each sound.

Write the following words, omitting pronunciations:

guest (gest)	bell (bel)	knock (nok)	hiss (his)
says (sez)	lamb (lam)	calf (kaf)	his (hiz)
cent (sent)	build (bild)	hinge (hinj)	said (sed)
scent (sent)	fence (fens)	has (haz)	come (kum)
head (hed)	tough (tuf)	hymn (him)	does (duz)

[1]The pronunciation symbols used in this book are from the Thorndike-Barnhart dictionaries. If your pupils are using a dictionary that employs other symbols, you will want to adapt the procedures to conform with those symbols.

Ask pupils how many sounds they hear in each word. As they respond, write the pronunciation after the word, explaining that it is the pronunciation given in the dictionary for that word. Then have pupils compare the number of letters in the spelling of the word with the number of symbols in its pronunciation. On the basis of this exercise, encourage children to generalize in their own words that (1) each pronunciation symbol always stands for the same sound; (2) no silent letters that occur in the spelling of a word are ever shown in the pronunciation of that word.

2. Write the words in the first list given below, omitting the pronunciations. Ask children to pronounce the three words and to listen to the beginning sound in each. Explain that this consonant sound is often called the g sound, and then write the pronunciation after each of the three words. Continue similarly with the words in the remaining lists, leading pupils to identify the j sound in the second list of words, the k sound in the third, the s sound in the fourth.

A consonant letter is used as the symbol for the sound it most commonly represents

got (got)	jam (jam)	kept (kept)	sit (sit)
gum (gum)	job (job)	keg (keg)	sell (sel)
gas (gas)	jump (jump)	kill (kil)	sun (sun)

Next, write the lists of words given below, omitting the pronunciations. As each word in the first list is pronounced, ask whether the letter g stands for the g sound or for the j sound. Then write the pronunciation after each word. Use similar procedures with the remaining words, leading children to note that the letter c stands for the k sound in the words in the second list and for the s sound in the words in the third list. Help pupils generalize that in dictionary pronunciations a consonant letter is used as a symbol for the sound it most commonly represents.

gem (jem)	cat (kat)	cell (sel)
hinge (hinj)	cup (kup)	dance (dans)
lunge (lunj)	cob (kob)	cent (sent)

3. Write the following words and pronunciations:

egg (eg)	nymph (nimf)	is (iz)
wreck (rek)	laugh (laf)	gnat (nat)
puff (puf)	since (sins)	badge (baj)

As each word is pronounced, ask such questions as "How many letters do you see in the spelling of the word *egg?* How many sounds do you hear when you say *egg?* What letter is used as the symbol for the consonant sound heard at the end of *egg?* What letters stand for no sounds in the spelling of *wreck?* What letter is used as the symbol for the first sound heard in *wreck?* for the last sound? What letter is used as the symbol for the last sound in the word *puff?* in *nymph?* in *laugh?*"

4. Write the following columns of words (without the pronunciations at first):

brick (brik)	flood (flud)	speck (spek)	crisp (krisp)
crumb (krum)	clock (klok)	skill (skil)	prince (prins)
grass (gras)	glove (gluv)	swell (swel)	mix (miks)
drill (dril)	pledge (plej)	stiff (stif)	film (film)

Recall that the letters *r*, *l*, and *s* stand for sounds that are often blended with other consonant sounds with no vowel sound in between. Pronounce the word *brick* and ask pupils how many sounds they hear in the word. What consonant sound blends with the sound represented by the letter *r?* Then write the pronunciation of the word *brick*. Continue with the other words in the first column and with the remaining columns, calling attention to the final consonant blends in the words in the last column. To conclude, point out that although the consonant sounds represented by the symbols l, r, and s are probably the most common "blenders," there are other consonant sounds that blend also, the sound represented by the symbol w, for example, as in the word *twig* (twig).

5. Write the words *when* and *quit*. As the words are pronounced, ask pupils to listen to the consonant blend at the beginning of *when*[1] and of *quit*. What consonant sound is the second sound in both blends (the sound that the letter *w* usually stands for)? Then after each word, write its pronunciation (hwen) and (kwit). Comment that in the spelling of many words the letters *wh* stand for the consonant blend (hw) and the letters *qu* for the consonant blend (kw).

6. Write just the pronunciations given below (the spellings of the words will be added later), and explain that these are pronunciations of words that pupils all know and use.

twelve (twelv)	quack (kwak)	wax (waks)
quick (kwik)	whiff (hwif)	quilt (kwilt)
whip (hwip)	wrist (rist)	squint (skwint)

Ask children to say each word by looking at its pronunciation. (By now most pupils will have inferred what the symbols for the short vowel sounds are. However, if necessary, explain that the vowel symbols in these words stand for the short vowel sounds.) As each word is pronounced, write its spelling before its pronunciation.

When all the words have been pronounced and written, encourage children to compare the spelling of each word with the symbols used to show its pronunciation. Reëmphasize the understanding that for every symbol we see in a dictionary pronunciation, we say a sound and that any one symbol always stands for the same sound.

7. Write the following pairs of words, omitting the pronunciations at first:

chill (chil)	shell (shel)	thin (thin)	sing (sing)
much (much)	rush (rush)	bath (bath)	clang (klang)

Ask pupils to listen to the sound at the beginning of *chill* and at the end of *much* as they pronounce these words.

[1]See the footnote on page 83.

Comment that because this sound is commonly represented by the letters *ch* in the spelling of words, the dictionary uses these letters as the symbol for this sound in pronunciations. Then write the pronunciations of *chill* and *much*. Continue similarly with the words *shell* and *rush* and with the words *thin* and *bath*. When presenting the pronunciation symbol ng in (sing) and (klang), remind pupils that the sound for which this symbol stands is never heard at the beginning of English words.

Write the pronunciations (omit the spellings at first) shown below and use procedures similar to those suggested for the sixth exercise.

catch (kach)	quench (kwench)	chunk (chungk)
think (thingk)	clash (klash)	thread (thred)
shall (shal)	tongue (tung)	young (yung)

8. To introduce the full pronunciation key, have pupils turn to it in the front of their dictionaries and comment that on this page they can find out what sound every pronunciation symbol represents. Call attention to the first symbol (a) and to the key words following it. Then ask children to listen to the vowel sound as they say the key words *hat* and *cap*. Explain that every time the symbol a is used in a pronunciation, it stands for the vowel sound heard in *hat* and *cap* (the short *a* sound). Continue with the symbols e, i, o, and u, which represent other short vowel sounds, making sure that pupils understand the function of the key words in each instance.

Call attention to the symbols d, l, and p and ask pupils to say the key words that indicate the consonant sound that each of these pronunciation symbols represents. Next, suggest that everyone find the entry word *plaid* in their dictionaries and note its pronunciation (plad). Then have the word *plaid* pronounced. Continue similarly with the entry words *salve, cleanse, sieve, myth, loll, sponge.*

The clue to the sound that any pronunciation symbol stands for is the key word (or words)

9. Ask pupils to pronounce the key words following the symbols ā, ē, ī, ō, and ū to find out what vowel sound each represents. Recall that these vowel sounds are often referred to as long vowel sounds. Then explain that the small horizontal line (a macron) used over a vowel letter to indicate a particular sound is an example of a diacritical mark and that pupils will soon learn to interpret other diacritical marks.

Write the pronunciations given below (omit the spellings at first) and ask pupils to pronounce the words that these pronunciations represent. As each is pronounced, write the spelling before its pronunciation. Emphasize again the understandings that (1) within any one pronunciation key the relationship between symbol and sound remains constant and (2) no silent letters are shown in the pronunciations of words.

cheese (chēz)	why (hwī)	knee (nē)
cage (kāj)	scheme (skēm)	comb (kōm)
phone (fōn)	own (ōn)	paid (pād)
rise (rīz)	freight (frāt)	flight (flīt)
view (vū)	cute (kūt)	few (fū)

10. After writing the words *dare*, *chair*, *bear*, and *where*, ask pupils to pronounce them and to listen to the vowel sound in each. When children recognize that the same vowel sound is heard in these words, call attention to the symbol that represents this sound (ã) in the full pronunciation key and have the key words pronounced (the diacritical mark ˜ is a tilde). Then after each word on the board write its pronunciation—(dãr), (chãr), (bãr), (hwãr).

Use similar procedures with the words *calm* and *car* to introduce the symbol ä; *call* and *corn* to introduce ô; *took* and *pull* to introduce u̇; *true* and *room* to introduce ü. (The diacritical mark ¨ is a dieresis; the mark ˆ is a circumflex.) Then write just the pronunciations that follow. As pupils pronounce the word that each represents, write the spelling of the word before its pronunciation.

barn (bärn)	could (ku̇d)	glue (glü)
care (kãr)	cool (kül)	cart (kärt)
war (wôr)	cough (kôf)	talk (tôk)

11. Write the words *her, earn, bird, word, hurt,* have them pronounced, and lead pupils to note that each contains the same vowel sound followed by *r.* Call attention to the symbol (ėr) that stands for this combination of a vowel and consonant sound, and have the key words pronounced. Then write the pronunciation after each word—(hėr), (ėrn), (bėrd), (wėrd), (hėrt). In like manner use the words *boy* and *noise* to introduce the symbol oi, and the words *cloud* and *crowd* to introduce the symbol ou.

Use the words *then* (ᴛHen) and *breathe* (brēᴛH) to introduce the pronunciation symbol ᴛH, making sure that pupils hear the difference between the voiced consonant sound that this symbol represents and the unvoiced consonant sound that is heard at the beginning of *thin* (thin) and at the end of *breath* (breth). Use the words *rouge* (rüzh) and *beige* (bāzh) to introduce the symbol zh. Write the pronunciations given below and use procedures like those suggested at the end of the preceding exercise.

girl (gėrl)	boy (boi)	these (ᴛHēz)
doubt (dout)	crown (kroun)	coin (koin)
smooth (smüᴛH)	church (chėrch)	earth (ėrth)

12. Write the following words with their pronunciations:

have (hav)	jour ney (jėr′ni)	At lan tic (at lan′tik)
niece (nēs)	neph ew (nef′ū)	ra di o (rā′di ō)
thought (thôt)	be ware (bi wãr′)	oc cu py (ok′ū pī)

Have the words in the first list pronounced and ask how many vowel sounds are heard in each word (one). Continue with the words in the second list, each of which contains two vowel sounds, and with those in the third list, each of which contains three vowel sounds. Recall that a word or part of a word in which one vowel sound is heard is called a syllable. Lead pupils to note how both the spelling and the pronunciation of each word in the second and third lists are divided to show the number of syllables.

Next, review the understanding that when we pronounce a word of two or more syllables, we accent one of the syllables more than the other or others. Have the words in the second and third lists pronounced again and ask which syllable is accented in each one. Call attention to the accent mark and discuss its function. Conclude by writing just the pronunciations shown below. Ask pupils to pronounce the word that each represents. As they do so, write the spelling of the word before its pronunciation.

can dy (kan′di)	dis tinct (dis tingkt′)	thir ti eth (thėr′ti ith)
beau ty (bū′ti)	ex haust (eg zôst′)	ex hib it (eg zib′it)
Ju ly (jù lī′)	knowl edge (nol′ij)	de tec tive (di tek′tiv)

13. To introduce the secondary accent mark, write the following words and their pronunciations:

birth day (bėrth′dā′)	rep re sent (rep′ri zent′)
gang plank (gang′plangk′)	Jan u ar y (jan′ū er′i)
snow flake (snō′flāk′)	un de cid ed (un′di sīd′id)

Lead pupils to note that the three words in the first list are compounds and have them pronounced. Did children notice that each word has two accented syllables, one of which is stressed more than the other? After pupils have identified the primary and the secondary accent in each word, remind them that these words illustrate a common pattern of accent in English compounds—a primary accent on or within the first root word and a secondary accent on or within the second root word. Then call attention to the secondary accent mark. Continue with the words in the other list, reminding pupils that many words other than compounds have a secondary as well as a primary accent.

14. To introduce the symbol ə (the schwa), which represents the vowel sound heard in the majority of unaccented syllables, write the following words on the board (the pronunciations will be added later):

The schwa sound and symbol

soda (sō′də)	precious (presh′əs)
linen (lin′ən)	mountain (moun′tən)
April (ā′prəl)	fraction (frak′shən)
common (kom′ən)	gorgeous (gôr′jəs)
minus (mī′nəs)	partial (pär′shəl)

As pupils pronounce each word, have them listen first to the vowel sound in the accented syllable (it is different in each word). Then ask them to listen to the vowel sound in the unaccented syllables of these words, leading pupils to note that it is the same in each word. Recall that this soft, unstressed vowel sound is called the schwa (shwä) sound. Write the pronunciation after each word and call attention to the schwa symbol (ə) and to the fact that any vowel letter or combination of vowel letters may stand for this unstressed vowel sound. Ask pupils to find this symbol in the full pronunciation key and to pronounce the key words.

Conclude by writing just the pronunciations of the words that are shown below. As children pronounce the word that each pronunciation represents, write the spelling before its pronunciation.

china (chī′nə)	challenge (chal′ənj)
amount (ə mount′)	elephant (el′ə fənt)
vacant (vā′kənt)	convenient (kən vēn′yənt)
anger (ang′gər)	potato (pə tā′tō)
extra (eks′trə)	dictionary (dik′shən er′i)
connect (kə nekt′)	pioneer (pī′ə nēr′)
million (mil′yən)	television (tel′ə vizh′ən)

The next group of procedures is suggested for providing enjoyable practice in using dictionary pronunciation symbols. At the same time these procedures will provide the teacher with a means of determining whether pupils have acquired the skills and understandings necessary to translating pronunciation symbols into spoken words. As pupils do the exercises, remind them to use the full pronunciation key in their dictionaries as a guide to the sound that any symbol stands for. If children are using Thorndike-Barnhart dictionaries or any others that have a short pronunciation key at the bottom of every right-hand page, call attention to the short key and explain its use as a handy key to vowel sounds and to a few consonant sounds.

Checking ability to interpret pronunciation symbols

1. Write the pronunciations given below and explain that ten of them are the pronunciations of words that name something to eat. Ask pupils to indicate which pronunciations these are by writing the number of each and the spelling of the word it represents (1. *cabbage*, for example). When everyone has finished, ask children what words the other pronunciations represent.

1. (kab′ij)	7. (ə plī′)	13. (chēz)
2. (sal′ə ri)	8. (süp)	14. (sel′ə ri)
3. (rīs)	9. (ap′əl)	15. (bek′ən)
4. (ches)	10. (sōp)	16. (tėr′ki)
5. (sam′ən)	11. (ūn′yən)	17. (plüm)
6. (trik′i)	12. (mak′ə rō′ni)	18. (skwosh)

2. Write or reproduce the following sentences and pronunciations, underlining the italicized words. Explain that only one of the pronunciations following each sentence is that of the underlined word. When pupils have decided which it is in each instance, ask them to write the word and its pronunciation on a piece of paper (1. *whose* (hüz), for example). In conclusion, have children pronounce the word that the other pronunciation stands for.

1. *Whose* book is this? (hōz) (hüz)
2. The room was very *quiet*. (kwīt) (kwī'ət)
3. It is ten degrees *below* zero. (bi lō') (bel'ō)
4. We saw a *warship* in the bay. (wôr'ship') (wėr'ship)
5. I had to *cancel* my appointment. (kən sēl') (kan'səl)
6. He gave me his *photograph*. (fə tog'rə fi) (fō'tə graf)
7. She wants a *definite* answer. (def'ə nit) (di fī'ənt)
8. Africa is a *continent*. (kən tent'mənt) (kon'tə nənt)
9. Who is the main *character?* (char'ə ti) (kar'ik tər)

3. Write or reproduce the questions given below. Tell pupils to look up the pronunciation of the word *dearth* in their dictionaries and to pronounce it. Then ask whether *dearth* rhymes with *mirth, hearth,* or *fourth*. Have pupils write the rhyming word after the number of the question (1. *mirth*). Suggest that pupils finish the exercise independently.

   1. Does *dearth* rhyme with *mirth, hearth,* or *fourth?*
   2. Does *gaol* rhyme with *roll, boil,* or *mail?*
   3. Does *tread* rhyme with *said, feed,* or *made?*
   4. Does *mould* rhyme with *could, told,* or *called?*
   5. Does *queue* rhyme with *chewy, see,* or *few?*
   6. Does *pique* rhyme with *cheek, sick,* or *like?*
   7. Does *geyser* rhyme with *razor, loser,* or *miser?*
   8. Does *phial* rhyme with *real, sail,* or *trial?*

4. Suggest that pupils play a game called "Which Is It?" Begin by writing the pronunciations (kôt) and (kōt) and asking, "Which of these represents a word that means 'something to wear'?" When children agree that it is (kōt), write the word *coat* before its pronunciation. Then ask what word the other pronunciation stands for. As pupils pronounce *caught*, write the word before its pronunciation (kôt). Continue with pronunciations and questions like the following:

   (shō) (shü) Which do you wear on your foot?
   (kol'əm) (sol'əm) Which means "serious or earnest"?

(stär) (stãr) Which can you see in the sky at night?
(pich'ər) (pik'chər) From which can you pour water?
(spek) (spēk) Which means "to talk"?
(hāl) (hwāl) Which is a huge sea animal?
(skat'ər) (skāt'ər) Which is a person who skates?
(bėrd) (brīd) Which is an animal with wings?
(ô'thər) (uтн'ər) Which is a person who writes books?

Deriving word meanings

The purpose of the procedures in this last section is to teach children how to use the dictionary to learn the meanings of words. It is important to keep in mind that when a child or an adult consults a dictionary for the meaning of an unfamiliar word, he is usually seeking the total meaning of a sentence or passage in which that word is used. For example, a reader will not understand what the sentence "The frightened man sought sanctuary in an abandoned farmhouse" means unless he knows what the word *sanctuary* means in this context. If he consults a dictionary, he must "tune" the appropriate definition of *sanctuary* back into the sentence. To do this, he must be able to (1) comprehend the definitions given for a word in the dictionary, (2) use context as a basis for selecting the appropriate definition if more than one is given, and (3) adapt the appropriate definition to fit the context. In general, the procedures in the remainder of this chapter are directed toward the development of these three major skills.

1. List on the board the words *grackle, katydid, verbena, gibbon, midge, merino, mongoose, linnet, nettle, cormorant, okra, okapi, osprey, petrel, cicada, tapir, yucca, gentian, aphid, snipe, chamois, fungus, phlox, mangrove.* Tell pupils that each one of these words is the name of an animal or plant, and suggest that they read the first definition of the entry words *animal* and *plant* in their dictionaries. Then have pupils write the words *Animals* and *Plants* as headings

Comprehending dictionary definitions

for two columns on a piece of paper. Next, ask whether a grackle is an animal or a plant. Suggest that pupils use their dictionaries to find out, and when they know, to write the word *grackle* under the appropriate heading. Have pupils continue independently with the remaining words. When the class has finished, ask which animals are birds and which are insects.

2. Ask children to leaf through their dictionaries and to notice the many pictures. Why do they suppose there are pictures in a dictionary? If they cannot think why, ask how they would explain what a cello or a parachute is to someone who had never heard of one. Suggest that children find the entry *cello*, read the definition, and notice how the picture helps us know just what a cello looks like—how big it is, how it is played, and so on. Repeat with *parachute*.

Using pictures and diagrams as aids to meaning

3. Have pupils find the entries *finch, lynx, marmoset, marmot* and read the definition for each. Then call attention to the picture and caption accompanying each entry, leading pupils to note the way in which the size of each animal is indicated. Next, ask pupils to use the definitions and illustrations to answer such questions as the following: "Which animal is the largest? the smallest? Which one is a monkey? Which one is found in South America? Is a woodchuck a marmoset or a marmot?"

4. Write on the board entry words for which part-whole diagrams are given—*bowsprit, cupola, periscope*, for example. Point to the word *bowsprit* and ask whether children know what it is and what it is a part of. Suggest that they use their dictionaries to find out. When everyone has found the entry, ask how the word is pronounced and call special attention to the picture in the form of a diagram. Lead pupils to note how the diagram helps the reader know exactly where a bowsprit is located on a ship or boat. Then ask children to look up the remaining entries independently and to write a sentence telling what each is a part of.

5. Ask pupils to find the entry *afar* and to read the definition. Then call attention to the sentence printed in italic type after the definition. Explain that this sentence, which uses the word *afar*, is called an illustrative sentence. By showing how an entry word may be used in a sentence, it gives the reader additional help with the meaning of an entry word. Next, comment that sometimes an illustrative phrase is used and that it serves the same purpose as an illustrative sentence. To illustrate, have pupils read the definition and the illustrative phrase given for the entry *pallid*. In conclusion, have children find and read the definition for each of the following entries: *ado, advisable, affable, pamper, pane*. Ask them to notice especially how the illustrative sentence or phrase in italic type makes the use and the meaning of each entry word very clear. Suggest that pupils write sentences in which they use each of these entry words.

Using illustrative sentences and phrases as aids to meaning

The preceding five exercises should acquaint pupils with the ways in which the dictionary gives meanings of words. Once children have become familiar with the dictionary as a source for learning word meanings, they should be given practice in interpreting dictionary definitions in light of a given context.

1. Write the word *cross* and recall with the class that many words like this have more than one meaning and that the meaning of a word is determined by its use in context. Then write the sentences "We had to cross the river," "That church has a cross on it," "She is never cross," and ask pupils to tell what the word *cross* means in each. Explain that when an entry word has more than one meaning, the dictionary numbers the various meanings to make it easier to find them. Then suggest that pupils find the entry *cross* in their dictionaries and note how many definitions are given for this word. Which definition explains the meaning of *cross* in each sentence on the board?

Using context clues to select appropriate definitions

2. Write groups of sentences like those shown below. For the first group, have pupils find the word *crane* in their dictionaries and read the definitions. Then ask someone to read aloud the definition of *crane* that explains its meaning in the first sentence, in the second, in the third. Continue similarly with the other groups of sentences.

> I had to *crane* my neck to see over the fence.
> The arm of the *crane* lifted the automobile out of the ditch.
> The *crane* flew away when I came near it.

> The duke declared his allegiance to the *crown*.
> Each bridesmaid wore a *crown* of daisies.
> The queen seldom wears her *crown*.

3. Write or reproduce the sentences given below, underlining the italicized words. Ask pupils to read the definitions given in their dictionaries for each underlined word. When they have decided which definition of a word explains its meaning in the sentence, have them write the number of that definition after the number of the sentence (for example, 1. definition 5).

1. The stones in this necklace are *paste*.
2. A driver learns to *gauge* the speed of an approaching car.
3. The king's *standard* fluttered in the breeze over the castle.
4. Your total does not *tally* with mine.
5. We carried the injured man on a *litter*.
6. The *gallery* stood up and cheered.
7. My mother's electric *range* has two ovens.
8. I had to *comb* the town before I found an apartment.

4. Ask whether pupils know that there are two words spelled *junk*. Suggest that they find these two words in their dictionaries and read the definition that is given for each. Which word, *junk*[1] or *junk*[2], is used in the sentence "The Chinese family lived on a junk"? Explain that words like *junk* that are spelled alike but are different words are called homographs. Whenever pupils see a small number after an

Using context to choose appropriate entry words

entry word, they know that it is a homograph and that there is at least one more entry word spelled the same way. If they do not find the definition they need after the first homograph, they must check the definitions after the other (or others). Ask pupils how many words are spelled *lap* in their dictionary. How many definitions are given for *lap*¹? for *lap*²? for *lap*³? Then write the sentences given below. Ask children which entry, *lap*¹, *lap*², or *lap*³, is used in the first sentence. Which definition of *lap*³ is the meaning used in the first sentence? Continue similarly with the other sentences.

> The waves lap against the rocks.
> Mother held the baby on her lap.
> My kitten is too young to lap milk.
> That horse was injured during the first lap of the race.

5. Write or reproduce the sentences below, underlining the italicized words and explaining that each is a homograph. Tell pupils to read each sentence and to use their dictionaries to decide which homograph (*shock*¹, *shock*², or *shock*³, for example) is used in the sentence. Then ask them to write that entry word with its number after the number of the sentence.

   1. The news was a great *shock* to me.
   2. We had fried *perch* for supper.
   3. Do you know how to play *cricket?*
   4. The *squall* nearly overturned our sailboat.
   5. The old man sat on the *stoop*.

6. Present a list of questions like the following in which each italicized word is a homograph. Ask pupils to use their dictionaries to help them answer each question. Suggest that after the number of each question they write *yes* or *no* followed by the entry word that helped them answer the question (for example, 1. no, *cape*²).

1. Are all *capes* something to wear?
2. Do all *flickers* have feathers?
3. Can cloth have a *nap?*
4. Can some people buy things with a *mark?*
5. Can you sail in a *smack?*
6. Can you sit on a *settle?*
7. Can you travel on a *pike?*

7. Comment that some homographs are not pronounced alike. To illustrate, have pupils find the entries *close*[1], *close*[2] and *row*[1], *row*[2], *row*[3]. After writing sentences like those given below, ask pupils to tell which entry word is used in each sentence and how that entry is pronounced.

Using context to choose appropriate pronunciations

She sat *close* to the fireplace.
Please *close* the door.
I helped *row* the boat.
A *row* started when everyone demanded his pay at once.
We sat in the third *row* of seats.

8. Have pupils find the entry word *moderate.* Call attention to the two pronunciations that are given for this one entry word and to the way in which each pronunciation is linked to a particular meaning of the word. Then ask what the word means in the following phrases and how it is pronounced in each phrase: *a moderate salary, a moderate rainfall, winds that moderate at sunset.* Continue with the entries *contract, contrast, separate, perfect* and phrases that use different pronunciations for each word.

9. To give practice in using context to choose appropriate pronunciations, write sentences like those that follow, underlining the italicized words. Comment that the pronunciation of each underlined word is determined by its meaning, as pupils will discover when they consult their dictionaries. When pupils have decided what each word means in the context given and therefore how it should be pronounced, ask them to copy the appropriate pronuncia-

tion after the number of the sentence. When children have finished, have them read each sentence aloud.

1. Mother is a *graduate* of Smith College.
2. We made rapid *progress* in arithmetic.
3. He sings *bass* in the chorus.
4. The men were lost in the *desert*.
5. Can you *estimate* the total cost?
6. This machine will *record* our voices.
7. The clerk gave me a *refund* of five dollars.
8. I know nothing about the *subject*.

If a child is to use the dictionary as an aid to word perception and as a part of the total reading process, he must be able to do more than comprehend definitions of an entry word and select the one that fits a given context. He *Adapting* must also be able to "tune" a definition back into the con-*definitions* *to context* text in which he encounters the unfamiliar word. With many dictionary definitions this is relatively simple, since all the reader has to do is substitute a definition for the unfamiliar word in context. Sometimes, however, he must transpose a word or two in the definition or in the context. Often he must add an ending or a suffix to fit the definition into context. At other times it is necessary to completely paraphrase the definition (or several definitions) of an unfamiliar word as well as the context in which the word appears. The next group of procedures is designed to help children master these four levels of difficulty in fitting dictionary definitions into sentence context.

1. Write the sentence "This is a replica of a famous painting," and suggest that pupils find the word *replica* in their dic-*Substituting a* tionaries and read the definition. Then ask them to restate *definition of an* *unfamiliar word* the sentence, using another word that means "replica" *in context* ("copy, reproduction"). Comment that to understand or explain the meaning of some sentences in which there is an unfamiliar word, we can often just substitute one of the definitions for the unfamiliar word.

To provide practice in fitting definitions into context by the technique of substitution, write or reproduce the sentences given below, underlining the italicized words. Suggest that pupils read the definition (or definitions) of each underlined word in their dictionaries. Then ask them to choose the definition that explains the meaning of the word in the sentence and to rewrite each sentence, using one of the definitions instead of the underlined word.

> Do not *divulge* our plans to anyone.
> The old *mariner* had been in many countries.
> The *vociferous* crowd demanded their rights.
> I find it difficult to *converse* with strangers.
> I saw a British *man-of-war* when I was in Boston.
> I am suspicious of people who *malign* others.

2. Write the sentence "I hope the news did not perturb you," and ask children to read the definition of *perturb* in their dictionaries. What does *perturb* mean in the sentence on the board ("disturb greatly; make uneasy or trouble")? Ask whether either part of that definition can be substituted for the word *perturb* in the sentence. When pupils agree that to do so makes an awkward, confusing sentence, ask how they would rearrange the words to fit them into a smooth, clear sentence ("I hope the news did not disturb you greatly"). Comment that it is often necessary to change the order of words to make a definition of an unfamiliar word fit smoothly into the context.

Transposing words to adapt a definition to context

Ask children to rewrite each sentence that is given below, using the appropriate definition of the italicized word. Tell the class that the words will have to be rearranged in each sentence.

> A *pugnacious* person seldom has many friends.
> A shark is a *marine* animal.
> This is an *insoluble* puzzle.
> The *floral* display was beautiful.
> The recipe says to *halve* the squash before baking it.

3. Write the sentence "The wind is veering to the south,"
and ask children to use their dictionaries to find out what
veering means in this sentence. What entry word will pu-

Inflectional
adaptation
of a definition

pils look for first? Why? Remind the class, if necessary,
that most words are entered and defined in their root forms.
Then ask which definition of *veer* fits the meaning of the
sentence on the board. What ending will have to be added
to this definition to make it fit the sentence (*-ing*)? Then
have pupils restate the sentence, using the correct form of
the appropriate definition ("The wind is shifting or turning . . ."). Use similar procedures with the derived form
morosely and the sentence " 'I'll never amount to much,' the
boy said morosely." Bring out that to adapt to context any
one of the words in the definition of *morose*, it is necessary
to add the suffix *-ly* to the definition.

To provide practice in inflectional adaptation, ask children to rewrite the following sentences, using a form of the
appropriate definition instead of the italicized words:

> This land was *reforested* five years ago.
> I have several *chores* to finish before I can go.
> He *conceded* that he had acted foolishly.
> The rebels won by *ousting* the king's men.
> He is the *canniest* man I know.

4. Comment that often we have to do more than change the
order of a few words or add an ending to fit a definition into
context. To illustrate, write the sentence "His remarks were

Complete
paraphrasing

not pertinent to our discussion," and ask pupils to read the
definition of *pertinent* in their dictionaries ("having something to do with what is being considered; relating to the
matter in hand; to the point"). In discussion, lead pupils to
see that with a definition like this, it is the general idea of the
definition that counts, not the exact wording. Then ask how
they would explain to someone what the sentence means
without using the word *pertinent*. Encourage several

pupils to try. Perhaps the class will agree that the following is satisfactory: "His remarks had nothing to do with our discussion."

Continue similarly with the italicized words in the following sentences:

Few people admire a *mercenary* person.
How do you expect me to carry this *unwieldy* parcel?
Because of the fog Mr. Bell did not recognize his *assailant*.
My grandparents were Swedish *immigrants*.
This *perforated* paper does not fit my notebook.

5. As the class discusses stories and articles that have been assigned, direct attention to the meaning of specific words. **Checking ability to adapt definitions to context** After pupils have used their dictionaries (or glossaries) to find out what a word means, have them restate the sentence in which the word occurs without using that word. The italicized words in the sentences below are examples of words that pupils may encounter. Restating the sentences below without using the italicized words reviews inflectional adaptation, transposition of words, and complete paraphrasing.

Deer are *herbivorous* animals.
My car collided with a *stationary* truck.
The colonists believed there was no way of *averting* war.
He *enumerated* the things we would need for our trip.
Who was Lincoln's *predecessor* in The White House?
The war *impoverished* my country.
When the storm *diminished*, the men *surveyed* the damage.

The procedures suggested up to this point lay the foundation for successful use of the dictionary. We should, however, continue at all levels to extend and strengthen the major dictionary skills that are initiated at about fourth grade. The next group of procedures suggests ways of helping pupils solve some problems that a reader is likely to encounter as he uses a dictionary.

1. To introduce special meanings of words and phrases and the way in which such meanings are given in most dictionaries, write the following sentences, underlining the italicized words:

> Two nickels are *equal to* a dime.
> She is not *equal to* climbing five flights of stairs.

Noting special meanings

After discussing what the phrase *equal to* means in the first sentence, ask what the same phrase means in the second sentence. Comment that the words *equal to* in the second sentence have a special meaning and that special meanings of words or phrases are often entered in a dictionary. Suggest that pupils find the entry *equal* in their dictionaries and note how the special meaning of *equal to* is indicated (it is printed in heavy black type and entered as one definition of *equal*). Explain that when a word has only one or two special meanings, these meanings are usually given along with the definitions of the word. To find the meaning of a phrase like *equal to*, one should look under the entry for the most important word in the phrase, in this case *equal*. If pupils are not sure under what entry word to look for some special meanings—*presence of mind*, for example—they may have to try looking under both important words, *presence* and *mind*, until they find the special meaning.

To give pupils practice in finding special meanings that are listed along with definitions of entry words, write the following, underlining the italicized words. What does the underlined word (or words) mean in each sentence? Have pupils restate the sentence without using it.

> I *dashed off* a letter and ran to the post office.
> Last year we had an *open winter*.
> She practices the piano *by fits and starts*.
> He asked me to give his *compliments* to my father.
> The commander told his men to *open fire*.
> I *took exception* to his remarks about our school.

2. Explain that some special meanings are printed as entry phrases below the definitions of an entry word, and to illustrate, have pupils find the entry *put* in their dictionaries. How many special meanings containing the word *put* are given below the definitions of the word *put?* Which of these special meanings have more than one definition? Ask pupils to restate each of the following sentences without using the italicized words:

> I was *put out* by his refusal to go with me.
> Mother *put up* ten quarts of strawberry jam.
> He *put down* every word I said.
> We can *put* you *up* for the night.
> The soldiers *put down* the riot in an hour.
> I *put in* three hours a day practicing the piano.
> Do not *put on;* we know you are not hurt.
> The ship *put about* to avoid the storm.

3. Write the following sentences and have them read:

> These plants may be harmed by frost.
> Cold is harmful to many plants.
> This dog is harmless.
> We escaped unharmed from the fire.

Determining meaning of derivatives and inflected forms

Ask what these sentences have in common (some form of the root word *harm*) and review the understanding that a root word retains one of its meanings in all words that are formed from it. Then have pupils find the definition of *harm* in their dictionaries, and ask them to restate each of the sentences using words from the definition of *harm* instead of the word *harm.* Bring out in discussion that once we know the meaning (or meanings) of a root word and of commonly used endings, prefixes, and suffixes, we should have no trouble understanding what words formed from that root mean.

4. Have pupils find the word *observe* in their dictionaries and discuss the definitions. Ask which meaning of *observe* is present in the italicized word in each sentence that follows.

The thief entered and left the store *unobserved* by anyone.
She insists on strict *observance* of all rules and regulations.
I looked through the telescope at the *observatory*.
The captain stationed an *observer* at each corner of the fort.
If you are *observant*, you may find a four-leaf clover.
"Nice day today" was the doorman's usual *observation*.

Comment that although these forms of *observe* can be found as separate entries in many dictionaries (have pupils check the dictionary they are using), a knowledge of the various meanings of the root *observe* makes it unnecessary for a person to look up each derived form. (As pupils progress, they should also learn to use their dictionaries to find the meanings of prefixes and suffixes.)

5. Comment that many derived forms are defined in terms of their root words, making it necessary for the reader to read the definitions of the root in order to understand the meaning of the derived form. To illustrate, have pupils find and read the definitions of several derived forms that are defined in terms of their roots—*exaggeration, exclusion, regrettable, luxurious,* and so on.

6. To help pupils find the meaning of irregular inflected forms of words, write the following sentence, underlining the italicized word:

The horse *trod* on the flowers as he whirled in fright.

Ask pupils to look up *trod* in their dictionaries. To find the meaning of *trod*, what does their dictionary tell them to do (see *tread*)? Have them find *tread* and point out that *trod* is given in bold-face type after the definitions of *tread*. This fact helps them know that they have the right entry word. Which definition of *tread* fits the meaning of *trod* in the sentence? Have pupils use the definition instead of the word *trod* in the sentence. Continue similarly with the sentences on the next page.

The wolf *slunk* through the trees.
He *sought* his fortune in South America.
Thirty buffalo were *slain* that day.

7. As soon as pupils are using dictionaries that employ labels
(*Old use, Slang, Scottish*, and so on), call attention to the
way the dictionary that is being used labels words, and
Interpreting provide practice in using labels. Questions like the follow-
labels ing may be used:

> What is a *kirtle?* a *goodman?* a *cruse?* Would you be likely
> to use these words today?
>
> In what kind of writing would you be likely to see these
> words: *courser, guerdon, Araby, fain, seagirt, eventide?*
>
> In what country or countries would you be likely to hear
> each of these words: *lift* (meaning "elevator"), *bonny,
> banshee, loch, bairn, mickle, lorry* (meaning "truck"),
> *tram* (meaning "streetcar"), *tramway?*
>
> Which meaning of the word *foot* is used in the sentence
> "He refused to foot the bill"? How is this meaning labeled?
>
> Would you be using slang if you referred to food as *chow?*
> if you said your dog was a *chow?* if you said the test was a
> *cinch?* if you said someone *razzed* you about your haircut?
>
> Which of the following are trade names: *Thermos bottle,
> zeppelin, X-ray, isinglass, Pyrex, Vaseline, Kodak, khaki?*

Any dictionary that pupils are using will have some sort of
explanation of what each label signifies. Make sure that the
class reads all such explanatory matter.

As soon as pupils are using dictionaries designed for
use in junior high school and in senior high school, attention
should be called to usage notes, synonym studies, and
etymologies. At no level of schooling should it be assumed
that most pupils will automatically use or even be aware of
the many helps included in a dictionary.

As has been mentioned, using a dictionary for the pronunciation and meaning of unfamiliar words is one of the major aids to word perception. As with any method of word perception (phonetic analysis, for example), real mastery of the skills involved comes only with abundant application in genuine reading situations. The procedures given in this chapter are suggested mainly for the purpose of *presenting* concepts, for *building* understandings, and for *initiating* basic skills that are fundamental to successful use of the dictionary. Our ultimate goal should be that students form the dictionary habit for life. If we are to realize this goal, teachers at all levels and of all subjects should encourage the use of the dictionary as an indispensable source of information about words—their meaning, pronunciation, and spelling.

Index

[Page numbers in boldface type refer to teaching procedures.]